The Real America in Romance
by John Roy Musick

Address:
HardPress
8345 NW 66TH ST #2561
MIAMI FL 33166-2626
USA
Email: info@hardpress.net

The real America in
romance ...

DUEL BETWEEN THE "MONITOR" AND "MERRIMAC."
(See page 234)
After an original drawing by Freeland A. Carter.

THE REAL AMERICA IN ROMANCE

Volume XII

SECESSION
The Age of Union

By
JOHN R. MUSICK

ILLUSTRATIONS BY
FREELAND A. CARTER

WM. H. WISE & COMPANY
NEW YORK — 1906 — CHICAGO

$\mathfrak{To}$

MY SISTER,

LIZZIE MUSICK,

WHO HAS GIVEN ME VALUABLE AID IN THE PREPARATION

OF THESE BOOKS,

THIS VOLUME IS DEDICATED

BY

THE AUTHOR.

PREFACE.

THIS volume ends the original series of THE REAL AMERICA IN ROMANCE, designed to give a complete history of the United States, in twelve complete stories, chronologically arranged. Throughout the series I have adhered to the original plan of making fiction subordinate to history, even at the expense of unity. I have been censured by some critics for deserting my fictitious characters in order to bring up the historical events by which they were surrounded, but as my design was to make the series beneficial as well as interesting, I have turned a deaf ear to all suggestions to sacrifice usefulness to smoothness.

It is doubtful if the time has yet arrived to write a fair and impartial history of the war of Secession, even as a historical romance. We are so prone to let prejudice warp judgment that we can hardly deal fairly with an opponent, even though that opponent be a brother.

I believe the great civil war was not a war for the freedom of the slaves, but for the preservation of the Union. Slavery was a secondary issue, merely a pretext to test the long and bitterly contested doctrines of State supremacy. The seeds of the great conflict were really sown in the convention which framed our constitution, and the prophetic eye of Washington early saw the danger. Calhoun and Webster found this fire smouldering in the memories of men, and by brilliant powers fanned it into a conflagration. It spread and at one time threatened the North more than the South. There was no way to decide this great question of constitutional law, save by the highest court known, an appeal to arms. Had not slavery formed the issue some other disputed point would. In 1861, the abolition of slavery was not contemplated by either the Republican party or President Lincoln. In his inaugural address, March 4, 1861, Mr. Lincoln said: " I have no purpose, directly or indirectly, to interfere with the institution of slavery in any State where it exists. I believe I have no lawful right to do so, and I have no inclination to do so." When the war had raged almost two years, President Lincoln late in September issued a proclamation, in which he gave notice that it was his purpose to declare the emancipation of the slaves on the 1st of January, 1863, to take effect immediately wherever a state of insurrection might exist, unless the offenders should lay down their arms. If the offenders had laid down their arms and returned to their allegiance to the Union, slavery would not have been abolished. Then it is certain that the first two years' war was merely for the preservation of the Union, and not for the freedom of the slaves. If the first two years were a war for the Union, and the fighting never ceased until the Union was preserved, it is reasonable to suppose that the whole war was for the Union, and not for the freedom of the negro, as most writers of late years declare. While the freedom of the slaves was one of the inevitable results of the war, it was not the cause. The soldier who donned the blue in 1861, did so to defend his country, and had no more thought of abolition of the slaves than did Mr. Lincoln, on whom it was forced as a military necessity.

The grand central figure of this great period of our nation's history is Abraham Lincoln. He was the brilliant orb illuminating the republic's darkest hour, and others in the North were but satellites borrowing brilliance from him. He planned those Northern campaigns, and issued the orders to his lieutenants to execute. He could be a soldier at headquarters; but he had too much human kindness in his soul to personally participate in such butcheries as Gettysburg and the Wilderness.

John Brown is still an enigma to the American

historian, and it is too early to place him. Writers call him a saint or a devil, according to their political persuasions. When time shall have sifted all the evidence, and our prejudices have had time to cool, I believe that we shall learn that John Brown was neither. A saint is not usually armed with a gun, nor does he violate law, murder, nor stir up wrath. Christ rebuked Peter for striking in self-defence, then how much more would he rebuke the bloody deeds of John Brown. Brown began his Virginia career as a fraud, entering the State under an assumed name, with a premeditated plan to violate the laws of the State and general government. When captured he had been as much an offender against the Union as any man in the Southern army during the four years of conflict; so he could not be called a patriot. It is better to lay aside foolish sentiment and look at these matters in a sensible light, even if we do shatter a cherished idol. Though once an admirer of John Brown, after years of careful study of the man and times, I can do no more than pronounce him a dangerous fanatic whom it were better to forget than to praise. In these days, when men are thirsting after notoriety, sounding the praises of a law breaker like John Brown, stimulates such fanatics as the Chicago anarchists to like deeds. Brown's motive may have been a good one, but a man has no more right to rob on the highway

for charity, than had Brown to adopt his means
for freeing the slaves. It is doubtful if his conduct did the cause he claimed to represent any
good. He was as much a detriment to the Republican party, as the anarchists of to-day are to the
labor party. While representing their conscientious principles, he was lawless and unscrupulous
in bringing about the desired reform. He neither
exercised prudence nor common sense in any of
his plans. His bravery was foolhardiness which
any true soldier would condemn. As none of his
sons took any prominent part in the war which
followed two years after their father's death, it
has led many to believe that their Kansas career
was more a war of plunder than sentiment. That
is a question, however, that we do not propose to
discuss in these pages.

Secession was brought about mainly by a few
extremists — abolitionists in the North, aristocrats in the South, the latter holding manual labor
in contempt, and regarding the man who toiled
as no better than the negro slave. This class of
southern aristocrats may be traced from the cava-
liers of the Cromwellian period. They early
learned to call the New Englanders Puritanic
fanatics. Yet we would not deal too severely with
the southern people. It is difficult to judge the
promptings of a man's heart if one is unfamiliar
with his surroundings. We should not forget that

slavery had existed from the earliest civilization down to 1861. Cruel masters were an exception. The slave was valuable property, whom the sensible master was careful to keep in good working condition. Naturally the abolitionists told only the worst side of the story of slavery. The effect of this system was worse on the whites than on the blacks, yet the man born and reared in the midst of such an institution could not be made to see it. He believed that the hated " abolitionists " envied him his riches, and was seeking to deprive him of them. He could not believe that the northern people were sincere. To him, all their pleading for the poor slave was sentimental hypocrisy, and his only design was to deprive him of his property from malice or envy. The underground railroads, and John Brown raids only confirmed him in this belief, and made him more stubborn. The South was greatly to blame, yet the southern people are our brothers; let us deal charitably with them. They took up the sword, and their social system perished by the sword, — let us be content. In military achievements, they were prodigies. They fought with a valor worthy of the best days of chivalry. When we consider that we enlisted almost two millions more than the South; that we lost in killed, wounded and from hospital deaths more than their entire forces; that with only one hundred thousand men in the field the last year of the war, they fought over a million, we really have not much to boast of. We may say what we please about generalship, military skill, yet the official reports of the adjutant generals, give the greatest skill, generalship and courage to the defeated. There were acts of cruelty on both sides, which had better be forgotten, and I have omitted all mention of them. In this volume and throughout this series, I have endeavored to teach the great moral principle of patriotism both North and South. Some day the South may concede that she was in the wrong, and the North that she failed to understand southern patriots. Each is a part of the grand whole. Southerners need not be ashamed of their record as soldiers; but numbers were against them, and even the South may come to see that it was best that its cause should suffer defeat.

In writing this series, I have tried to get at the truth, and have selected such matter as to me seemed most reliable. No one knows better than the historian how difficult it is to sift the truth from the great mass of error. Official records and documents are usually supposed to be correct; but in them one finds such irreconcilable contradictions, that the historian is at a loss which to choose. This is especially true of the official reports of the commanding officers in the late war. For certain statements in a former volume of this series a critic takes me to task, because I adopted the generally accepted statements of nine-tenths of the standard historians against an isolated favorite authority of his, and in a private letter expresses his amazement that I should prefer Bancroft, Prince, Dr. Robinson, and like authority to his "one book," which differs a hair on some immaterial points. In this volume, from the multiplicity of worthy witnesses on both sides, I have been frequently at a loss which to choose; but have in every case taken what to me seemed most authentic, without fear or favor.

Mark Stevens, a brother of Arthur Stevens, hero of the story "Humbled Pride," and son of Albert Stevens, a soldier of the war of 1812, is the chief actor in this volume. About this fictitious family, whose ancestors are traced to the cabin boy on board the *Santa Maria*, coming with Columbus on his first voyage in 1492, I have tried to weave the history of the United States. As every life has a plot of its own, each man having a destiny marked out for himself, so have I given to the Stevens family each a different career, at the same time preserving inherent family characteristics, chief of which are honesty and patriotism. I believe that if those principles were taught at every fireside, our country would never again be threatened with dissolution.

JOHN R. MUSICK.

KIRKVILLE, MO., January 15, 1894.

TABLE OF CONTENTS.

CONTENTS.

LIST OF ILLUSTRATIONS.

UNION.

CHAPTER I.

LOVE AND MADNESS.

ABOUT the middle of the after-noon on a bleak October day, a close carriage driven by a negro coachman, drawn by a pair of blooded but jad-ed horses reached Crum-mels Junction. Crummels Junction in the ante-bel-lum days was much like the ordinary junctions of to-day. People who travel much, never cease to wonder why the crossest depot agents that can be found are always located at junctions, where there is nothing but a depot, a store and a saloon, but such seems to be the case. The carriage crossed the track, which seemed to require all the strength of the horses, for the rails and ties were above the embankment, and the section manager apparently

1

had taken special pains to have that crossing particularly inconvenient and dangerous to anything
lighter than an ox cart.

The cold, raw wind sweeping across a stretch of
bleak prairie, dotted here and there with houses,
wood sheds, hay stacks, and rail fences, howled
about the store, saloon and depot in a mournful
manner.   There was not a tavern or public house
at Crummels, and the travellers in the carriage
evidently did not expect to tarry long at this uninviting spot.

The vehicle was an elegant conveyance and, had
the air been balmy, would have brought all the
inhabitants of the junction out to gaze on it in
open-mouthed wonder.   The negro coachman drove
it as near to the platform as he could and, alight-
ing with the good manners of a well-bred servant
in an aristocratic household, opened the door of
the carriage saying:

" Heah ye are, massa !"

A young man, well muffled, alighted from the
carriage to the platform, and assisted a tall lady,
heavily veiled, to get out.   Another gentleman
appeared, and the two half led and half carried
from the coach a feeble young creature, who,
though she was closely veiled, one could see was
an invalid.

Her head drooped, and she seemed only half

conscious. As soon as she was on the platform, the woman who had preceded her came to her side and in a low affectionate tone said:

" Do you feel stronger, dear?"

The invalid made no response, but stared at her with her great eyes through the veil. Those large and beautiful eyes, sad to say, were expressionless. The blank stare of insanity or delirium beamed from them. She saw nothing real and her poor, tortured mind could scarce recognize those friends who were doing all possible for her comfort.

" Let us go into the depot," said one of the men, shivering with cold.

" Do you see any one in there, George?" the tall lady asked.

" No, the place seems almost if not quite deserted; but I suppose some one will be here before the train arrives." They entered the depot waiting-room,—one of those diminutive affairs always found at out-of-the-way stations, over which the most ill-natured and inaccessible agent presides. The floor was freshly swept; there was a fire in the round, large stove, three of the most inconvenient benches which a depot architect's ingenuity can invent, were fastened to the walls. The walls were ornamented only with unreliable railroad maps, timetables and misleading railroad advertising. There was a square box, two-thirds full of sawdust, well moistened and stained with tobacco juice.

The sad little party did not give the apartment a detailed survey. Three of the party looked fatigued, and the poor young lady, or rather girl, for she was scarcely more, had an air of settled melancholy and indifference.

"Here is a seat for you," said the young man called George, with a sigh. "It is the best we can do."

"Come, dear, sit down——there now, lean your head on me if you are tired," the lady said to the invalid.

George went to the office to see when the train left, and found the ticket window closed.

"Isn't the agent in there, George?" asked the other young man.

"No, Charles."

"Well, if you will look around you may find him," said Charles with a grim smile. "Probably he is helping unload freight, or upon a side track coupling cars, or over across the railroad helping a farmer kill hogs. Or maybe he has gone to another town with a team to carry some passengers."

George felt very much inclined to utter some unpleasant remarks about the agent; but as his pitying gaze alighted on the unfortunate object of his journey, his eyes grew dim with moisture, and he heaved a sigh. Waiting at a depot is never pleasant, and at a country junction, such as Crummels, it is particularly unpleasant. It seemed as if the management of the road had determined that no one who passed that spot should ever forget it.

"Are you tired?" asked the young man called George, going over to where the woman and invalid sat.

"Oh, yes," was the answer with a half-drawn sigh; "but we must make the best of it; can you learn nothing of the train?"

"No; the genius who presides over this important post seems invisible," said George bitterly. There was a spice of satire in his words, yet they were full of sadness. Hopes and ambitions crushed, a heart overburdened and bowed beneath its weight of sorrow, were all expressed in his low, sad voice. George with his hands clasped behind his back, began walking back and forth across the floor of the narrow depot. Charles went out to the platform and instructed the colored driver to go back about a mile to a farm house, feed the horses, and wait until the train came, then to return for him.

"I am going to stay with them until they are off," he added.

"Yes, massa—I'll come."

The negro was anxious to be gone, for the chill

winds seemed to pierce his bones, and he turned
the horses about and sped away. While all this
was transpiring, George was sadly pacing the narrow confines of the depot asking himself when and
how this would all end. The poor young girl,
whose white face rested on the shoulder of her lady
attendant, had closed her eyes as if to sleep, but
only to see visions more terrible than a sane mind
can imagine. Suddenly a rude, heavy tramp was
heard outside, the door was swung open, and a
man with red face, blue cap, and pencil behind his
ear entered. He closed the door with such a bang,
that the poor girl, whose nerves were already
shattered, started up with a half-uttered shriek,
and it required the soothing words and caresses
of her companion for several moments to quiet
her.

But what did the station agent care for a nervous
girl? He seemed to have more business than the
general manager of the road. Drawing a great
bunch of nerve-shattering keys, he dashed one
into the lock of the side door and, opening it, entered, banged the door after him, and threw up
the ticket window, as if to give the outside world
a view of the great man at work. He sat at a
desk and proceeded to count some money which he
took from his vest pocket with an air of importance
of which the treasurer of the United States might

well be proud. Men have an idea that inaccessibility is evidence of greatness, and there is not a more inaccessible man than the manager of a country depot station. The smaller the station the more inaccessible.

"When will the train come?" George ventured to ask.

The brow of the superior being corrugated, and he went on counting a pile of one-dollar bills, acting as if he had a very dim idea that he had been spoken to; but he waited until the money was in the safe, and he had turned the knob, and then answered, "I don't know," so sharply that, had George been

"WHEN WILL THE TRAIN COME?"

alone, he would have walked to the next station. This important task done, the agent bustled out of his narrow box-like office, slammed the door of the stove, as though he was afraid George would steal a stick of wood, or run away with the lining. Although George was wealthy, and the care of his horses cost him more than the agent's salary, the agent seemed to regard him as a three-card-monte man, and his entire party as intruders.

Going out, the agent closed the door with another bang which aroused the invalid, and once more brought forth a cry of dread and fear. George was inclined to follow him and punch his head, but checked this impulse. He went out on the platform, and saw this superior being helping a woman, evidently his landlady, hang out clothes in the back yard. This task done, he fell to splitting stove wood out of old railroad ties.

Night drew nearer, it became more drear, and the station agent entered, lighted a greasy lamp in the waiting-room, chucked more wood in the stove, and lighted a lamp in his own apartment.

Uncomplaining and patient, the young woman sat with the afflicted maiden at her side, trying to keep her wandering mind to the realities of life. This was impossible, for the vagaries of delusion constantly haunted her. At times she saw what seemed starry heavens, which were accompanied by indescribable horrors, so that she wanted to fly. There was ever present a demon of fear. She heard voices calling her from out of space, and, turning, found no one. She had the most unaccountable nightmare, in which she was tormented by fiends and goblins. At times, her tormentors assumed the shape of the devil, and at others of a sea serpent. Sometimes she seemed to go off into space, eluding their grasp. This was accompanied by a sense of suffocation, a feeling as of one coming out from the influence of ether. Raising her pale, yet beautiful face to the woman on whose shoulder she had been resting, she asked:

" Has he come?"

" Who, dear?"

" The doctor—the one who is to drive away these demons."

" Not yet, be patient, dear—all will be well."

" Oh, you say so, Lucy, yet you don't know—you can't know."

" Won't you try to sleep, dear?"

" No, this is no hotel. Call the servant—where is Maria?"

The station-agent came back again. He was in his element, for the train was two hours late, and he sat working at his telegraphic instrument as if the world rested on his shoulders. The patient George listened to the constant click of the instrument, and would have given ten dollars to know what was going over the wires. Occasionally the station-agent laughed at something the instrument said, and just as George began to think the news of the world was being stored in his massive brain, a young country lout in blue drillen roundabout, his pants in his boots, entered, wiping his nose on his mitten. The agent turned and, in a most commonplace manner, said:

"Hello, Jack, there is goin' to be a dance at the hop yard at Baylis Siding to-night, and they want us to come up on No. 4."

"How d'ye know, Charley?" the lout asked.

"Susie just now told me."

George now realized that the agent, all these long hours that he had been watching the varied expressions of his calm and mysterious face, had been chaffing with the female operator at the next station. The big country bumpkin took a chew of plug tobacco and said:

"I guess I will go and brush up a little and put on a clean shirt before No. 4 comes." To which the operator responded:

"Be sure to be on hand, Jack; we'll have a daisy time at the dance."

Great consolation this bit of information was to George, who was waiting with greatest of anxiety to know how soon they could leave this miserable place. He turned away from the narrow window and glanced at the two females sitting in the corner. His brother Charles who had been promenading a few moments on the damp platform entered the station and in a subdued tone asked:

"Can you get anything out of that idiot?"

"No; he's too much interested in a dance that

comes off somewhere to-night, to pay much attention to the business of the road."

Then George turned his sad gray eyes in pity
on the unfortunate maiden, and asked:

" Do you think she can stand it much longer?"

" I don't know."

" Oh, it is awful! My God! why should the
train be late at this time, above all others?"

" I don't know, George. This has been one of
the most unfortunate events of our lives."

" Yes; it seems like a horrible nightmare." He
folded his arms across his breast and walked back
and forth, softly, so as not to disturb the unfortunate maiden. Then he came to his brother's side
and said:

" Charles, try and console mother; if possible,
reconcile her to this step. It is the best that could
be done."

" I know it, George."

" Mother is a true Christian. Tell her to put
her faith in Him who comforts the afflicted."

" I will, George, though I don't just now feel
very religious," and he cast a savage glance at the
window of the ticket office.

George muttered some unintelligible words between his teeth and said something about horse-
whipping a puppy for his impudence, then went
out on the platform to try to pick up an acquaint-

ance with the man who ran the horse-power
threshing machine. He was more communicative
than the station agent, for he did not live in such
an exalted atmosphere. There is no man who
knows more than the junction agent, about everything, if you only possess the gift of drawing him
out. Though only four trains a day stop at his
station, and they halt only long enough to let off
some unfortunate wretch whom circumstances
force to get off, however reluctant he may be to
do so, the agent is in his element for a brief moment. He addresses the conductor as " Jim," or
" George," or " Billy," and asks, with a show of
interest as deep as a division superintendent, where
he passed " No. 1," and if " No. 6" is going to
be on time. He may even ask something about
railroad stocks in a manner that would convince
one that he was bulling the market, when in reality he might not have eleven dollars left from his
last month's salary.. Such an agent was at Crummels Junction, and had not George been weighed
down with grief and humiliation, he might have
resented the fellow's impudence.

After a few moments on the platform, George
took a glance down the long railroad track along
which it was hoped the train would come, and
strained his ear to catch the sound. Already it
was night, and the damp fog, which had settled

like a pall over the entire landscape, seemed to cut off the entire world, and no sound save a farmer calling hogs, or the barking of dogs reached the ears of the young man. With a sigh, he entered the depot, shivering with cold and damp. The patient Lucy was still supporting the delirious maiden.

"Is it coming?" she asked.

He shook his head.

"Are you tired, Lucy?"

"Yes."

"Let me sit by her while you walk about, and rest yourself."

"I think we had better not disturb her now."

"Is she asleep?" he asked in low, cautious voice.

"I don't know——"

At this the afflicted maiden started up, saying:

"What is it? what did you say? Is she coming? I have told you all the time she would; but you would not believe me. George—George— what are you thinking about?"

"It is all right," George said.

"All right—that is what you have told me all the time; but didn't I see her put the poison in the cup? Where is Maria? she saw her too. Maria, Maria!"

"Hush, dear, Maria is not here," Lucy said in

a low, soothing tone. "We are travelling now, we are going soon."

"Are we going home, Lucy?"

"Yes, dear."

"Now you won't deceive me, will you?"

"No, no, dear."

"Oh, Lucy, I want to go home—I want to go home—why did they ever take me away? There are no serpents nor insects there, such as I see here, day and night,—oh—there is one on my hand!"

"No, dear, it is not——"

"Take it off!"

Lucy made a gesture, as if brushing something away, and the invalid said:

"There, see, Lucy, you have taken off my hand! —put it on again."

"It is all right, dear," Lucy responded, carefully caressing her hand, and soothingly assuring her that she would be cared for.

"I am so glad, Lucy, that we are going home at last. Oh, it has been so long—so long since I left my home—I have suffered so much—where is Maria?—Has the doctor come yet?"

"Be quiet, dear, we have strangers about us now."

"Sing to me, Lucy."

Lucy, whose voice was choking with grief,

whispered that she could not sing, and as a mother soothes an affrighted child, so she quieted the nerve-shattered maiden, coaxing her to be quiet until the train came, when they would go.

For the hundredth time, George had gone to the platform to look for the train and came back disappointed.

" Can I get tickets now?" he asked, going to the window.

" Yes; how many do you want?" growled the agent.

" Three."

" Return-trip tickets?"

" Only two of us will return—one will not!" and his voice was almost choked with grief. The tickets were stamped and handed to him. He put down a golden double eagle and received his change. Then he sat down near his female companions, and bowing his head on his chest, closed his eyes.

People who travel soon learn to dread junction waiting. Nowhere in the world does time hang so heavily as at the station; but when one has an invalid with whom it is important to reach their destination as quickly as possible, time hangs with double weight upon them. George was almost in a state of unconsciousness when his brother Charles said :

"George, it's coming."

"At last!—thank God!" he ejaculated, starting up.

There was a little bustle in the depot.   A dozen people had entered to see the train come in. Most of them were country boys in brown home-spun and slouched hats who stood with hands in their pockets, and in open-mouthed wonder gazed at the monster as it went puffing by.   Through this crowd of idle loafers, they conveyed the un-fortunate maiden, who shrank from sight of every one, and seemed liable to go frantic at the slight-est noise.

George heard the agent accost the engineer familiarly with:

"Hello, Roxy, you're late."

"Yes."

"How long before No. 4 will come?"

"In half an hour."

"Glad o' that, we're goin' up to the dance."

"Where?"

"At Baylises Siding."

"Wish I could go."

It required the united efforts of the three rela-tives to get the unfortunate maiden through the noisy crowd and hissing steam to the cars.   The conductor was shouting:

"All aboard!"

"Do you run a sleeping coach on this train?" asked George.

" No."

Sleeping coaches at this time were very uncommon. They were shown to the rear car, which was reserved for ladies, and found seats upholstered with dark leather, but more comfortable than the benches of the depot. The elegant red velvet plush seats and reclining chairs which make railroad travel a luxury to-day were not common then.

They got comfortable seats, and George said:

" Lucy, I will sit by and watch over her to-night. Take this vacant seat behind us and try to get some sleep."

Charles, who had followed them into the train with bandboxes and travelling bags, bade George adieu, kissed Lucy and the invalid affectionately, and then darted out as the car began to move. The louts on the platform uttered diabolical and senseless yells as the train rolled away.

" What is it? George—George, are you here?"

" Yes."

" What is it?"

" We are going now!"

" Home?"

" Yes, home!" he answered with a suppressed sob.

2

Then he thought that only two of them would come back, and a moisture gathered in his eyes. "It's for the best—I know it's for the best," he said.

At his side the unfortunate being crouched, sometimes covering her head, and shivering with fear. The conductor passed through taking up the tickets. When George, worn out from excessive watching and anxiety, closed his eyes for a moment, he was startled by a movement on the part of the girl at his side. Looking at her, he found her sitting bolt upright staring about her, with her great, insane eyes, as if she were seeking some one, or looking for an opportunity to fly.

"Lie down; place your head on my shoulder," he said in a low, gentle tone.

She obeyed and, nestling her head on his broad shoulder, as she had so often done in childhood, she whispered:

"George, are we going home?"

"Yes."

It almost broke his heart to deceive her; but he could not tell the truth. Yes, George lied. The home to which he was taking her was one from which all shrink with dread. He had ever been her favorite brother, for he was almost fifteen years her senior, and she had looked up to him in early childhood with the utmost confidence. In all her career of fantastic madness, even though she denied father and mother, George was to her the same George of her early childhood, ever trusted, ever noble and grand. His voice soothed her alarm and drove away those demoniacal creatures of " bromide," when no other would.

"George, am I going home?"

"Yes."

Then she was quiet for awhile. Only the sullen roar of iron wheels on the damp cold rails fell on their ears. The seat before them was occupied by a large middle-aged bald-headed gentleman, who half lay and half sat in it. Over the back of the seat could be seen his bald cranium, bare and white, glistening in the dim light, and when the train stopped as it occasionally did, the snoring of the sleeper attested that his slumber was profound.

The sleeper was in blissful ignorance of the fact that a madwoman was in the seat behind him, and in his dreamland wanderings had forgotten railroad travel and all its inconveniences.

George never slept. Once or twice he was dozing, but at the slightest rustling of his sister's silk dress, he was aroused. He found her sitting up again leaning forward with fingers ready to pluck something, and, to his mortification, found the bald head of the sleeper in front the object of her diseased fancy.

"Come, come, sister," he said soothingly, "don't do that! lie down," and he drew her head on his shoulder.

"George, am I going home?" she asked again.

"Yes."

"I don't believe it. This is not the road."

"We will come to the right road."

"Where is Maria? I want Maria."

"Don't you remember you became angry at her and said she should not come with you?"

"Yes, I believe I did; but how am I to do without a maid?"

"Lucy will be your maid," he answered. "Come now, try to go to sleep."

"I can't—when I try, there is something that comes crawling all over me."

"It is nothing; it is only your imagination. Don't you know I won't let you be harmed?"

She was again soothed, and this time he thought she slept. He was so tired that he could scarcely keep his eyes open; and despite all his anxiety and watchfulness, had once more begun to sink away into slumberland, when the rustling of the silk dress at his side awoke him. Again she was sitting up leaning over the seat in front. That bald head before her seemed to have some special attraction, and fingers and thumb were held as if to grab something. He was only in time to prevent her giving the sleeper's bare pate a nip which would undoubtedly have aroused him.

" You must not do this,—you must not. "

" Why? "

" You must not wake the stranger. "

" But I saw it crawling there! "

" What? "

" The bug or spider. It's on his head, and I want to pluck it off; look and you will see it. "

" No, no; it's only your imagination. Do lie quiet. Don't disturb the stranger. "

" Stranger? why, brother, he is no stranger. "

" He is. "

" Isn't that brother Charles? "

" No; Charles was left back at Crummels Junction. "

" Is that so? well, I had forgotten. I thought it was him, and that the spider might bite him. "

Then she laid her head down against her brother's shoulder and slept a long time. Fatigue had at last overcome the abnormal activity of her brain, and she did not awake until broad day. The train was still flying along through a wooded country. The trees and fences were dripping from the dampness, and as they were whirled past farm houses, they saw evidences of life. At one a man was feeding some hungry pigs, at another a farmer was seen washing his face in a tin basin by the rainwater barrel. He took a towel and wiped his eyes, then stared at the train. A little further on they saw a negro boy riding a colt, which was frightened at the train and trying to run away. On, on and on they whirled, across a creek spanned by a bridge and through a grove. Next they sped through a village without stopping. They saw a negro woman standing on the rear porch with a broom in her hand, and a red bandanna handkerchief about her head. There were people in the streets, in stores and at the depot.

On they sped like the wind and a few moments were among the stony hills. The train whirled on, and as the hour grew later, they saw men and negroes going to the villages in wagons, on horseback or on foot. The face of the country had changed.

Soon there was evidence of approaching a larger town or city. Lucy, who had been awake for some time, asked George:

" Is she asleep? "

" No. "

" Did she sleep during the night? "

" Yes, some. "

At this, the invalid started up and asked:

" What is it? "

" We will soon be there, dear, be quiet. "

" Lucy, take my place in this seat, " said George.

She did so. The sick girl had by this time attracted the attention of nearly all in the car. George went to the conductor, who was entering at the front door, and held a short consultation with him. On returning, the bald-headed man, who had waked up, heard him say:

" The conductor says we will find carriages at the depot to take us. "

" How far is it? "

" We will be there in ten minutes. "

" I am so glad. "

George was both glad and sorry. He was like one going to the funeral of a near relative, glad when it would be over, yet filled with grief while it was transpiring. He was a young man, tall and handsome, with a strong and vigorous frame, but care had furrowed his cheeks, and there were flecks of gray in his hair, which could not have been seen six months ago.

At last the train ran into the depot, and the invalid was assisted from the coach. The two young women sat in a great crowded depot, while George went out to hunt for a conveyance. He found one and came back. There was a lunch room near, and he said:

" Lucy, won't you have a bite of breakfast and some coffee? "

" No. "

"Don't you feel faint?"

"Yes; but let us get this over with."

She asked the invalid, who sat staring into vacancy, if she would not have some breakfast, and she shook her head. The carriage was ready, a trunk and travelling bags were placed on it, and the three were soon ensconced in the vehicle, speeding out of the town.

"Charles, Charles," called the invalid.

"Don't call, dear; it is not Charles."

"Isn't that Charles with Pete on the box?"

"No, dear."

"Then tell Pete to go back."

"It is not Pete; see, we are going to your new home."

At this moment, the carriage made a sweep round the bend in the road and came in full view of a large, elegant building several stories in height, with vast wings and windows, and beautiful grounds ornamented with trees. There was ease and elegance evinced there; but the windows had iron gratings like a prison. At sight of it, George's head fell. The carriage rolled up a beautiful drive to the front of the building, and the party alighted. A negro slave showed them into the institution, and on the right was an office where the president and principal physician, a large, well-preserved man, past middle age, with black eyes and iron-gray hair, was found sitting at his desk. He rose on their entrance, for by the air and rich dress of the people, he saw at once that they were of the wealthy class. It only needed a glance for him to see his patient, and he said:

"She is tired, let her sit in this easy-chair." When she was seated he asked of George, "How long has she been in this condition?"

"It is about three weeks since we noticed any change, doctor."

Then the doctor opened a book, in which he wrote a history of the young maiden and her disease. When he had done so, Lucy, whose anxiety to understand the cause overcame all medical propriety, asked:

"Doctor, what is it?"

The lips of the doctor were compressed a moment, and then he said:

"Bromide."

"Can she be cured?"

"There is a hope." He got up, muttering something about "accursed quackery," and rang a bell. A lady with a mild, kind face appeared, and to her the new patient was consigned, the doctor merely saying:

"Take her to the hospital ward."

They accompanied her through long corridors, where there were iron doors, which closed with a bang. They passed gibbering, chattering idiots and wild-eyed lunatics, until a quiet wing of the institution was gained, where they were met by another sweet-faced woman, a professional nurse. With her, George and Lucy held a conversation, in which the latter, with tears streaming down her cheeks, said:

"Be good to her, give her all the advantages you can, and you shall be well paid for your trouble." Some jingling coins fell in the nurse's hands. The parting was heart-breaking. How could it be otherwise, when the poor sick girl, scarcely more than a child, begged them not to leave her in this strange place? But necessity compelled them to do so, and they went away.

Three weeks later the newspapers all over the land published one of the most sensational stories of which the American press can boast. As the reader will see from the following clipping from one of the daily papers, the names were suppressed. This was obviously done to shield the officials in charge of the institution, who must have been guilty of the grossest negligence. One of the newspaper statements was as follows:

"LOVE AND MADNESS.

"A PAIR OF LUNATICS ELOPE FROM AN INSANE ASYLUM AND WED.

"A fact has just leaked out, which rivals anything in romance. The novelist might cudgel his brain for years,

AWAY THEY FLEW, PURSUED BY THE ANGRY MALE ATTENDANT, WHOSE HORSE
FELL AND DISLOCATED HIS SHOULDER.

and never invent a story more exquisitely fantastic. It seems that an insane asylum, less than a thousand miles from this city, is the theatre of this remarkable episode. A few weeks ago, a young man, suffering from some nervous complaint, aggravated by quack treatment, until he was laboring under delirium, was confined in the asylum. He soon evinced some signs of recovery and was given the privilege of the grounds. One day, while with his attendant, he met a young and very beautiful female patient. Insane people have strange freaks, and it is supposed that with these two lunatics it was a case of love at first sight. How they wooed each other in the asylum, where the male and female wards are kept separate, and where they could hardly see each other, unless when with attendants, is a mystery which the investigation now in progress may clear up. Perhaps he, Romeo-like, met his insane Juliet on the balcony while the nurses slept, as did Capulet. Be that as it may, they certainly met more than once, and their plan of escape had method in it, even if it was madness. The two, being children of wealthy parents, had, among other privileges, saddle horses, and one day while riding about the grounds, the insane Romeo espied his Juliet mounted, and riding with her attendant, and at a preconcerted signal the lovers dashed out at the open gate like the wind, and away they flew along the road, pursued by the angry male attendant, whose horse fell down and dislocated his shoulder. On they sped for ten miles to the house of a local minister, whom they asked to marry them. Here the cunning peculiar to madness was exercised, and the good parson who performed the ceremony had not the slightest idea he was wedding a pair of lunatics. Having imposed on the good parson, the youngster paid him ten dollars in gold, and, with his bride, set out—Heaven only knows where, when they were overtaken by the authorities of the asylum, and taken back. It is said that these young folks are both from wealthy and respectable families, and

under ordinary circumstances the wedding would have
been unobjectionable.   As it is, however, the indignant
friends and relatives of these romantic patients have removed them from the institution, and the atmosphere in
that locality is growing decidedly warm, in the nature of
a legal investigation."

CHAPTER II.

JACKSONVILLE, Florida, is famous all over the world. To the pale-faced northerner it is the Mecca of his hopes, and yet in the ante-bellum days it was scarce known outside the State. It is not two score years since there was a corn-field on the site of Bay Street, now the chief avenue of a city of over seventeen thousand inhabitants, which from 1880 to 1890 increased in population 124.85 per cent. Jacksonville was once known as "Cow Ford." There the "King's Road" in the old days, crossed the river, and connected the northern settlements with St. Augustine. During the war, it ran to decay. It was strongly fortified, and was clung to desperately by the Confederates. The Union troops occupied it several times, and on the third assault a fire broke out, which did much damage. At the close of the great struggle, the grass stood waist high in the streets, and the cattle had taken refuge from the sun in the deserted houses. Since Florida became famous as a health resort and winter garden, northern people have swept in so resistlessly that so far as its artificial features are concerned, the city has grown up according to the New England pattern, though the foliage, climate and sun are the antipodes of those of the North.

It is not the Jacksonville of to-day, but the town or village which nestled there in 1858 and 1859 to which we call the attention of the reader. It was a small, insignificant spot, yet as the topography of the country never changes, one may judge something of its characteristics then, by seeing it now. It was a frosty morning in January, when the wheezy little coast steamer ran up the river to the village of Jacksonville. Thin flakes of ice had formed in the little pools along the shore, and the pale young man who stood on the deck, drew the folds of his cloak closer about him, and grumbled:

"If this is the tropical region, where winter never comes, I see but little change after all."

In vain those who had been there before told him that this was an exceptional winter for Florida, that this "cold snap" would last but a few hours; he still grumbled and vowed he would find warmer weather or cross the line. The scenery along the shore was drear and uninviting. Here and there, in the forest gaps, the negroes had kindled huge fires, and were grouped about them, toasting their heads, and freezing their backs. Now and then the traveller caught glimpses of beautiful thickets; or long stretches of field carpeted with thick growths of palmetto, while in other places might be seen the distant pine barrens, and log cabins swarming with black-skinned negroes.

Mark Stevens was entering the " Sunny South" for the first time. Of northern climes and middle States he was thoroughly familiar. He was a native of Kentucky; but the principal part of his boyhood and young manhood had been spent in Massachusetts. His pale cheeks and thoughtful mien betokened the student. He had completed a course at Harvard, and, as his health had suffered from over-exertion, he had taken the advice of some friends and gone South. Mark's parents still lived in Kentucky. He had relatives in Massachusetts and some distant relatives in Florida, whom he expected to meet. Reuben Stevens was a wealthy planter in Florida. His son Alec, a wild, harum-scarum young fellow, yet kind-hearted, and generous, was with Mark one year in college, and made him promise to come to Florida and visit them. He was now on his way to make that visit, and as he entered the gateway of the great peninsula, he paused for a moment to reflect upon its history. Fact and fancy here wandered hand in hand. The airy chronicles of the ancient fathers hovered upon the confines of the impossible. The austere northerner and the cynical European murmur incredulously at the tales of modern writers who grow enthusiastic over the charms of this new winter paradise. Yet what of fiction should exceed in romantic interest the history of this venerable State? What artist could paint foliage whose splendors would equal that of the virgin forests of the Oclawaha and Indian rivers? What " fountain of youth" could be imagined more redolent with enchantment than the " Silver Spring," which is to-day annually visited by fifty thousand tourists? The subtle moonlight, the perfect glory of the dying sun as he sinks below a horizon fringed with fantastic trees, the perfume faintly borne from the orange grove, the murmuring music of the waves along the inlets, and the mangrove-covered banks are beyond words.

This American Italy lies in the latitude of northern Mexico, the desert of Sahara, Central Arabia, Southern China, and northern Hindostan; but its heats are tempered by the Gulf of Mexico on one side, and the Gulf Stream, which flows along the eastern coast for three hundred miles, on the other. Over the level breadth of ninety miles between these two waters, constantly blow odorous and health-giving ocean winds, and under their influence, aided by the genial sun, springs up an almost miraculous sub-tropical vegetation. It is the home of the pal-metto, and the cabbage palm, the live-oak and the cypress, the mistletoe, with its bright green leaves and red berries, the Spanish moss, the ambitious mangrove, the stately magnolia, the *smilax china*, the orange, the myrtle, the water-lily, the jasmine, the cork tree, the sisal-hemp, the grape, and the cocoanut. There the northerner, wont to boast of the brilliant sunsets of his own clime, finds all his past experiences outdone. In the winter months, soft breezes come caressingly; the whole peninsula is carpeted with blossoms, and the birds sing sweetly in the untrodden thickets. It has the charm of wildness, of mystery; it is untamed; civilization has not stained it. No wonder the Seminoles fought ferociously ere they suffered themselves to be banished from this charming land.

The vessel landed, and Mark was conducted to one of those old-fashioned southern taverns by a negro slave, while two or three more carried his luggage. The sea air and frosty morning had quite chilled his frame, and he asked to be taken to a room at once where there was a fire. There were fire-places in nearly all the rooms, but no fire. Two negro boys brought pine sticks to his apart-ment, and a fire was soon kindled. His room was carpetless. There was a bed, two or three large arm-chairs, an old-fashioned mantel on which were a pair of old-fashioned candlesticks, a pair of fire tongs, a centre table, and a quaint old bookcase, in which were four or five odd-looking volumes.

" Won't you have breakfast?" the landlord asked, entering the room.

" Can you serve it here?"

" Yes."

" I am so infernally chilled, I don't want to leave the fire."

" I guess it's a leetle airish on the river this mornin'."

" I thought you never had winter here?" growled Mark.

" Wall, we do sometimes have a cold snap; but this'll be gone afore mo'nin'. Ye'll see it warm enough in a few hours."

" I hope so."

Breakfast was served as Mark requested in the room. His host came and sat at his side, and talked with him in the interval about the north and the ever-interesting question of slavery and the " doings in congress." The landlord was a typical southerner, who declared if the " Abolitionists succeed, we'll secede." Mark was tired, and the landlord, who was a kind-hearted man, saw his condition, so he left him, advising him to lie down and take a nap. He took the advice and extended his nap late into the day. He had supper and dinner together, and again went to bed to sleep until sunrise.

The Jacksonville landlord proved to be a weather prophet. There was a wonderful change in a few hours. To Mark it was remarkable. Transferred from the trying climate of the North into the gentle atmosphere of the Florida peninsula, seemed like being transported to fairy land. The sun was shining brightly and the balmy breeze of summer was wafted in at the open casement. After breakfast he went out on the veranda and, seating himself in an arm-chair, gazed over the pretty square in Jacksonville. His face was fanned by the warm January breeze, and the chippering of the birds mingled with the music of a negro's banjo over in a shanty. The lazy, ne'er-do-well black boys, sporting in the sand, so abundant in all the roads, had the unconscious pose and careless grace of Neapolitan beggars. Occasionally a dusky Indian maiden, with her almost Grecian features, and long, straight hair, was seen crossing the road, with a face beautiful in its duskiness, as was ever the face of olive-brown maid in Messina. This is the South, slumbrous, voluptuous, round and graceful. Here beauty peeps from every door yard. Mere existence is a pleasure, exertion a bore. Through orange-trees and grand oaks, thickly bordering the broad avenues of the village, gleamed the wide current of the St. John's river.

Mark sat gazing listlessly, dreamily upon the enchanting vision before him, when he was suddenly startled from a revery, painful, but sweet, by a merry peal of rippling laughter, and, turning his eyes in another direction, he saw two lovely girls, shy, blushing and mischievous, coming slowly along the street. They could not have been over eighteen years of age, perhaps not so old. Mark saw that the one nearest him had golden hair flowing in sunny waves about a pair of beautiful shoulders. Her face was slightly averted at first; but anon she turned the gaze of a pair of large blue eyes full upon him. If the peal of merry laughter was like rippling music to his sad soul, the face was like a burst of sunshine at midnight. The face was wondrous fair, every feature was exquisite in its perfection, regularity and the beauty of its curves. The form was symmetrical, and as she walked by, it was with the grace of a queen whose every motion might be set to music.

Mark stared at her longer than good manners would have warranted. She blushed slightly, her head drooped, and she passed on, like a bright dream which, once gone, is forever beyond recall. He thought of her, he dreamed of her, and in his imagination wove bright castles for his nameless love. How foolish he was—he knew her not— and perhaps would never see her again. He spent a whole week in Jacksonville before Alec arrived to take him a twenty-five-mile ride to the plantation of his father, and did not see the bright being again. Had he known her name, he might have inquired for her.

One bright day, Alec arrived in a two-wheeled gig, quite suitable to Florida roads. He was the same harum-scarum care-for-naught, but good-hearted fellow, Mark had known three years before at college. Leaping from his vehicle, he came bounding up to the veranda where Mark sat, crying:

"Hello, Mark! Mark, old boy, what are you doing here? Why didn't you hire a nigger to bring you out?"

"I was taking a rest, Alec."

"A rest! by Jove, I believe you. Say, old boy, how long have you been here?"

"A little over a week."

"A week—great guns—over a week! Why didn't you send me word sooner, and I'd a been after you in no time?"

"As I said, Alec, I was a little tired, and I

wanted to rest; besides I found this country an excellent study———."

"Study!—by thunder, you've been studying too much; that's what ails you. Why, you are as pale as a ghost. Did you break down before you got through?"

"No, I graduated with honors," Mark answered proudly; "but I was sick a long time afterward," he added sadly.

"And you came here to recruit———"

"Yes."

"By George, you couldn't a come to a better place, my boy. Well, it's too much of a trip to start back to-day. I'll stay over until to-morrow, and then we will start early."

This arrangement made, the mules were removed from the vehicle to the stable by a pair of lazy negroes, and Alec and Mark took a walk about the village, talking over their old college days, and laughing at some of their merry frolics more easily remembered than Greek lessons.

"I am glad you came, Mark. It's just the thing to do. We'll bring the color back to your cheeks. Such hunting and fishing as we will have, you never dreamed of in your philosophy."

They sat up until late that night, and, like school boys, both slept in the same bed and talked each other to sleep. They got an early start next morning and, with Mark's lightest trunk strapped on behind the vehicle, rolled away along the sandy road, which was a constantly shifting panorama of scenery.

Rounding a bend in the road, they came upon a scene which might have made a fortune for an artist. Before them could be seen the deep, glossy green of a thrifty orange grove, where nestled enough well-set young oranges and white blossoms to make glad the heart of the owner. In the foreground was a mule, whose characteristics were a meek and lowly carriage of the head, a general lack of adipose tissue and a gait that would have made Jehu weep. Adorning her lank person was a harness, mostly collar, by which she was attached to an ancient buckboard. On the seat were two persons, whom they failed to recognize because of the broad rims of their sun-hats. Each held a child, and the gentleman was supplied with a small tree with which he evidently entertained some hopes of animating the statue-like mule. A lunch basket, wraps and fishing-rods were strongly suggestive of a picnic excursion. The little group of persons gathered near consisted of a white-haired man who looked on the turnout with the proud gaze of ownership, a lady in a sun-bonnet, who took equal satisfaction in a brood of nine chickens she was feeding, and a man with a hoe resting on his shoulder, who resembled an exaggerated exclamation point. About three-fourths of his height was given up to a pair of spider-like legs, and the other fourth to a set of ribs and a pair of drooping shoulders from which dangled arms reaching well down to the knees. An elbow in his neck thrust his head far in advance of his body. He had a weazened face, pinched features, and a shaggy brown beard. This man is known to farhe all the world over by two euphonious titles— "Before taking," and "Florida Cracker."

Passing over a slight eminence, this interesting group was lost to their view, and they toiled on through the deep sand. A landscape indescribably beautiful lay about them. On every side was a picture. On one side woods, thickly pillared with tall pines and richly carpeted with their long brown needles. Yellow, white and purple wild flowers lifted their bright faces to be kissed by the slanting sunbeams that fell through the scanty foliage overhead. It seemed as if summer had come in a day. Not two weeks before Mark had seen thin flakes of ice near the coast, and not fifty miles away, he was in the midst of perpetual blooming Spring. Mocking-birds, blue-birds, butcher-birds and song sparrows vied with each other in entertaining their feathered friends of less vocal talent. Robins ran on the ground silent, big

and brilliant butterflies flitted to and fro, and the
wind soughing through the pines, breathed a tran-
quillizing lullaby over all. In other directions,
through clearings, lakes of various sizes and shapes,
having neither inlet nor outlet, yet clear as crystal,
gleamed in the morning sun. The graceful slopes
reaching to their banks were
covered with mingled forests
of pine and groves of orange-
trees. Orchards of peach,
plum, persimmon and other
fruit trees, with large vegeta-
ble gardens in which negro
slaves were at work, told why
this country was called the
" winter garden" of the frozen North.

" FLORIDA CRACKER."

They arrived at Alec's
home before nightfall. It was
one of those palatial houses of
the ante-bellum days. Before
the war, the wealth of the
South was in the country, where the rich plantations were supported by slave labor, where each
planter was a petty feudal lord with his dusky
subjects. Mr. Reuben Stevens was a typical southerner. He had only emigrated from the cotton
districts of Georgia because he believed the devel-

opment of orange groves in Florida would pay better. He was a cavalier of the old type; one who believed that slavery was a divine institution, and yet he was one of the kindest men in the world. He would protect one of his dusky subjects with his life, and when they were sick, he and his amiable wife nursed them. Those who have travelled in the South will bear me out in the statement that there does not exist more hospitable people than the people of the South. They are easily touched by a story of wrong or oppression; they are patriotic as they understand patriotism; they were, as a rule, kind and indulgent masters with their slaves. Only the worst side of the picture of slavery was presented by the Abolitionists. Some masters assigned their slaves tasks, and all over the task was their own, and many of the thriftier darkies accumulated considerable money in this way. The author knew many masters, who, after President Lincoln's proclamation, freed their slaves, gave them nice little homes of thirty or forty acres of land, mules and wagons, and set them up in their new life.

Uncle Reuben Stevens, as he was known, was a kind master and loved by all his slaves, save one or two vicious fellows incapable of gratitude.

The old planter, with his Panama hat on his

head, stood in shirt sleeves on the broad piazza, when the young men drove up.

" Well, this is Mark Stevens, is it?" said Uncle Reuben, grasping Mark's hand with an assuring welcome.

" Yes, sir, and I suppose we are distantly related."

" Oh, yes, all o' the same branch. My folks came from Virginia. Sit down; Alec, send Cater to put up the mules."

Alec called a negro who was playing with a hound on the grass, and sent him to unharness the mules.

" Sit down, Mark; let me see;—is your father livin'?"

" Yes, sir; he still lives in Boone County, Kentucky."

" What's his name?"

" Fernando."

" Yes, warn't he in the war of 'twelve?"

" Yes, sir, he was a major and fought at New Orleans."

" Yes, yes, I remember now. I was thar myself. I tell you, boy, we did some good shootin' that day. I was with the Tennessee troops and he with Kentucky; but we were stationed close enough together to swap jokes."

" I don't suppose you did?"

"Some of the boys said some pretty sassy things. I tell you the Americans showed spunk there. What was your grandfather's name?"

" Albert."

" That's it. He and my father were brothers, I reckon, well we are all of one branch, why I trace my family back to Captain John Smith."

" Farther than that, father," interposed Alec. " It goes clear back to Columbus."

" Oh, Alec, you always want to overdo the thing. But, Mark, was your father in the war with Mexico?"

" No; my brother Arthur was."

" Where is he?"

" Living in Boone County; married a Mexican wife, and is now one of the richest planters in the county; but I believe he is going to Mexico to live."

" Foolish to do it. Well I warn't in the Mexican war. Didn't take much stock in it. Shouldn't wonder we have to whip the Abolitionists yet. Hope you and Alec didn't imbibe any o' the doctrine o' the North while at college."

Mark hoped there would be no war between the North and South. At this moment Mrs. Betty Stevens came out to form the acquaintance of Mark and scold Uncle Reuben for talking politics while the young man was tired. The colored cook soon had supper ready, and the journey had given Mark a splendid appetite. Alec, with a glow of satisfaction, noted Mark's increased appetite, and said ·

"I told you we'd bring the color back to your cheeks, my cousin."

Next day Alec planned a fishing excursion.

"You must come back to-night, Alec," said his mother. "Clara and Richard will be here to-night, with Miss Elsie Cole from Charleston."

"I wish Dick had come this morning to go with us. I tell you, Dick is a jolly good fellow; but if Elsie is coming, I'll be back."

The young men set out on a buckboard on their fishing expedition. The scenery was somewhat similar to the day before. A thick jungle of semi-tropical trees and plants was penetrated, and they came to a huge spring, boiling from the earth in a volume sufficient to form a stream twenty feet wide and deep enough to row a boat upon. On all sides was a great "bay head," with its wealth of palmettoes, cactuses, live-oaks, ferns and flowers like an immense conservatory. The trees were festooned from their highest branches to the ground with the graceful gray Florida moss and a tangled network of vines. Here and there a great monarch had fallen and, unable to reach the earth, rested in the outstretched arms of his comrades, who pityingly wove a shroud of trailing plants about him. The boys, leaving mule and buckboard among the trees, launched a skiff and, climbing into it, glided noiselessly down the stream, until they suddenly came into a lake, several miles wide, fringed for many rods with lily-pods, reeds and the wonderful " Cypress Knees," looking wonderfully like so many champagne bottles set in the water to cool. White herons and other water fowls glided along the margin, or floated gracefully overhead.

The boat had come to a stop, and while Mark was contemplating the scene, Alec with all the keen instincts of a sportsman was busy preparing his rod, line and bait. A swish, a swirl in the water, a rush, a clicking reel, the slender rod bent almost double,—and a big black bass lay flopping in the boat at Mark's feet. He awoke to the realities of sport. In a short time they had an abundant supply, and started homeward.

The sun had set, and the new moon was looking down upon them out of the liquid blue of a cloud-less sky that Italy herself might claim. The crescent moon and her infinite number of starry companions shone with that softened splendor only seen in southern lands. The air was heavy with dew-kissed orange buds. Night birds were flitting by; katydids gossiped merrily, and from the lake came the deep tones of an alligator, very much like the hoarse croaking of a bull-frog. As they jour-

neyed on, a weird and novel sight came in view—
a large pine forest on fire. The trees were ablaze
from the ground to the top branches, and great red
tongues leaped and danced fantastically in the
air. Leaving the blazing forest, they came to a

A SWISH, A SWIRL IN THE WATER, A RUSH, A CLICKING REEL,
THE SLENDER ROD BENT ALMOST DOUBLE.

quaint nook in which stood a negro's cabin.
There were no windows, but the door stood wide
open, showing an immense log fire over which the
" old mammy" bent, preparing the evening meal.
There was only one room in the house, scantily

furnished, with "yarbs" in abundance hanging from the rafter overhead. There were big darkies, little darkies and middle-aged darkies. A young negro man was picking an old banjo and singing "Nelly Grey." They still heard his not unmusical voice when the lights of the old mansion house came in sight, and they drove hastily forward.

"Here we are!" cried Alec leaping out at the great front gate. "Cater, Cater come here."

"Yes, massa."

"Take this mule out and put him in the barn."

"Git many, massa?" asked Cater straining his eyes to look into the basket.

"Yes, more than you would catch in a week, you can't fish."

"Bet I kin, massa. Cater'll show ye some time,—golly, ain't dis a whopper!"

"Carry them in to Liza, Cater, and then come and get the mule."

"Golly, ain't dey heaby, massa? Dem's all whoppers."

"Hurry up, Cater; the mule is hungry and so are we."

"Is that Alec?" asked a voice which the young men recognized as Uncle Reuben.

"Yes, father."

"Come right in. Dick's come with the gals.

Go in the back way and slick up a bit, for them Charleston gals are monstrous fine."

The young men soon arranged their toilet. Mark seemed to evince eagerness.

"You never saw my cousin Clara, did you Mark?" asked Alec.

"No."

"She's a beauty; you can fall in love with her; but you must let Elsie Cole alone. I'll get jealous there in a minute."

"Never fear, Alec, I'll not rob you of your sweetheart," said Mark with a sigh which might have been interpreted as meaning that he had had his love's romance.

They met the young folks in the large parlor, where Dick, a tall, handsome young fellow, and two young ladies were awaiting them. Alec did the presenting and right gracefully too.

Mark glanced at Elsie Cole, then started back covered with confusion. She was the vision of his last week's dreams, seen but a moment from the veranda of the Jacksonville hotel.

4

CHAPTER III.

SAINT OR DEVIL.

THE confusion of Mark Stevens was so great that all present observed it. The effect on Elsie was strange. She recognized the young man as the person who had given her an impudent stare at Jacksonville, and for whom she had entertained no other thought than that he was some impudent fellow from the North. Alec noticed Mark's embarrassment and said:

"By Jove! have you folks met before?"

"If I mistake not I saw these young ladies in Jacksonville about two weeks ago," said Mark.

"We were there," said Elsie, "and if I mistake not you sat on the hotel veranda and stared at us."

"Don't talk that way, Elsie," put in Clara.

"Well, Clara, you said he stared at one just like an impudent northerner."

"But I did not know he was a Stevens then."

"Oh!" said Elsie with a curve of her pretty lip. "I suppose his being a Stevens makes a difference. Are the Stevens family infallible?"

" Yes. "

" Thank you, cousin Clara," put in Mark, whose face was flaming crimson. "One may well be proud of a relative that always comes to help a fellow out of a bad scrape."

" Come, come, you folks get out to supper," interrupted Uncle Reuben. "Let us not have a quarrel the first meeting."

" We are not quarrelling Mr. Stevens, I was just rebuking your kinsman for staring at us," said Elsie.

" I appeal to Uncle Reuben, who has not lost his gallantry, if I was not justified."

It was Elsie's turn to blush, and look confused, and Uncle Reuben answered:

" He's got ye, Elsie. By Gineral Jackson, I'd not think much of a young man's taste who wouldn't stop and stare a second on such faces as yours."

Aunt Betty came to the rescue by declaring that Uncle Reuben ought to be ashamed of himself, and the party were soon in the ample dining room seated at the table. The young people from Charleston were vivacious; conversation never flagged, and Mark soon overcame his temporary embarrassment, and before the evening was over was one of the merriest of the happy group.

Alec noticed with some degree of uneasiness

the interest which Mark seemed to take in Elsie. He gave his attention to both young ladies, but Alec thought he devoted most of his time to Elsie. That evening Alec said:

"Well, Mark, what do you think of her?"

"Who, Alec?"

"Elsie."

"She is a very pretty girl."

"Yes and as good as she is beautiful. I'll tell you a secret, Mark; now don't tell anybody for the people might laugh at me;—I like that girl. I just want to put you on your guard, Mark; I love her."

"Are you betrothed?"

"No——"

"Well, have you ever proposed?"

"No, I never had a chance. That is, I mean I never could pluck up courage when I had a chance. I've tried to, but when I get at it I always feel just like a fool, and quit."

"Is Dick a rival?"

"Oh, no, she's Dick's own cousin,—his mother's niece, you see, but that makes her no relative of mine."

Mark felt little interest in Alec's love affair; but his friend went on telling him that Dick had said he didn't believe she cared a fig for him, but he knew better. Dick was not in the way; but he feared Mark might be.

"Fact is, Mark, you are a plaguy fine-looking fellow, and it would just be my luck for Elsie to take a fancy to you, and it might cause me a thundering lot of trouble."

Mark Stevens could not refrain from smiling; but his answer did not alleviate the anxiety of Alec. Long after the other members of the household had sunk into slumber Alec tossed restlessly on his bed unable to sleep. After heaving sighs which would run up into the third notation he muttered:

"I do wonder, now, if I have played the very devil with my chances by bringing Mark here. Well, I don't care; Mark's a good fellow; I like him, and if Elsie prefers him to me, let her have him."

With this sensible conclusion he fell asleep.

Weeks rolled on. Mark Stevens evinced more pleasure in the society of the young ladies than with the gentlemen. He went on picnic excursions with them, while Dick and Alec were hunting and fishing. There could be no question that Mark was a great favorite with the girls. Josie Stevens, Alec's sister was about the same age as the visiting ladies, none of whom exceeded seventeen or eighteen. For awhile, Mark seemed an equal favorite of all, but at last, by law of instinct or mutual attraction, it became evident that Elsie and Mark were partial to each other. They were seen walking and talking together often, her blue eyes seemed brighter when with him, and her cheek glowed with a warmer tint when at his side.

"Alec, if you don't watch, you will be cut out!" declared Josie to her brother.

"Why?"

"I saw Mark and Elsie talking very low last evening, as we came from the lake. They were walking behind us, some distance, and Clara says that she believes he squeezed her hand."

Alec sighed and then, like the generous fellow that he was, said:

"I like Mark better than a brother, and he's worthy of her. If she prefers him to me, I have nothing to say, only God bless them."

The winter passed and the time came for Mark to go to Virginia where he had some business to transact. On the night before his departure he and Elsie once more walked alone in the delightful orange grove. Her small hand rested gently on his arm, her beautiful face was upturned to his, half seriously half roguishly, but ravishingly beautiful. Their voices were low and tender. The heart of each was throbbing violently, and she finally said:

"You are going away in the morning?"

"Yes, Elsie; but I hope to see you again before many months."

" Where are you going?"

" To Harper's Ferry, Virginia."

" I thought your home was in Kentucky."

" It is; but I am not going home; I am going to meet Mr. Smith at Harper's Ferry. I don't know the nature of the business. A friend has written me to meet Mr. Smith. That friend is an old college classmate, and I am going on his honor and judgment. But I shall see you again, Elsie."

" Why?" she asked, sighing.

" I must. Please say I may come to visit you at Charleston. I can say something to you there, which I cannot say here."

" Perhaps you had better not say it at all," and she glanced archly at him from the corners of her eyes.

" We have passed many pleasant hours in each other's society, Elsie. Let us hope they will not be the last."

She hoped they might not, and then began praising the beauty of Florida and talking of Ponce de Leon and his fountain of youth. He thought there was but one fountain of youth and that was in the honest love of a fond heart, which never grew old. She again warded off the subject by saying the gray hairs of a father or mother enhanced their beauty, in the eyes of a loving child. Mark, all the while he was making or trying to

make love to Elsie, felt that he was serving his
cousin Alec a mean trick. His conscience smote
him in more ways than one. He wanted Elsie to
know he loved her; he wanted to know whether
he was loved in return; yet he would have been
horrified at the thought of a betrothal.

Their interview that evening was unsatisfactory
to either party. Alec took Mark to Jacksonville
next day. The old college friends had for several
days been a little cool toward each other; for Alec
thought Mark had treated him badly. As they
rode along the sandy thoroughfare, Alec said:

"It was all right, Mark. I hoped you wouldn't
take Elsie away from me; but you have; yet it is
all right. She is a lovely girl, Southern, too. You
are a handsome fellow, and I can't blame you for
loving her. When is it to be, Mark?"

Mark started, and answered:

"Alec, we are not betrothed."

"Not betrothed! then what in the name of
General Jackson were you doing so much courting
for?"

"I don't know," he sighed, looking guilty. "I
like Elsie,—I believe I do—but"—he hesitated.
"Alec, I am miserable—if you knew my heart, you
would pity me. I don't intend to be a villain—I
don't want to; but circumstances seem driving me
to crime, ruin and wretchedness."

Alec's eyes opened wide in wonder, and he gave his unfortunate relative a fixed stare, as if he feared he was losing his mind. He had never seen him until they met at Harvard, and after he left the college, almost three years before Mark's visit, he had not heard from him, until he received the letter in which he stated that his health was shattered and he was coming South to rest and recruit. Mark had always seemed to live in an atmosphere of mystery, that was sometimes puzzling and aggravating to Alec, who was like an open page to be read by everybody.

"Well, Mark, if she likes you I—I shan't blame you. We've been good friends, and I'd do anything for a friend," said the noble Alec.

"Thank you, Alec; you are the best friend I ever had, and God forbid I should ever wrong you. I don't know that Miss Cole cares for me; but if she did not,—if she preferred you to me, I should not blame her. Alec, you are better than I."

"Oh, nonsense!—a great harum-scarum good-for-nothing fellow like me better than you?"

"Yes, you are."

"No; but let us change the subject. Mark, what are you going to Virginia for?"

"I don't know. Mr. Sewall of Boston wrote me to call on Mr. Smith near Harper's Ferry and he would explain."

"Mark, I'll bet it's an abolition scheme."

Mark thought not, for the question of slavery seemed about to take a long rest.

"But you used to declare in our debates at college that slavery was a curse to our institutions, and that you wished there was not a slave in the United States."

"I did; yet the abolition of slavery cannot be brought about suddenly, without violence. I would favor gradual emancipation. The abolitionists want to obtain by violence, what cannot be obtained by law."

"That's so, Mark; and I heard that there was a plot on foot to set all the niggers in the South free. To rouse the slaves to an insurrection and have them murder their masters."

"Such a thing could not be accomplished. It would only result in the suffering of the slaves. Masters now lenient would become severe and distrustful."

Jacksonville was reached and the cousins bade each other adieu, and Alec drove sadly away, while Mark stood on the veranda of the hotel gazing after him.

"Noble fellow!" he sighed. "Would to heaven I had such a heart! but I am either a fool or a knave. Ah, fate, fate, you have played me some scurvy tricks."

Mark retired early, for he expected to start on his northward journey early in the morning. We need not give an account of that journey, as it would prove uninteresting to the reader. He reached Harper's Ferry in due time, and at once began to inquire for Mr. Smith.

"Mister Smith? dun know any sich a man, stranger," said an old Virginian in blue-drillen trowsers and straw hat. "Maybe they kin tell ye at the post-office or over at Sheppard's store."

At the former place, he learned that a stranger named Smith had just come into the neighborhood and hired a farm a few miles from Harper's Ferry. He was a queer old case everybody declared, and always had a suspicious gang about him. Yet they all seemed civil and polite. Mark resolved to call upon the mysterious farmer as soon as he could, and he set out next day for the home of Mr. Smith. It was late in the evening when he reached the house of the pretended farmer.

The cloudless June day was almost done, and the farmer was resting from his toil, if he toiled at all. He was sitting on the broad piazza of an old-fashioned Virginia mansion. Mark advanced to the gate and the man rose. He was tall and rather ungainly looking. His beard was long and almost white; his eyes were restless and stern.

"Are you Captain Smith?" Mark asked.

"Yes, sir," was the answer, after a moment's hesitation.

"I have a letter here which may explain itself to you."

Mark gave him Sewall's letter, which he read carefully and then, glancing keenly at the young man, seemed to size him up, as a recruiting officer would a candidate for enlistment.

"You are Mr. Mark Stevens, who graduated at Harvard?"

"Yes, sir."

"Are you willing to follow the commands of God Almighty?"

Mark gazed at him as if he had met a lunatic. He was speechless with astonishment, while the old man went on.

"Your fame has gone forth. We know you are on our side, young man, and there is a great work to do; let us do it. Don't you believe that one should do his duty?"

"Certainly."

"Are you willing to die for your country and your principles?"

"Yes."

"Give me your hand. Come in."

Mark was bewildered and mystified. He entered the old-fashioned Virginia house, where he met half a dozen white men who seemed to have no particular business, and with them fully as many negroes. There existed among the blacks and whites a certain degree of social equality quite disgusting to a man of Mark's taste.

Captain Smith did not fully explain his business then. He was a shrewd man and moved with the utmost caution. He sounded Mark carefully as to his views on the question of slavery and found him strongly opposed to it, but at the same time he did not favor violation of law. He was opposed to anarchy or insurrection. If they had laws, observe them.

" Well, you say you want to go home to Kentucky. Go, and return here in the fall. I'll be ready to tell you all then."

" Mr. Smith, I can hardly understand what you want with me," said Mark. " This mystery is to me inexplicable. If you require any act of lawlessness from me, I assure you I will not take any hand in it."

Mr. Smith, or Captain Smith, as he called himself, answered:

" I ask nothing of you save what will be approved by God Almighty."

" I must be the judge of what my God deems lawful."

" Have you faith in the author of that letter?"

" Yes."

"Then believe in me."

Mark went home, after having first promised Mr. Smith to keep secret their interview. Mark's health and spirits were fully restored. He kept up a correspondence with his southern friends Elsie, Clara, Jack and Alec, and promised on the next winter to return.

In the fall of 1859, there was a brighter hope of peace than the country had known for years. The vehement discussion of the slavery question had somewhat subsided; there was a lull in the border war in Kansas; the Mormons were quiet; difficulties between the United States and Paraguay, in South America, had been settled; troubles with Indians on the Pacific coast were drawing to a close, and the filibustering operations of Walker in Nicaragua were losing much of their interest. The summer had passed away like a peaceful dream, and such wholesome topics as the Pacific Railway, Homestead and Soldiers' pension bills, and other measures for the promotion of peace and national prosperity were engaging the attention of the people. The slavery agitators seemed to be quiet, and it was hoped the question might be at rest; but all the while ambitious if not unscrupulous men were at work fomenting discontent and using every effort to kindle civil war.

It was late in October when Mark returned to

Virginia, determined to have an end of the late mystery with Captain Smith. He found the plain, unassuming, strange and incomprehensible old man at the farm house. He was told to wait until the morrow and he would outline his plans and business to him. On the morrow he led Mark to the forest above the bluff of Harper's Ferry and said:

"Here we can talk alone and understand each other. Sit down on that stone, my friend." When Mark was seated, he asked, "Do you believe that slavery is against the law of God?"

"I do."

"I knew I was not mistaken. Slavery curses our land, and I feel that I am ordained by Heaven to free these toiling millions. First, I shall commence here!" and the speaker swept his hand over toward the valley below him. "I will liberate these first."

"How, Mr. Smith?" asked Mark.

"Mark Stevens, it is time that we let the mask fall. Let us understand each other fully. You are a mystery to me and I to you. Call me, when alone, Brown, not Smith. I am John Brown, the hero of Ossawattomie, Kansas, of 1856. Have you never heard of that battle?"

Of course Mark had, and he gazed in amazement at the man before him. Old John Brown was thoroughly hated or admired at the time of this story, and friends and foes both tended to give him a liberal advertisement. He had participated in the Kansas troubles and it is said by his enemies that he murdered and plundered. That he took human life cannot be denied, perhaps not for the sake of plunder, but from the extreme fanatical bent of his mind. Brown was a native of Connecticut, and at this time in the sixtieth year of his age. He espoused the cause of abolition very early in life, and was enthusiastic and brave. If history is to be believed, he was unscrupulous as to the methods by which he sought to gain his ends. He had been active in the midst of the troubles in Kansas, and had suffered much; and he believed himself to be the destined liberator of the slaves in the American Republic.

"We have established Freedom in Kansas, and we can do it here," he said.

"How?" asked Mark.

Then he explained that with a few white followers and twelve slaves from Missouri, he had gone into Canada West, and at Chatham a convention of sympathizers was held in May, 1859, whereat a "provisional constitution and ordinances for the people of the United States" was adopted, "not," as the instrument declared, "for the overthrow of any government, but simply to amend and repeal." This was, of course, a part of the scheme for promoting the uprising of the slaves for obtaining their freedom.

Mark listened carefully to the wild plans of Brown, and when he had concluded asked:

" How do you propose to succeed, Mr. Brown?"

" The blacks will rise in a body and flock to my standard. Do you see that?" he asked pointing to the United States arsenal.

" Yes."

" We will seize that first, and arm every negro, and free Virginia."

Mark looked at him a moment incredulously and said:

" Mr. Brown, you must be mad. Such a thing is impossible."

" All things are possible with God."

" But God does not ordain any such work."

For the first time in his acquaintance with John Brown, he saw his face flame with a passion. The old man's eyes gleamed from under his shaggy eyebrows, as he cried:

" Does not God ordain me for this work?—I know it—I know it! I shall go down in history as the liberator of slaves."

" Mr. Brown, you are a mistaken man. Your faith will be shattered when you see how your plans fail. You do not understand the negroes as

5

well as I. They will not flock to your standard. You people of the North count too much on the intelligence and patriotism of the black man. While I believe he should be free, while I believe his slavery is a curse to the land, yet I have no confidence in the negro's fidelity and intelligence. You forget that he is of an inferior race, and that his only enlightenment from barbarism has been in his slave state. It would take one hundred years of freedom to bring the negro to the point in perfection you now believe he has attained, even if he ever reaches it. You will hardly be able to muster a score to your side, when you strike a blow for freedom."

"I am called of God——"

"No, no, Mr. Brown," interrupted Mark. "Again you are deluded. God does not call upon you to commit murder. Christ said to Peter, 'Put up thy sword,' and He healed the ear of the high priest. To succeed, you would have to shed rivers of blood. Thousands of ignorant, half-savage negroes would be turned loose to murder and plunder their masters. I hope you will forbear so mad a project."

Pleading with a man of Brown's temperament was in vain. He had so long brooded over the subject of slavery that he saw but one vision, that of freedom of the negroes. He had only one idea.

To him there was but one wrong, and to right that wrong any amount of wrongs might be committed.

John Brown is a study for the impartial historian. With those who lived in his day he was a saint or a devil, a man ordained of God to bring about the redemption of the black race from slavery, or a dark-hearted, ambitious murderer. The sooner the American people get over their prejudice on one hand, and foolish admiration of John Brown on the other, the sooner will they come to a just and true apprehension of the man. He was neither a saint nor was he a devil. He was more nearly a madman than either. John Brown's whole soul was wrapped up in the liberation of the slaves, his motive was good; but his means were foolish and diabolical. He was no Christian; for he killed and incited others to do the same. He was no soldier; for a good general would never have allowed himself to be caught in such a trap, as he was at Harper's Ferry. To tell the real truth, John Brown's act was a piece of stupendous folly, which must cause any fair-thinking man to smile. Just what he intended is a mystery. Before his capture, while seizing Harper's Ferry, he declared his intention to " free the slaves." After his capture, he stated that he never intended a general insurrection. John Brown violated the laws of Virginia by inciting the slaves to rise against their masters; he violated the laws of the nation in seizing United States arms; he committed murder while resisting arrest; was tried, convicted and hung. When we come to look calmly at the cold facts in the light of reason, with eyes unprejudiced and mind unbiased by the nonsensical sentimentality of the abolitionist, John Brown deserved his fate, as much as the Chicago Anarchists, or any other failures at a revolution. That he was a martyr to the freedom of the negroes, there is cause for dispute, for it may be doubted if his death had anything to do with their freedom.

While Brown was trying to convert Mark Stevens to his mode of thought and action, his son, John Brown Jr., was in Canada. His father had sent him there to enlist the active support of the better class of colored men who had escaped from bondage; in fact to recruit soldiers for their cause. He had been quite successful, and had just returned to their home in Ashtabula County, intending to rejoin his father near the scene of action, when the combat took place. It was the intention not to make the attack for some months; but when Mark Stevens, on whose support Brown had calculated, refused to enter into his scheme, the liberator determined to strike at once.

Mark Stevens was perplexed as to what he should do. Although born and raised in Kentucky, and the son of a slave-holder, he had been an advocate of abolition. He was a strong admirer of the new Republican party, which had freedom of mankind for its platform; but he dared not enlist under the banner of this madman. He dared not raise his hand against the laws of his land to bring about a reform.

"Two wrongs cannot make a right," he thought. Besides the plan must fail. Brown's only hope of success was in a general uprising of the negroes, and Mark knew negro character too well to believe any concert of action on their part possible. Many loved their masters too well to slay them, even though they might desire their own freedom.

Mark went to the house of Mr. Beverly near Harper's Ferry, a gentleman of strong common sense, who was cool, unprejudiced and capable of advising in such a matter. He reached his house Sunday, October 16, 1859. Brown and his spies had been watching him, and Mark was really in danger. Those men fresh from the battlefields of Kansas did not hold life in the highest esteem.

He held a long consultation with Mr. Beverly as to what he should do in the premises. Mr. Beverly was a Republican, but a law-abiding citizen, and he could not favor such a scheme as John Brown's.

"He must be arrested," said Mr. Beverly. "It

will not do to permit so dangerous a man to be at large.   We will inform on him in the morning."

But John Brown acted on that very night.   One by one, his followers had been stealthily congregating, and pikes, guns and ammunition gathered together for striking the first blow at Virginia and arming the slaves.   The refusal of Mark to take part in the insurrection, and the fears that he might betray his plans caused him to act at once. Under cover of profound darkness, Brown, at the head of seventeen white men and five negroes, entered the village of Harper's Ferry on that fatal Sunday night, put out the street lights, and seized the armory and the railway bridge, and quietly arrested and imprisoned in the government buildings the citizens found in the streets at the earliest hours of the next morning, each one being ignorant of what had happened.   The invaders seized Colonel Washington, living a few miles from Harper's Ferry; with his arms and horses, and liberated his slaves, and at eight o'clock on Monday morning, the 17th of October, Brown and his followers (among whom were two of his sons) had full possession of the village and government works.   His action was as much an act of open rebellion as the attack and capture of Fort Sumter. When asked what his purpose was, and by what authority he acted, Brown replied:

"To free the slaves, and by the authority of God Almighty."

He thought that when he struck this blow the negroes of the surrounding country would rise and flock to his standard. He believed that a general uprising of the slaves of the whole country would follow, and that he would win the satisfaction of being a great liberator. He was mistaken. While the martyr to their liberty was offering up his life and the lives of his sons at Harper's Ferry, a dozen miles away, the negroes were singing, playing the banjo and dancing, not caring a fig for Brown and his sentimental notions.

Mark was sleeping soundly, when Mr. Beverly came to his room and cried:

"Awake, Mark! for Heaven's sake, wake and fly for your life! Brown has already struck."

Hurriedly dressing, Mark raised his window and looked down on the village not a fourth of a mile away, but all was utter darkness. Only the wild tumult of voices and deep, stern tones of John Brown in command told of danger.

"The madman has done his work," thought Mark, as he hurried away from the house, went to a farmer's, mounted a horse and riding to the nearest telegraph station, telegraphed the news all over the country. Governor Henry A. Wise, at once ordered out the militia, and by noon a com-

pany of the State Guards was at Harper's Ferry.
Mark returned to the town with the militia and
from an eminence saw the puffing of smoke and
heard the sharp crack of musketry. Brown and
his forces were driven into the fire-engine house,
where they defended themselves with great bravery.

On Monday evening, Colonel Robert E. Lee
arrived at Harper's Ferry, with ninety United
States marines and two pieces of artillery. The
instructions .of President Buchanan were to use
caution. The last orders from Secretary Floyd to
Lee was to, " Give 'em h——l, colonel."

When Colonel Lee arrived on the scene, he
found Brown with his band and the prisoners he
had taken, in the engine-house. It was a small
house inside the grounds of the arsenal, exactly
like an ordinary fire-engine house in cities——with
large folding-doors. The Virginia militia had
been deliberating upon the best means of assault;
but when Colonel Lee arrived he assumed command, and the first step he took was to send Lieutenant J. E. B. Stuart forward to demand a surrender. He accordingly walked into the enclosure,
and approached the engine-house, waving a white
handkerchief, and, when he got to the door, called
out that he wished to see Captain Smith; for up
to this time but few knew that the insurrectionist
was in reality John Brown of Kansas fame. At

Lieutenant Stuart's call, Brown came and opened
one fold of the door a little way.   Behind it was
a heavy rope stretched across, better security than
a bar, as it would yield if a
battering ram of any sort were
used, but would not give way.

Brown had a gun in his
hand, and below appeared the
head of a big bull dog, which
kept snarling at Stuart, and
causing him to feel unpleas-
antly.   No sooner had the
Lieutenant seen the insurgent,
than he remembered him and
asked:

"You are Ossawattomie
Brown of Kansas, are you
not?"

JOHN BROWN.

Old John Brown gazed at him keenly from
under his grizzly, shaggy eyebrows, and coolly
answered:

"Well, they do call me that sometimes, Lieutenant."

"I thought I remembered meeting you in Kansas," the lieutenant gravely said.   "This is a bad
business you are in, Captain.   The United States
troops have arrived and I am sent to demand your
surrender."

"Upon what terms?" he asked without displaying the least sort of excitement. .

"The terms are that you must surrender to the officer commanding the troops, and he will protect you from the crowd, and guarantee you a fair trial."

Brown shaking his head answered:

"I can't surrender on such terms. You must allow me to leave this engine-house with my comrades and the prisoners, and march across the river to the Maryland side: there I will release the prisoners, and, as soon as this is done, your troops may fire on and pursue us."

Lieutenant Stuart answered that he had no authority to agree to any such arrangement, and was ordered to demand his surrender on the terms first proposed.

"Well, Lieutenant," Brown answered, coolly, "I see we can't agree. You have the numbers on me; but you know we soldiers are not afraid of death. I would as lief die by a bullet as on the gallows."

"Is that your final answer, Captain?" asked the Lieutenant.*

"Yes."

Stuart turned sadly away and went back to Colonel Lee, saying they refused to surrender.

---

* Historical account in Cooke's "Surry of Eagle's-Nest."

"THE UNITED STATES TROOPS HAVE ARRIVED, AND I AM SENT TO
DEMAND YOUR SURRENDER."

(See page 73)

After an original drawing by Freeland A. Carter.

"Take that ladder and batter down the door," commanded Lee of the marines. As they approached the door, Brown and his party opened fire and two or three fell. The fire was returned and for several moments the conflict raged. One of Brown's sons lay dead on the floor, another lay dying in his father's arms; yet with one hand he felt the pulse of his dying child, held his gun with the other and coolly issued his commands. The door was battered down and after a brief struggle the whole party was captured.

Brown was tried for treason, convicted and hung on December 3d, 1859, and ever since his enthusiastic admirers have sung:

"John Brown's soul goes marching on."

CHAPTER IV.

CALHOUNISM.

It is easy, after events have transpired, for would-be philosophers to see what means brought them about; but it requires a sage or prophet to penetrate into the future. The war of 1861 had its origin in the constitutional convention. Washington and Hamilton foresaw the danger of State supremacy, when they urged a strong centralized power. A Union of sand was dangerous, and they knew it. Thomas Jefferson and his school, equally as patriotic as Washington and Hamilton, nevertheless from their bitter experience with monarchies and centralized power, advocated different principles in the doctrine of State supremacy. This doctrine, however, was first fully promulgated by John C. Calhoun and may be attributed to him. This famous doctrine gave warning of the notable fruits it was bearing long before it culminated in the tempest of carnage and blood. We can see its effects as early as 1812, when the New England States refused to obey the order of the general government for troops to defend the northern frontier; again in the revolt of South Carolina under Jackson's administration. Again and again the republic was warned of its danger, until the sages of the day predicted that State supremacy was a nice point of constitutional law which must be settled in the highest court, a resort to arms.

The time for that appeal was coming. When James Buchanan was inaugurated the fifteenth president of the United States on the 4th of March, 1857, and chose for his constitutional advisers, Louis Cass, secretary of state; Howell Cobb, secretary of the treasury; John B. Floyd, secretary of war; Isaac Toucey, secretary of the navy; Jacob Thompson, secretary of the interior, Aaron V. Brown, postmaster-general, a new era in the history of our country dawned. It was the beginning of a great political and social revolution in the republic which entirely changed the industrial aspects in many of the States of the Union.

It was during the administration of Mr. Buchanan that the preliminary skirmishes, moral and physical, which immediately preceded the war, occurred. Both parties were then putting on their armor and preparing their weapons for the struggle. There were two wings of the democracy at this time. One leaning toward an anti-slavery policy, advocating gradual emancipation, and the other

declaring slavery a divine institution. The doctrine of Calhounism was possibly advocated in
the main as a means for the promulgation of
slavery; but in the nomination of Mr. Buchanan
the two branches of democracy harmonized. In
their resolutions, put forth as a platform of principles, they approved the invasion and usurpation
of Walker in Nicaragua, as efforts of the people of
Central America " to regenerate that portion of the
continent which covers the passage across the in-
teroceanic isthmus." They also approved the
doctrine of the " Ostend Manifesto," by resolving
that " the Democratic party was in favor of the
acquisition of Cuba."

One of the most vital preliminary skirmishes,
though wholly of a moral nature, to the great civil
war began just about the time of the accession of
Mr. Buchanan to the presidency.

This skirmish is known in history as the " Dred
Scott decision." Dred Scott was a young negro
owned by Dr. Emerson of the United States army,
living in Missouri. When the doctor was ordered
to Rock Island, Illinois, in 1834, he took Scott
with him. There Major Taliaferro of the army
had a female slave, and when the two masters were
transferred to Fort Snelling (now in Minnesota)
next year, the two slaves with the consent of their
masters were married. They had two children

born in the free-labor Territory, and the mother was bought by Dr. Emerson in order to keep the family from being separated. He brought the parents and children to Missouri and sold them to a New Yorker. Scott sued for his freedom, on the plea of his involuntary residence in a free-labor State and Territory for several years, and the circuit court of St. Louis decided in his favor. The supreme court of Missouri reversed the decision of the inferior court, and the case was carried by an appeal to the supreme court of the United States, presided over by Chief Justice Roger B. Taney, a Maryland slave-holder. A majority of the court was composed of men in sympathy with slavery, and their decision, about to be given in 1856, was, for prudential reasons, withheld until after the president's election.

The chief justice who rendered the decision took a step which so firmly established the institution of slavery on the government, that nothing save arms could free it. He declared that any person "whose ancestors were imported into this country and held as slaves" had no right to sue in any court of the United States. The only question upon which the court could have legitimately decided was the question of jurisdiction; but the chief justice, with the sanction of a majority of the bench went outside to declare that the framers and supporters of the Declaration of Independence did not include the negro race in our country in the great proclamation that " *all* men are created equal;" that the patriots of the Revolution, and all their progenitors " for more than a century before," regarded the negroes as beings of an inferior race, and altogether unfit to associate with the white race either in social or political relations, and so far inferior that they had no rights which a white man was bound to respect, and that the negro might lawfully be reduced to slavery for the white man's benefit.

Chief Justice Taney then hurled a firebrand into the camp of friend or foe which kindled the destructive war that followed, by declaring that the Missouri Compromise Act and all other acts for the restriction of slavery were unconstitutional, and that neither congress nor local legislature had any authority for restricting the spread of the institution all over the Union. Although a State or Territory might be supreme and independent of the general government in all other things, it had no power to settle the question of slavery according to the Dred Scott decision.

There was civil war in Kansas in the earlier part of 1856. As is always the case, outrages too terrible to mention were committed by both parties. Lawlessness has ever hovered on the frontier and under the mask of Free-State or Proslavery many depredations were committed. During 1856, the war in Kansas assumed an alarming aspect. The actual settlers of Kansas from free-labor States outnumbered the emigrants from elsewhere, and a regiment of young men from Georgia and South Carolina, under Colonel Bufford, fully armed went into the territory for the avowed purpose of making it a slave-labor State "at all hazards." They were joined by armed Missourians, and for several months spread terror over the land. They sacked the town of Lawrence, and murdered and plundered people in various places. Steamboats ascending the Missouri River with emigrants from free-labor States were stopped, and the passengers were frequently robbed of their money, and persons of the same class, crossing the State of Missouri, were arrested and turned back. Lawlessness reigned supreme in all that region. Justice was bound, and there was general defiance of all mandates of right. The civil war in Kansas was more wasteful than bloody. It was a war more for personal gain than for principle. Robbery and horse-stealing were practised more than military movements. Assassinations were common and conflicts few. Neither side did anything praiseworthy. John Brown, with twenty-eight emigrants, fought H. Clay Pate of Virginia with fifty-six armed men, on the

6

prairie at Ossawattomie. An early account of the fight reports Brown as defeated, and says he retreated. It also gives the number of border ruffians or proslavery men at six hundred. Later histories say Brown gained a victory. It was very insignificant either way. The term border ruffian might be applied alike to the free-soil and proslavery men. Finally, John W. Geary, afterward a major-general and governor of Pennsylvania, who succeeded Shannon as chief magistrate of Kansas, by judicious administration of affairs there, smothered the flames of civil war, and both parties worked vigorously with moral forces for the admission of Kansas as a State of the Union, but with ends in view diametrically opposed. Though the war in Kansas never fully subsided until it was swallowed up by the great rebellion, there was a lull in hostilities after John Brown left the Territory, and human life became more safe. Most of the killing was done by assassination. Men were called to their doors at night and shot down by unknown assassins.

The fugitive-slave law now began to bear bitter fruit, and it soon became one of the most prolific causes of the continually increasing controversies between the upholders and opposers of the slave-labor system. It was made more objectionable from the evident intention of the friends of the institution everywhere to nationalize slavery, and the alteration of the familiar meaning of the vital doctrine of the Declaration of Independence, by the judicial branch of the government, while the executive branch was ready to lend his tremendous power · in giving practical effect to the system, which awakened in the breasts of the people of the free-labor States a burning desire to wipe the mark of human bondage from the escutcheon of the Republic. Seizures under the fugitive-slave law were becoming more and more frequent, with circumstances of increasing injustice and cruelty. The business of arresting and remanding to hopeless slavery, men, women and children, was carried on all over the free-labor States, and the people stood appalled. By that dreadful law, every man, under certain conditions, was compelled to become a slave hunter; and every kindhearted woman, who might give a cup of cold water, or the shelter of a roof to a suffering negro, bleeding from intolerable bondage, incurred the penalty of felony. The law became a broad cover under which the kidnapping of free persons of color was extensively carried on, and many men, women and children, born free, were dragged from their homes and consigned to hopeless bondage.

The abolitionists were by no means blameless. They were constantly irritating the proslavery people and inciting their negroes to run away. Many a poor negro with a good master was living comfortably and contentedly at home until the disturber came to put the idea of escape into his head. Then came flight and misery. There is no impartial historian in America who has dealt with this subject. No historian will deal impartially with it for the next hundred years—if ever. The author fears that his feeling against the slaveholder may mislead him to some extent, yet from personal observation he knows that only the worst examples of slavery were recorded in history. Those rare examples were made to represent the conditions of human beings in bondage. While they were rare exceptions of cruelty and degradation, they showed only to what ends the system might go — not what it was. The abolitionists placed a barrier between master and man and often increased the severity of the former, and misery of the latter.

On a cold day in January, 1856, two slaves, with their wives and four children, all thinly clad, escaped from Kentucky into Ohio. They crossed the frozen river to Cincinnati, closely pursued by the master of three of them on horseback. In Cincinnati, they were harbored by a colored man. Their retreat was discovered by the pursuing master, who repaired to the house with the United

States marshal and his deputies, and demanded their surrender.

They refused to do this; and then after a desperate struggle, the door was broken open and the fugitives were secured. They had determined to die rather than to be taken back into slavery. The mother of the three children, in despair, tried first to kill her offspring and then herself. When she was seized, she had slain one of her children. A coroner's jury decided to hold the mother for murder under the laws of Ohio; but it was discovered that the fugitive-slave law had been made so absolute by the terms of its enactments and the opinion of the chief justice of the United States, that a State law could not interfere with it; so the mother and her surviving companions were taken back into slavery.

Many have seen in this construction of the fugitive-slave law and the Dred Scott decision, an inconsistency in the enemies of the Union. On the one hand, they were States-rights men, strong believers in State supremacy, when the working of that doctrine was to their own advantage; but when the authority of a State was attempted to be exercised against a woman who had murdered her *own* child, the government was strong enough to take her across the river and restore her to her master.

In 1848, a year after the Mormons settled in the valley of the Great Salt Lake, the United States acquired the territory from Mexico. Under the leadership of Brigham Young, the successor of Joseph Smith, this region had developed rapidly and in 1850 a territorial form of government was organized, with Brigham Young, spiritual head of the church, as governor. The population was rapidly increasing, owing largely to the efforts of Mormon missionaries in foreign countries, and the question of Utah's admission to the Union as a State was earnestly agitated. The Mormons were charged with being in a state of rebellion against the government. President Buchanan deprived Young of the office of governor of the territory and put Colonel Alfred Cumming, a superintendent of Indian affairs on the Upper Mississippi, in his place.

An armed force of twenty-five hundred men, under command of Colonel A. Sidney Johnston, was sent to Utah. Fearing military excesses, Young and his people prepared to hold the army east of the Wasatch Mountains, and when it entered the territory early in the autumn it was assailed by Mormon cavalry, who destroyed several supply trains and seized eight hundred of the oxen at the rear of the army. The troops, thus crippled and caught among the snows in the mountains, went into winter quarters. Governor Cumming proclaimed the territory of Utah to be in a state of rebellion. The spring of 1858 found the Mormons willing to submit to national authority, and arrangements were made for the peaceable entry of the army, but not until a promise of pardon to all who would accept national authority had been made, and the Mormons had abandoned their city and removed south, with the avowed determination of burning every building and reducing Utah to its former condition of barrenness, if pursued. However, they were not molested. The troops passed quietly through the city and encamped in Cedar Valley, about forty miles southwest, and the people returned to their homes.

The Republican party had been rapidly acquiring strength. It was not an abolition party in the sense that is usually supposed; that is, it was not the intent of the party, nor its leaders to forcibly free all the slaves in the South, though the Republican party was in sympathy with the cause opposing slavery. The great leaders of the party favored first checking the spread of the disease, and then gradually extinguishing it. Just how they would do so, the wisest among them could not determine; but they trusted to God to help them out of the difficulty.

One thing is certain, — such notable men as Lincoln and Sumner never desired bloodshed and war. That idea was inculcated by foolish fanatics like John Brown, the surviving members of whose family took scarcely any part in the war after it began. There was talk of purchasing the slaves at the expense of the government, of gradual emancipation and many theories proposed, none of which was acceptable to the southern people, who, believing firmly in the idea of the abstract right of slavery as well as the doctrine of State supremacy, prepared to resist the rising tide of Republicanism.

One author said: "It was the dream of the chiefs of the Great Rebellion to dissolve the Union and set up a great slave empire." We hardly believe that. The South was not fully organized when the time came, or between Lincoln's election and his inauguration they would have throttled the government. It might have been the dream of a few; but they must have been few indeed. 1860 came, and, being a presidential year, the State-rights Democracy determined that they would nominate a man of their proclivities or divide the party. The history of the convention which met in the South California Institute Hall, in Charleston, is interesting to the scholar, but has no place in a novel like this. Jefferson Davis was a prominent candidate of the State-rights Democracy, while Stephen A. Douglas, the Union Democrat, was the favorite of his class. The Democratic convention, after adjourning to meet in Richmond, and again adjourning to meet in Baltimore, finally split, and one faction nominated Stephen A. Douglas, and the other faction John C. Breckinridge. A third faction, or party, called Constitutional Union Party, nominated John Bell.

The Republican party nominated Mr. Abraham Lincoln for president, with Mr. Hannibal Hamlin for vice-president. The party could not have made a wiser choice for the head of its ticket. Lincoln was a man who came from among the people. He had drunk the cup of poverty to its bitter dregs. He had lived in a slave State where he knew the curse that slavery was to the poor whites. He knew the curse of slave-holding aristocracy. Neither Lincoln nor his party intended the freedom of the negroes. Their platform never hinted at it, and subsequent events prove that Lincoln was averse to the act. It was forced upon him in the third year of the war, when he was compelled to do so, first warning the States in rebellion.

Had the Democratic party not been divided, the Republicans would probably have been defeated, for although Lincoln received 180 electoral votes to 84 for Breckinridge and 12 for Douglas, he did not receive one-half of the popular vote. Be that as it may, he was fairly and honorably elected, and

the loyal Democrats of the Stephen A. Douglas
school resolved to support him, while the State-
supremacy Democrats once more revived in full

force the famous doc-
trines of Calhoun, and
were loud in their de-
mands for d i s u n i o n.
The plans taken to force
States out of the Union
w e r e   unjustifiable.
W i l d ,   i n c e n d i a r y
speeches   were   m a d e
everywhere,   calculated
to drive the people to
the most desperate meas-
ures.   One orator named
Yancey,   of   Alabama,
during the canvass is re-
ported as having said:

ABRAHAM LINCOLN.

"Organize   commit-
tees all over the cotton States; fire the southern
heart; instruct the southern mind; give courage
to each other; and at the proper moment, by one
organized, concreted action, precipitate the cotton
States into revolution."

Calhounism, or State-supremacy was the rock
on which dashed the ship of state, ending in the
war, all sages, statesmen and philosophers to the

contrary notwithstanding. The seed of secession sowed by Calhoun was independent of slavery. Slavery became only a means for testing the theory, and had it not been tested by slavery it would have been tried by a minority holding some other view. It was a question of unwritten constitutional law which had to be settled by blood. No court was high enough to appeal to for a decision, save the appeal to arms. A close student of our government will see at once that there was some excuse for the error. Like all questions it had two sides. The North was the side that prevailed. A southern brother was on the side which failed, consequently we were right and he wrong. As historians we have been unduly harsh with our southern brother, though as soldiers we showed great magnanimity to him when conquered. Had there been no slavery to uphold the South, perhaps men might never have put in force the celebrated doctrines of Calhoun. Had there been some local question in the North which affected that section as did slavery affect the South, who knows but that the North might have adopted the same theory and become the secessionists?

Before the articles of confederation, Virginia was as independent of Massachusetts or any other colony, as is Mexico of Peru; but the confederation of States united them for mutual protection, and then came the constitution, making the Union still stronger. Mr. Calhoun treated the union of States simply as a copartnership, from which any member of the firm might withdraw at will. There is direct evidence to prove that the extremists of South Carolina and elsewhere had been making preparations for revolt for many years, and that the alleged violations of the fugitive-slave act and the election of Mr. Lincoln were made occasions for stirring up the " common people " to support and do the fighting for them. The testimony of the speakers in the convention at Charleston, that declared the secession of that State from the Union, seems clear and explicit.

" It is not an event of a day," declared Mr. Robert Barnwell Rhett, one of the most famous declaimers of his class; " it is not anything produced by Mr. Lincoln's election, or by the non-execution of the fugitive-slave law. It is a matter which has been gathering head for thirty years. In regard to the fugitive-slave law, I myself doubted its constitutionality, and doubted it on the floor of the senate when I was a member of that body. The States, acting in their sovereign capacity, should be responsible for the rendition of slaves."

Mr. Francis S. Parker, another member of the convention, declared:

" It is not a spasmodic effort that has come suddenly upon us; it has been gradually culminating for a long period of thirty years."

Had he added, ever since Mr. Calhoun began teaching and preaching his doctrines of State sovereignty, he would have been more correct.

The South was now in a fever of the wildest excitement. There were many loyal men in the South who opposed secession until they were absolutely driven into it by the politicians and leaders. Long before secession was declared, there were secret orders and minute-men. There were midnight musters and enrolments. Arms were secured and every effort made for a terrible war.

When the election of Mr. Lincoln was certified, the political leaders in South Carolina were eager to begin the contemplated revolution. To be prepared for immediate action, an extraordinary session of the legislature was assembled at Columbia on the 15th of November; and as the news of the result of the election went over the land, the governor of the State received congratulatory dispatches from other commonwealths wherein the politicians were in sympathy with the secessionists. " North Carolina will secede," a dispatch from Raleigh said. " A large number of the Bell men have declared for secession; the State will undoubtedly secede," said another from the capital of Alabama.

Another from Milledgeville, Georgia, said, " The hour for action has come. This State is ready to assert her rights and independence."

The men sending those telegrams perhaps only gave their individual opinions, yet they claimed to bind the whole State by them. The South Carolina legislature was committed to separation from the Union; and on November 12, 1860, an act was passed authorizing a convention. The legislature also formulated the doctrine of " State sovereignty," or State supremacy, in a resolution that declared that a " sovereign State " of the Union had a right to secede from it, adopting as its own the doctrine that the States of the Union are not subordinate to the national government; were not created by it, and do not belong to it; that they created the national government; from them it derives its powers; to them it is responsible, and when it abuses the trust reposed in it, they, as equal sovereigns, have a right to resume the powers respectively delegated to it by them. This is the sum and substance of the doctrine of State supremacy (" State rights," as it was commonly called), which confines patriotism to the narrow dimensions of a single State, sets limits to the American citizen, and opposes a fundamental principle upon which the founders of the republic securely built our noble superstructure of a free, powerful and sovereign commonwealth. It seems to oppose the plain meaning of the preamble to the constitution, which declared that the *people* (not the States) of the whole country had given vitality to that fundamental law of the land, and to the nation.

CHAPTER V.

MRS. ANDERSON'S RECRUIT.

NEVER did the ship of State so need a master at the helm as in the dark hours which marked the close of Buchanan's administration. Oh, for a Washington, Jackson, or Jefferson to throttle the threatened fraternal strife before it could gain dangerous proportions!

Mr. Buchanan was ill fitted for the exalted place he held. Never did a man have a greater opportunity to immortalize himself than Buchanan, but he failed to avail himself of the opportunity, and his name is the insignia of weakness, while his memory is darkened with obloquy. We suspect that in after years, when the American people have had time to cool down, it will be found that we have done Mr. Buchanan an injustice. He was a weak man, incapable of grasping with great questions. He was a lawyer, and a good lawyer too. In fact, Mr. Buchanan was too much of a lawyer to be a good practical statesman. He depended upon precedents, while " honest old Abe Lincoln " depended on common sense. While Mr. Buchanan was ransacking the law books and studying the constitution for some legal escape from the dilemma, the South was preparing and arming for battle. Had Mr. Buchanan been a farmer in youth, instead of a college student; had he been compelled to wrestle with the world for existence in early life, he would have realized that exigencies arise in the lives of nations as well as people, where common sense counts for more than law or precedent, and instead of burning midnight oil to see if there were any way in the constitution whereby he might put an end to the trouble, he would have taken firm steps to check the rising tide of war in the bud, by arresting the ringleaders.

Some accuse Mr. Buchanan of being a traitor to his country, but I would prefer to place a mantle of charity about his shoulders, and call him " weak." Mr. Buchanan was a native of a free-labor State, and had never lived in a slave State; so he could hardly have been in sympathy with them; but he was surrounded by bad advisers. He trusted men who hourly betrayed him. Men very close to him in the government were using office as a means of fomenting the discontent. Indeed some of these acts were tending as if by every possible means to ruin the credit of the government; yet in the beginning, he trusted these men as his constitutional advisers. A weak man like Buchanan could not do otherwise than he did. He was surrounded by public and secret enemies of peace, he lived in an atmosphere of secession and unconsciously breathed it. Many of his regular army officers, on whom he had a natural desire to depend, were secretly endeavoring to aid the South in the work of secession. South Carolina, at a quarter before one o'clock, December 20, 1860, passed the following ordinance of secession:

"We, the people of the State of South Carolina, in convention assembled, do declare and ordain, and it is hereby declared and ordained, that the ordinance adopted by us in convention, on the 23d day of May, in the year of our Lord one thousand seven hundred and eighty-eight, whereby the constitution of the United States was ratified, and also all acts and parts of acts of the general assembly of the State, ratifying amendments of the said constitution, are hereby repealed, and the union now subsisting between South Carolina and other States of America, is hereby dissolved."

The cry at once went forth, " The Union is dissolved! " It was echoed and re-echoed in the streets of Charleston, and hurried on the wings of lightning all over the republic. The people in

Charleston were wild with excitement. All business was suspended and huzzas for " Southern Confederacy" filled the air. Women appeared in the streets with secession bonnets, the invention of a northern milliner in Charleston. Flags waved; church-bells pealed merrily, and cannon boomed; and some enthusiastic young men went to the grave of John C. Calhoun, in St. Philip's church-yard and, forming a circle around it, made a solemn vow to devote their " lives, their fortunes, and their sacred honor, to the cause of South Carolina independence." A drunken rabble ran through the streets crying, " The old union is gone to h—l."

Before night, the ordinance of secession was engrossed on a sheet of parchment; and at the appointed time, in the evening, Institute Hall was crowded with eager spectators to witness the signing of the instrument. Back of the president's chair was suspended a banner of cotton cloth, on which was painted a significant device. At the bottom was a mass of broken and discolored blocks of hewn stone, on each of which were the name and arms of a free-labor State. Rising from this mass were two columns made of perfect blocks of stone, each bearing the name and arms of a slave-labor State. The keystone of an arch that crowned the two columns had the name and arms of South

Carolina upon it, and it bore the figure of Calhoun. In the space between the columns was a palmetto tree, with a rattlesnake coiled around its trunk, and on a ribbon the words, "Southern Republic." Beneath all, in large letters, were the significant words, *"Built from the ruins."*

As time went on, and other States either passed articles of secession, or sent South Carolina assurances that they would enter into a confederacy for the dissolution of the Union, Charleston harbor became the theatre of stirring events. John B. Floyd, Buchanan's southern secretary of war, was gradually weakening the physical power of the government by stripping the arsenals of the North of their arms and ammunition, and strengthening the secessionists by filling the arsenals of the South with an abundance of weapons. He did not obey the orders of General Winfield Scott, the chief of the army, when, so early as the end of October, he observed signs of incipient insurrection in South Carolina, and recommended the strengthening of the forts near Charleston. And when, at the close of the same month, Colonel Gardener, in command of the fortifications near that city, attempted to increase his supply of ammunition, Floyd removed him, and in November placed Major Robert Anderson, a meritorious officer in the war with Mexico, in his place. That

Kentuckian surprised and disappointed Floyd.
Perceiving at once by various acts, the designs of
the southerners to seize the fortifications in the
harbor, he urged his government to strengthen
them with men and munitions of war, especially
Fort Moultrie, in which there was but a feeble
garrison; but his constant warnings were un-
heeded, even when he wrote:

"The clouds are threatening, and the storm
may burst at any moment. I need not say to you
how anxious I am, indeed determined, so far as
honor will permit, to avoid collision with the
people of South Carolina. Nothing will, however, be better calculated to prevent bloodshed,
than our being found in such an attitude that it
would be madness and folly to attack us."

He continually urged the war department to
give him more strength, and send him explicit
instructions; and when he found his warnings
treated with ominous silence, he wrote:

"Unless otherwise directed, I shall make future
communications through the regular channel —
the general-in-chief." Little did Major Anderson
dream that he was addressing an enemy of the
Union.

The secretary of war found Major Anderson a
strong Unionist for his purpose; but it was too
late to displace him, so he left him to his own

feeble resources, satisfied that the military companies then in process of organization in South Carolina would be able to seize the forts of Charleston harbor in good time. Moultrie was weak, and many of the little garrison in Sumter were known to be southerners. The latter fort was by far the stronger and more important work; and as evidence hourly increased, especially after the passage of the ordinance of secession, that the South Carolinians intended to seize Fort Sumter, Anderson being commander of all the forts in the harbor, resolved to transfer the garrison of Fort Moultrie to Sumter. It was a delicate undertaking, for the southerners had watch-boats out upon the waters. Of course he did not entrust his secret to the secretary of war, for Floyd was even then supplying the Confederates with arms from the arsenals of the general government.

Only three or four of Major Anderson's most trusted officers were aware of his intentions. He resorted to a stratagem to get the women and children into Fort Sumter first. They were taken in a vessel, with ample provisions, to Fort Johnson on James Island, where, under pretext of difficulty in finding quarters for them, they were detained on board until evening. Three guns fired at Fort Moultrie were to be the signal for immediately consigning them to Fort Sumter. The movement was regarded by the people of Charleston as a natural and prudent measure of Anderson, who, they knew, believed they were about to attack Fort Moultrie, and so all suspicion was allayed.

The sun had set; an almost full-orbed moon was shining brightly, when the greater portion of the little garrison of Moultrie embarked for Sumter. The three guns were fired; the women and children were quickly taken from before Fort Johnson to Sumter, and the movement was successful. Two or three officers remained at Fort Moultrie to spike the guns, and cut down the flagstaff, that no secession banner might float from the peak from which the national flag had so long fluttered. When the soldiers and their families, with many weeks' provisions, were safely within the granite walls of Fort Sumter, Major Anderson wrote to the secretary of war:

"I have the honor to report that I have just completed, by the blessing of God, the removal to this fort, of all my garrison, except the surgeon, four North Carolina officers and seven men."

Floyd had already received intelligence of the act by a telegram from the Confederates, and he was surprised that his plans as to Anderson had failed. Governor Pickens sent a boat to Sumter with a demand to Major Anderson to evacuate the fort and return to Moultrie. This he promptly yet firmly refused to do, and he was denounced as an enemy of the South.

Floyd sought to have Anderson removed; but Buchanan refused to do so, and Floyd resigned from the cabinet, and was succeeded by Joseph Holt, a Union Kentuckian, who wrote to Major Anderson that his movement in transferring the garrison from Moultrie to Sumter, "was in every way admirable, alike for its humanity and patriotism, as for its soldiership."

Major Anderson's course was approved by Northern people everywhere, for they saw in it nothing but devotion to their cause; but Major Anderson and his little band of soldiers, were in extreme peril from the hour when they entered Fort Sumter. His friends knew that he was exposed to desertions within and foes without, and all were anxious.

Mark Stevens, one of the characters of this story, was an acquaintance of Major Anderson. His brother Arthur had served with Anderson in the Mexican war, and the strong friendship which sprang up between the two soldiers, was kept up after Arthur, the volunteer, was discharged.

While Major Anderson was transferring his forces from one fort to another, and undergoing trials of patience and temper almost unendurable, Arthur was on his way by rail to New York city.

He had taken a lively interest in the political

situation. Mark had been in Charleston during the autumn and witnessed something of the excitement. He had heard the most excited speeches of the extremists with calmness; yet every word they uttered was contrary to his political sentiments; but Mark kept a close mouth, for he had many friends in Charleston. Elsie Cole was still the great object of attraction to him. He loved Elsie desperately, though no avowal had as yet passed his lips. Mark was a mystery to all who knew him. Alec, an unfavored suitor for Elsie's hand, often asked himself why Mark did not propose. He was sure all was clear sailing.

Mark reached New York and, having transacted his business, was almost ready to go home, when one day, boarding the uptown stage, he saw sitting opposite him, a pale, small lady, whom he thought he had seen before. He noticed that her gaze was fixed upon him, and a half smile of recognition started two or three times upon her face, but faded away, as if in doubt.

"Who the deuce is she?" he asked himself again and again. He tried to look out of the stage window on the busy throngs hurrying along Broadway; but he found his glance again and again reverting to the little pale lady. They had gone several blocks before he finally determined to know who she was.

"I beg pardon," he said politely, bowing to the unknown; "it may seem rude in me; but I have surely seen you before. Are you not from Kentucky?"

"I am, and you are Mr. Stevens, are you not?" she asked.

"I am Mark Stevens."

"I thought you must be one of the boys, as I recognized a family resemblance."

"May I make so bold as to ask your name?"

"Anderson."

"I knew Major Anderson; are you his wife?"

"Yes, sir."

Mark shook her hand, and she, recognizing in him a friend and acquaintance, made room for him at her side. They had attracted some attention from the people in the stage; but Mark paid no heed to the other passengers.

"Mrs. Anderson, is your husband still in the South?"

"Yes, sir; he is in Charleston."

"Charleston? why, it is thought that the first blow will be struck in Charleston."

"Yes; I have great fears; but," she added in a low tone, "let us not talk here. It is too public. Will you come to my house? I want to consult with you."

"Where do you live?" he asked.

She hastily wrote her address on a card and handed it to him.

"When shall I call?" he asked.

"Any time this evening. I need your counsel, and must talk with you. Be sure and come."

He promised, and she motioned for him to pull the strap and stop the stage. Mark did so, and the brave little woman got out. He rode two blocks further, then alighted from the vehicle and went to a public house, where he ordered a meal. After supper he called on Mrs. Anderson.

The little lady was pale but calm. She was an invalid and certainly the last person one would expect to engage in a hazardous enterprise. Mrs. Anderson was the daughter of General Clinch of Georgia, and a more devoted wife, or a more sympathetic woman never lived. Mark found her surrounded by her children whom she was endeavoring to amuse.

She warmly greeted the young man, and asked about his father and mother and the remainder of the family, especially his brother Arthur, who had married a Spanish lady. He told her that Arthur had gone to Mexico to live. His father-in-law, Señor Rodrigo Estevan, had died leaving a vast fortune to be divided between his son and daughter.

"He has left in time to escape a terrible war, Mr. Stevens."

"Do you think there will really be war?"

"Undoubtedly!"

"I hope not; yet I am willing to do all I can for my country's cause, if it comes to blows," he said.

"I want your assistance, Mr. Stevens."

"You can have it in anything, Mrs. Anderson."

"I have resolved to go to my husband."

"And you want me to accompany you? I will do it," said Mark, as hope of meeting Elsie once more rose in his mind. There was an impassable barrier between him and Elsie, yet it was so pleasant to be with her, to gaze on her face and listen to the music of her voice, that he could not resist the temptation though it seemed a sin to think of her. To him that voice was the unforgotten music of some delightful dream recalled in after years.

Mrs. Anderson dispelled his pleasant delusion by saying:

"I did not send for you with that design, Mr. Stevens; but there is a man in this town who was a sergeant under my husband in Mexico. I want to find him."

"What is his name?"

"Peter Hart. He is brave, faithful and shrewd, perfectly devoted to my husband, and I want to take him to Major Anderson."

" Have you seen this Peter Hart since you came to the city?"

" No, sir, nor have I communicated with him in any way; but to-day I incidentally learned that there was a man named Peter Hart on the police force."

" If that be true, it will be the easiest matter possible to find him."

" Yet you will have to exercise some caution, Mr. Stevens, for New York is not entirely free from southerners. If they should learn that I was preparing to visit my husband, I would in all probability be prevented."

" Leave the matter of finding Peter Hart to me, Mrs. Anderson. I will manage it so carefully, that should it turn out to be some other Peter Hart than the one you want, he shall not suspect why I want him."

Next day Mark went to the chief of police and inquired if there was a man on the force named Peter Hart. There was. Was he an Irishman? That was his nationality, the bald-headed clerk answered. Next Mark asked if he could see officer Hart. When he was off duty, he could, and he took the policeman's address and went to look him up as soon as he was at liberty.

To his ring at the door of the small house, a stout Irish woman appeared. Was this the home

of Mr. Hart? "To be sure it was."   Was he in?
He was, the Hibernian female answered.   Could
Mark see him?   "Indade," he could, and then
she called, "Paythur, here's a gintleman as wants
to see ye."

Peter Hart appeared in the hall, and Mark expressed a wish to ask him some questions, and the
policeman, supposing that he had some grievance
to lay before him, suggested that he had better go
to the station.

"But this concerns you personally, Peter," said
Mark.   "Do you know Major Robert Anderson?"

"Do I know the major? why, sir, I know him
as well as me own wife Maggie.   I was his sergeant when we fit the Mexicans."

"Then you are acquainted with his wife?"

"Know her like a book."

"She wants to see you, Peter, on some very
important business."

"Faith, I'll go at once," Peter declared.

That evening, accompanied by his wife, Peter
Hart called on Mrs. Anderson.   The meeting was
very cordial and friendly.

"I have sent for you, to ask you to do me a
favor," said Mrs. Anderson.

"Anything Mrs. Anderson wishes, I will do,"
was Hart's prompt reply.

" But it may be more than you imagine," added Mrs. Anderson.

" Anything Mrs. Anderson wishes," the brave fellow declared.

" I want you to go with me to Fort Sumter."

Peter looked at his wife a moment, and promptly responded: " I will go, madam."

Then the earnest woman added:

" But, Hart, I want you to stay with the major; you will have to leave your family and give up a good situation."

Again Hart looked at his wife and, receiving an assenting glance, replied:

" I will go, madam!"

Mrs. Anderson, not willing to take away the husband without his wife's consent, turned to Mrs. Hart and asked:

" But, Maggie, what do you say?"

" Indade, ma'am, an' it's Maggie's sorry she can't do as much for you as Paythur can," was the reply of the warm-hearted woman.

" Then, Peter, be ready to start in twenty-four hours," said Mrs. Anderson.

Mark interposed a mild remonstrance.

" Mrs. Anderson, will you be strong enough?"

" I must be strong enough."

" Do you make this journey with the advice of your physicians?"

"I do it against their advice," she declared; "but Robert is there penned up in the fort. I must see him; he needs Peter Hart's aid, and he shall have it."

Mark Stevens decided to accompany them to Charleston, for he wished to see Elsie once more before the chasm between them widened into impassibility.

Twenty-four hours later, Mrs. Anderson, contrary to the advice of her physicians, started by railway for Charleston, accompanied by Peter Hart in the capacity of a servant, and Mark Stevens as friend and protector.

As the train thundered along the iron rails, Mark Stevens, who occupied the seat behind Mrs. Anderson, leaned his head against the cushion and, closing his eyes, tried to sleep; but strange fancies came into his head and drove slumber away. Why was he making this journey? In one sense it was a crime to even think of Elsie Cole. When he remembered his relative, the tender-hearted Alec, desperately in love with Elsie, and yet willing for his friend's sake to yield her to him, Mark thought himself the greatest villain on earth. He had played the traditional dog in the manger; but even with the knowledge of how he had wronged poor Alec, he seemed drawn by some irresistible force to further crimes for which he despised himself. This journey could only result in additional misery, yet he could not forego it.

" No, no," his weaker self seemed to plead with his better self, " let me go and bask in the sunlight of those bright blue eyes once more; let me hear the music of that voice again; let me dream just a little longer, then I will awake and shake off this guilty vision. It is so sweet to dream on, that I cannot awake just yet."

Self-condemnation, the ruin to which he was rushing, the misery he was entailing, not only for himself but for the being who had for months been the bright vision of his fancy, could not drive the subject from his mind. Mark was selfish even against his own interests. For the pleasure of a few days he would endanger life, honor and happiness.

It is ever thus. Pleasure is always deceptive, so alluring that one runs great risks to enjoy the present. Mark had always been a dreamer, and as he lay back in his seat, he seemed to mingle the present, past and the impenetrable future into one glorious picture the central figure of which was Elsie Cole.

As the train thundered on, the sullen roar seemed a lullaby to Mark's waking senses. He slept; he dreamed. As usual, the vision of his dreams was a fairy-like creature. She seemed an angel hovering over him with the sweetest smiles.

8

On either side of her were two dark clouds, on one of which was painted the past, on the other the future.

She wore sweet, entrancing smiles and whispered peace to his soul. That dread, that long doubt of years was removed by a single whisper, and he clasped her in his arms. Imparadised in a vision of glory, he seemed wafted from the world to happiness unknown to mortals on earth; but such joys are always delusive. He awoke to find himself on the train, still thundering southward on a doubtful mission.

According to authentic history, from Thursday night, the time of her departure, until Sunday morning, when she arrived at Fort Sumter, Mrs. Anderson neither ate, drank nor slept. When they reached the State of Virginia, her ears were constantly greeted with ominous words and threats against her husband.

"Old Bob Anderson at Sumter won't surrender to General Beauregard," said one of the Virginians, who had but just come aboard the train. "We'll see about that when we get him."

"That we will," another declared.

The pale little woman shuddered as these words fell on her ears; but she did not allow them to suspect that she was the wife of Major Anderson, whom they were talking about in severe words.

"I HAVE BROUGHT YOU PETER HART," SHE SAID.

"Anderson is a southern man," said one. "He was born in Kentucky and is, or has been a slave-holder. Why does he cling to the Union?"

"Oh, it's some false notion of duty to the nation."

"Well, that false notion of his may cost him very dear."

She had difficulty at times to suppress her rising indignation; but she controlled herself, and the train thundered on. She gained considerable information which was valuable to her husband, for the Confederates talked quite freely. Having reached Charleston, on Sunday morning, after some difficulty she procured permission to visit Fort Sumter with Peter Hart. As the little boat touched the wharf of the fortress near the sally-port, and the name of Mrs. Anderson was announced to the sentry, the major, informed of her presence, rushed out and clasped her in his arms with the exclamation in a vehement whisper, intended for her ears only:

"My glorious wife!"

"I have brought you Peter Hart," she said. "The children are well; I return to-night."

She then partook of some refreshments, and after resting a few hours, returned to New York, where she was for a long time threatened with brain fever, the result of excitement and her long, toilsome journey. This devoted wife and fearless little woman, had given her husband a most faithful friend and assistant under all circumstances, in the fort, during the three months of severe trial that ensued. She had done what the government would not or could not do,—not *sent* but *taken* a most valuable reinforcement to Fort Sumter. A recruit, as history shows, that saved the fort from burning two or three times during the siege.

CHAPTER VI.

MARK AND ELSIE.

THE suburban home of Mr. Henry Cole, father of Elsie, was a neat cottage of the familiar southern type, which nestled near the bosom of a grove of sweet gum and pine trees, in a little village about three miles from Charleston. In the grove sang a mocking-bird family. Around the house were a few acres of ground, which were carefully cultivated. In one corner grazed a group of beautiful Minerva-eyed Jerseys. At one side of the house, hives of bees were placed near a flower garden, sloping down to the street, which passed in front of the house several rods distant. At the foot of the hill was a bubbling spring, whose sparkling waters supplied the needs of the household. A superb English mastiff eyed with dignified glance the casual visitor, whose coming was apt to be announced by the bark of two of the finest dogs in the country; one a Newfoundland, and the other a white English bull-terrier. The interior of the cottage was simple and unassuming.

118

Bric-a-brac and trumpery "articles of bigotry and virtue" were wanting. The places they usually occupy were taken up with wide windows and generous hearths. There was a library of choice books in the house, for Mr. Cole was not only one of the leading lawyers of Charleston, but a man of considerable literary attainments; but this summer cottage, as he called it, was neither a library, a museum, nor an art gallery, but a delightful home.

He had two sons and a daughter. One son was an officer in the army; one had graduated in the naval academy and was in England on business; while his daughter, the peerless Elsie, was at home. She was the idol of her parents, and, had she not possessed remarkably good sense, would have been spoiled. Mr. Cole was wealthy and influential. He not only enjoyed a very lucrative practice, but owned half a dozen cotton and rice plantations and several hundred slaves. In 1860 and 1861, no man in South Carolina was better or more favorably known than Henry Cole. He had served several terms in the State Legislature, and had been "talked of for congress." While Mr. Cole was decidedly Southern in sentiment, he lacked that peculiar speech, which in those days was necessary to make him popular. He was conservative in his views, and when it came to the discussion of questions of secession, he counselled moderation. In a speech shortly after Lincoln's election he said:

"My heart is with South Carolina, for her destiny is mine. On her soil I was born, in her territory I found my wife, in Charleston my children were born, and I love my dear native State next to my God and family. As to slavery, an institution tolerated since the Christian era began, I believe it must be right. As for the negro, I know his condition in slavery is better than when free. Give him his freedom, and he becomes a worthless, drunken vagabond. The northern people envy our wealth and prosperity, which they see consists in slaves, and they have worked up their sympathies for the downtrodden African race, until they believe they have a religious cause at stake. Some may be sincere; but the masses are instigated by envy. Nevertheless, fellow citizens, they dare not touch a slave. They have elected Mr. Lincoln president"—at this some one in the audience cried, "Yes, by fraud"—"I am not sure it was as much Republican fraud as Democratic folly. Had we not become divided, the Republican party would have dwindled away, the craze have blown over, and, like the Know-Nothings, the Whigs and Federalists, the Republicans would have quietly passed out of existence. But Mr. Lincoln has been elected; let us give him a chance.

Let him take his seat. If he breaks the constitution, or abrogates the decisions of the supreme court, then we can easily impeach him.

"If South Carolina does secede, I will go with her; but I warn you that only war and misery can follow such an act. We have a powerful North with unbounded resources, and the South must be the battle-ground. They can grow up and import soldiers faster than we can kill them. This fair city, these lovely plantations, and our beautiful homes will be ruins ere the war is over; and the chances are that humiliation, defeat and the loss of every slave will be the result."

Mr. Cole's remarks were greeted with marked disapproval. No sooner had he quit the stand, than a young South Carolinian mounted it and began in an eloquent way to "show up" the fallacy and sophistry of his remarks. He asserted that if they lay supinely on their backs until Lincoln was seated, and had their hands tied, they would be powerless. Let Lincoln once get in control, and they would find an armed host in the South, and the abolition of slavery declared. Better be cautious and, as Patrick Henry of old said, resist while they could. The doctrines of the immortal Calhoun had established the proof of State-supremacy and he who was not with South Carolina was against her. He who was against South Carolina was an enemy.

Mr. Cole was an even-tempered man, and did not become angry at the tirade. He was as loyal as the speaker before him; but he foresaw what the inevitable result would be, if war should follow.

But as time went on, and as the southern States, one by one went out, and formed the Southern Confederacy, he became an enthusiastic supporter of the new republic, and was chosen colonel of one of the provisional regiments which had been organized. He displayed as much military genius as he had legal ability, and his regiment was thoroughly equipped and well drilled long before the shot was fired on Fort Sumter, and when General Beauregard came to Charleston as commander of the Confederate armies, he was among the first to apply for an assignment.

The war was still brewing. Since the 9th of January, 1861, when Major Stevens, in command of a Confederate battery on Morris Island, fired on the *Star of the West* sent with supplies for Fort Sumter, and drove her from the harbor, all had been comparatively at peace, though drilling and mustering was constantly going on, and all preparations were being made for war.

It was near the close of day, in the first week of April, which in that semi-tropical land was like summer, that pretty Elsie Cole stood at the gate gazing down the broad street, which, after leaving the village, gradually became a country turnpike. The excitement in the city was so great, that Colonel Cole had removed his family to this quiet nook, where they might for awhile be free from the shock of war.

Merry, light-hearted Elsie had little thought of the coming storm. She was like a sunbeam, dispelling gloom wherever she went. Some who were intimate with Elsie thought she had never known a sorrow, or that no cloud had ever passed over her sky; yet there were times when she was sad, and sighed as if there had been a dark period somewhere in her life. Those melancholy moments came when she was alone. On this evening her face had lost some of its sunlight. Was it because her brothers were away, or that her father was in danger?

She had a rose in her hair, and as she stood leaning against the gate post which was overgrown with creeping vines, she looked the very picture of loveliness.

A carriage driven at a brisk pace came down the quiet street. The clattering of hoofs and roll of wheels first attracted her attention, and, glancing up, she discovered that the negro coachman was driving toward the gate. Her large blue eyes grew round with wonder as the door was thrown open, and a young man leaped from the vehicle.

" Elsie!" he cried.

" Mr. Stevens! where did you come from?"

For a moment it would have been difficult to tell whether she was more astonished than delighted at the appearance of the stranger. In the dimming light of the departing day, her face flushed to the hue of the rose in her hair.

" I came from the North," Mark answered.

" From the North, and dare come here?" and she tried to assume a haughty expression, but failed.

" Yes, Elsie; I must come and see you once more, before——"

" Before the war begins?"

" Yes; for it now seems inevitable."

" Have you come to the South to join the noble race of Stevens who have sworn to die for their country? It was like a Stevens for you to do so. Your name can claim the honor of firing the first gun of the war. It was Major Stevens, a relative of yours, who fired the first shot at the *Star of the West.*"

" I do not wish to discuss the war," said Mark. " Let us forget the past and cease to speculate on the future. The present is too glorious to think of either, Elsie. To be with you, to hear your voice, to gaze into your eyes is a joy which I would not have alloyed by dread for the future."

"Don't be sentimental, Mr. Stevens," said Elsie, as they walked toward the vine-clad cottage.

"Then let us talk of other matters. Where is your cousin Dick?"

"He is in England."

"When did he sail?"

"A few weeks ago."

"I suppose he will return soon?"

"I don't know."

"And Clara?"

"Didn't you see her in Charleston?"

"No."

"Surely you did not stop long."

"Only long enough to change, and hire a coach to bring me here."

"She is in Charleston and would have been glad to see you."

There was a beautiful vine-clad veranda in front of the house, with a rustic seat on which she asked him to be seated. The twilight hours flew by as silent and free as birds on the wing. The sable cloak of night pinned with millions of glittering stars, had already been flung over the earth, and the disk of the rising moon began to appear over the distant city. There is a charm in a southern night, with all its voluptuousness, that seems to enchant one. Those who have experienced an evening in South Carolina never forget it. The balmy breezes, the soft southern skies and the voluptuous foliage all bespeak richness, splendor and generosity. But the South is not now what it was before the war. Almost thirty years have not sufficed to restore the ravages and devastation of four years.

"Did you come from Kentucky?" Elsie asked, plucking a flower.

"No, not direct. I came from New York."

"I read in the paper this morning that Major Anderson's wife had come. I hope she will persuade him into surrendering."

"Why?"

"Because it will save bloodshed."

"Do you believe Beauregard will fire on Sumter?"

"As sure as the world moves. The people don't like the actions of Anderson. His removing his troops from Fort Moultrie into Fort Sumter is regarded as an act of open hostility."

"But was it not prudent?"

"If he expects to resist, it was; but he should surrender and save bloodshed."

Mark had it on his lips to answer that it was his duty as a soldier to defend his fort as long as he could; but he refrained from saying anything. He could not find it in his heart to quarrel with Elsie, no matter how much they might differ.

After several moments' silence and deliberation, he said:

"Elsie, I have come to pay a short visit to my friends in Charleston, more to you than to any other. I will not discuss the present political trouble. Friendship is dearer than all, Elsie, and though persons may differ it is no reason they should quarrel. I leave soon, perhaps never to return. We may never meet again on earth; let our last meeting be pleasant."

She assented, and both being sensible agreed to refrain from discussing the situation at all. Mark remained until late. Colonel Cole came home before he left and shook the hand of the young Kentuckian warmly. He wore the uniform of his rank; but there was nothing offensively partisan in his conversation. He talked of the coming trouble as a matter of news, and seemed to regard it more as a calamity than a blessing to the South.

Mark met Mrs. Cole, a mild, sweet woman of forty-five or fifty, whose cheek was furrowed with care, and whose hair was becoming streaked with gray. Both father and mother joined Elsie in extending a warm invitation to the young man to return every day during his stay. He accepted gladly. In fact, had they forbidden his coming, he could not have refrained from doing so.

Next day he was standing on the piazza of the

city hotel, when his attention was drawn to a fresh arrival, consisting of a spruce rockaway carriage drawn by a fine pair of spirited horses, which were driven by a self-possessed, good-looking young gentleman. As he drew up at the door, the clerk, bar-tender, porter, hostler, and "boots" were at the side of his carriage in a jiffy, obsequiously assisting the young man to alight and bring in his baggage. Giving these worthies a cool survey, as if he would judge by their appearance whether the remainder of the establishment occupied a satisfactory standard of respectability, he threw the reins to the colored hostler and sprang to the ground. Casting a rapid glance at his baggage to see that all was right, he turned upon his heel and for the first time saw Mark. Fixing his eyes upon him for a moment, he made a rush at him, and, grasping his hand with a vigor that recalled to Mark's mind all he had ever read of the thumb screws of the inquisition, he cried:

"How are you, my dear fellow? What? don't know me! Well, that's a good joke, as sure as you are my old friend and cousin Mark Stevens, whom I have roomed with, ate with and fought with for a whole year and a half at Harvard. Why, you precious old muff! Oho! you do remember me, do you?"

Mark recognized him at once, when he heard

his voice. It was his chum at school, Alexander Stevens, his cousin and rival.

Though a few months had made quite a change, yet he could now recognize in the newly polished individual before him the harum-scarum, devil-may-care boy of school days. Before he had time to mumble out his surprise, Alec in his roistering way continued:

" But come in, come in! I must get the dust out of my œsophagus, my throat, gullet, or whatever you have a mind to call it. Ah!" said he as his eye caught the glitter of the contents of the bar, " 'is this a dagger which I see before me, the handle toward my hand? Come, let me clutch thee'—what'll you have, *mon cher?* As for me, give me brandy in the virgin state, I thank you. Water is very good for navigable purposes, some one says, but for a constant beverage give me pony brandy. Come, name the nectar. Under what disguise will you imbibe a modicum of the invisible spirit of wine? If you are not familiar with its nomenclature, call it a cocktail, hey!"

Mark, who had had hardly time to get in a word edgeways until now, managed to say that his habits, religion and constitution all combined would not permit his taking anything stronger than lemonade. Alec made a wry face and, shivering, declared that Mark had surely become

9

wholly Yankeefied in the last few months; but nevertheless he declared that he was willing to allow his friend to indulge his whim to its utmost on this their first meeting.

Who does not feel his heart leap with joy in meeting such a friend and relative as Alec Stevens? War, storm, and disaster, even rivalry in love made no difference with him. He was still the rattle-headed chatterbox, possessed of a gift of word and an endless flow of language, that would run Webster's unabridged dictionary to the very last syllable every day in the year if enough listeners could be obtained. It seemed almost impossible for him to desist, when he had fairly commenced talking, and should he be fortunate enough to get a fellow cornered for a long evening, he would inundate him with conversation and be in his most delightful element.

His happiness at this meeting was fully reciprocated by Mark. He shook hands with him half a dozen times within twenty minutes, and then they could be content with doing nothing less than joining arms as they walked the piazza, reviewing the cherished reminiscences of their first acquaintance. He insisted so stoutly on Mark's taking dinner with him, that he was forced to do so.

"You see, my boy, I have a great deal to say to you and a very limited time to say it in, as the fiat has gone forth that I depart from this burg in the morning at precisely ten A.M. There sounds the loud hewgag. Let us grub. I am as ferocious as a vulture, and if there is any thing in this world I like when I am hungry, it is victuals and drink. Come——"

At the stroke of the gong, they joined in the general rush for the dining-room door, and by dint of good generalship secured seats in the vicinity of the most tempting viands, where, after they became firmly settled, Alec continued his conversation.

"It is barely possible you may have some curiosity to know why I am in Charleston, and it is also quite possible that you may guess," remarked Alec, as he proceeded to make use of the best of the viands placed before him. "You might guess that I was an officer recruiting for the southern army, or on some secret mission from Jeff Davis."

"Aha!" grunted Mark, his mouth full of beefsteak.

"But I am not. Then again you might think that I am here on a certain love affair in which I am so unfortunate, and somebody else is so successful——"

"Ahem! pass the biscuit, please."

"But I am not," answered Alec, as he passed the plate of biscuit to his friend. "I have degenerated into a negro hunter."

"Why, Alec, I thought you were opposed to the traffic."

"Well, on general principles I am; but Aunt Aggy is old and weak. She is not long for this world. Father has bought her children one by one in order to have them near the poor old thing; but one boy named Eph for a long time disappeared. He had been sold to a rice planter, and we did not know where he was, until by accident we learned that Eph was near Charleston. Father, with his great heart overflowing with sympathy, resolved to send his wayward boy with sufficient of the filthy lucre to purchase Eph, and take him home where he might make glad the kind heart of his mother."

"Your mission is a noble one, Alec," said Mark. "But won't you stop on your return?"

"Why, Mark, do you want me to?"

"Of course I do."

"You know you and I are so unfortunate as to both love the same girl———"

"Don't allow that to interfere with our friendship."

"It shall not, my good fellow, so far as I am concerned. Win Elsie, and I wish you much joy, and hope you won't forget me when it comes to naming babies. Again, I more than suspect that this big rumpus which is coming on will find us holding different opinions. It won't affect my friendship. Nothing will."

"Alec," said Mark, grasping his friend's hand, "you are a noble-hearted fellow and ten times more of a man than I!"

"Hush, hush! There is no need of that. I am only a wild, rattle-brained fellow; but I like you, Mark; I can't help it. You always have been a little mysterious to me; but all the same I like you. If you really wish me to stop on my way back I will do so; but, Mark, you never loved Elsie more than I. I may be wrong, for she loves you; but I can't help it, though it makes me feel like a fool."

"I want you to stop, Alec, and stay as long as I do. I am going away, and I feel that we will not meet again soon."

Alec declared he would stop, hoped Mark would not grow sentimental, and promised if he could help it, not to interfere with him and Elsie.

"But, Mark, I want to warn you to go in, or I shall not wait always. Win that girl, you can—I may never do it; but as sure as you leave Charleston without having popped the question, I will lay siege. Now I have been fair with you, and given you a clear road for a long time. If you don't take advantage of it, don't blame me."

"I won't."

Mark was miserable that night and almost wished he was dead. While unable to win Elsie himself, he was standing between the best man in the world, and the truest woman. But for him, she might love Alec, and to him, she was lost.

Next morning, Mark called on his friend after breakfast.

"Aha!" cried Alec in a loud, cheery voice. "Good morning, old chap! how d'ye feel this morning? Let's go and get a cigar."

They adjourned to a cigar store, in front of which was a wooden Indian, to procure a weed. The man behind the short, dingy counter passed a box out to them, and Alec, taking one, said:

"Here's a light. Those cigars cost about twenty-five cents a hundred, and were made in Pennsylvania, or I am no judge. What a humbug! Real Havana! They have the poorest cigars in Charleston imaginable. Now, this roll of leaves, for instance, is more of cabbage, and less of *nicotina*, than is desirable. I am exceedingly fond of savory cauliflower, *broccoli colewart kraut-salaat*, and other plants of the genus *Brassica*, but then I don't like them put up this way, by any manner of means."

"When do you start, Alec?"

"Within an hour and sixty minutes, my cherished friend and cousin, and now, by the way, as

I have half a dozen letters to post and wish to get twice as many, let us go to the post office. The carrier does not know me well enough to bring the mail to me."

Sauntering leisurely along the sunny side of the street, they came to the post office, and Alec called out his name. One was handed out by the putty-faced individual who presided within.

"If this isn't provoking!" said Alec. "Only one solitary epistle, when I expected a dozen at least. If they can't keep a better and fuller assortment of this kind of literature on hand, I've a mind to lease a room across the street and start an opposition post office, where I will supply nice printed letters in any quantity at two cents apiece."

The individual who glanced lightning at Alec through the orifice made no response. Alec remarked that the envelope was a dainty, perfumed affair, and the writing in a neat, feminine hand. Opening it, he cried:

"Hello, what is this? How did she know I was here! Why, Mark, here's an invitation to a ball at the home of Major Stevens, my uncle, on the evening of the eleventh, given in honor of the nineteenth birthday of cousin Clara. Look here, Mark, I'll bet my head for a football, there is one for you. Ask that hatchet-faced Lord Byron, if he can't treat you as well as me."

Mark did so and found a similar invitation for himself. This made Alec more determined to stop on his return. "It will be just one week," he said. "I will be here by that time and for once we will shake off dull care and enjoy ourselves. I will buy Eph and send him home to his old mother, with the horses and rockaway, and then I can go home by rail."

Alec departed at the time agreed upon, and Mark hastened to assure his cousin he would be present at the ball. Most of the intervening time was spent with Elsie, and Mark was a score of times on the point of declaring his love, but from a sense of right refrained from doing so. They walked and rode together, sang together, played duets, and she never seemed more nearly perfect. Sweet, happy days were those, days which Mark to the hour of his death will never forget. While all about him was a furious uprising, wild excitement, maddening speeches, the marshalling of clans for the conflict, he was living a life of bliss and peace,——a sweet dream, without a single care. Oh, that such a lot could be his, forever, though guilt at times made him almost hide his face in shame.

The Confederacy had been formed out of the seceded States, and on February 9, 1861, Jefferson Davis and Alexander H. Stevens were elected

president and vice-president of the new republic.
Fort after fort in the South had been surrendered
by their regular commanders, until the South had
almost complete control of the principal strong-
holds in that territory. Floyd had planned and
executed matters with a firm hand. Southern congressmen and United States senators were resign-
ing their seats. On the 29th of January, Kansas,
over which there had been so much dissension,
became the 34th State of the Union. Lincoln had
been inaugurated on the 4th of March as fourteenth president of the United States, and he was
taking vigorous measures to stop the progress of
the uprising.

While lounging about the rotunda of the hotel,
Mark learned much of what was going on. He
heard one man say that their agents and friends in
New York had telegraphed them that the steamer
Atlantic had sailed with troops and supplies for
Fort Sumter on the 7th. He also learned that
there was a rumor that troops were soon to gather
at Washington, and that the government of South
Carolina had been notified that provisions would
be sent to Major Anderson by force if necessary;
but Mark hardly realized the danger. He was too
much lost in the mazes of a happy dream to dread
a coming shock.

The evening of the 11th came, and the palatial

mansion of Major Stevens was a scene of brilliance.
The élite and beauty of Charleston, that proud city
of the South, were there. Major Stevens was admired by all. He had commanded the battery
that fired on the *Star of the West,* was a brave and
determined man and known by all to be an honorable, upright gentleman. His daughter Clara was
quite a favorite, and the young people anticipated
an excellent time. Mark was there among the
first. Alec had come back; but Mark, with Elsie
leaning on his arm as he passed through the brilliant halls and art galleries beneath gilded chande-
liers, seemed to have almost forgotten his cousin.

"Well, Mark is enjoying himself," Alec said
with a sigh. "It's at the cost of my happiness;
but I don't blame Mark. Let him go in and win
her,—I would. If he don't do it, I will. I promised Mark a clear field while he is here, so he
had better make hay while the sun shines."

Mark was enjoying just a little while longer the
music of a voice which reason had taught him he
was never more to hear, was basking in the sunlight of a pair of lovely eyes he was soon to see
no more. The crowd was gay. The room was
brilliant with uniforms and glittering epaulettes.
General Beauregard himself was present early in the
evening, but urgent duties called him elsewhere.

The home of Major Stevens overlooked the bay.

and far in the distance Fort Sumter loomed. Mark, in his love, bewilderment and self-condemnation, had almost forgotten the country and the brave men in the distant fort.

When music rose in its softest strains and with voluptuous swell, he joined in the dance with Elsie. Once she left him for a few minutes for a Confederate colonel; but he sought her as soon as the set was over, and when they were again apart from the others, he said:

" Elsie, I want to be with you all the remainder of the evening."

" Why?" she asked.

" Because I leave early in the morning, and—and——"

" We may never see each other again!"

" That is exactly what I mean, Elsie. I go perhaps never to return."

They went into the conservatory where the light of a southern moon fell gently upon them. For a long time both were silent, and then he said:

" Elsie, I hope you realize our situation."

"I do," she sighed. It was a favorable omen, yet how dared he propose? He a loyal unionist, about to engage in a desperate struggle, could not avow his love for this pretty rebel even had he been otherwise at liberty to love. After a long silence, he said:

"Elsie, you have two brothers and a father, who will probably engage in the coming struggle. You appreciate what it is, and for your sake I hope it may not come."

By an effort she threw off the spell, which seemed bowing down her spirits, and said:

"Let us not be gloomy. Nothing is so bad as it seems. Did you notice Captain Taylor, how attentive he was to Cousin Clara? Now she don't care a fig for him, and he is almost breaking his heart for her. I would not allow myself to be so ridiculous."

"Were you ever in love?"

"Oh, Mr. Stevens, what a question!" she cried, her eyes growing round with wonder.

"It is a question that admits of an answer by yes or no."

"It is a question that provokes one to falsehood. One in love never admits it, save in the most sacred confidence to a special friend. If one has never been in love,—but this is all nonsense."

"Do you ever feel melancholy?"

"Sometimes."

"Do you believe in presentiments?"

"I hardly know."

Before they could say more, Alec came hurriedly forward; his face flushed with excitement.

"Mark, you here? I have been hunting you and Elsie. Have you heard the news?"

"ELSIE, I HOPE YOU REALIZE OUR SITUATION."

"What news?" both asked.

"General Beauregard has demanded the surrender of Fort Sumter, and if it is not surrendered by four o'clock they will fire on the fort."

"Heaven forbid!"

"It is true. The soldiers have been summoned to their posts, and four thousand new troops have entered the city."

Mark now remembered having noticed a considerable stir among the soldiers and citizens. Elsie, who had been inclined to make light of the prospect of war, shuddered with dread, when she found it so near a realization. "I am going down to the battery to see what all that whooping and yelling means," cried Alec. "Come along, Elsie, you had better go home. There will be trouble soon, for the big shells from Sumter may reach Charleston."

Alec was gone in a moment, and Elsie, shuddering, said:

"Let us go in."

As they passed along the narrow garden path toward the house, he said:

"Elsie, I regret this."

"Will it drive you away?"

"Yes." Then, after a moment's silence, he asked, "Will you think of me when I am gone?"

"Yes."

They entered the house, where all had been joy and gayety a few moments before; but people were now dispersing. Men were hurrying down to the batteries in their ball dress, and crossing over to James Island.

Mark consulted his watch and found that it was after three o'clock. He would just have time to reach the battery before the fearful blow was struck. The city was ablaze with torches, and although the throngs were silent, there was uneasiness in their manner.

"Elsie, I must go. I don't know why; but I shall die if I don't," said Mark.

"Will you come back?"

"I hope to, Elsie!" he whispered in her ear. "Forgive me,—it is wrong, I know it. God knows I would not say this if I could help it; I ought never to have come here; but I could not help it;—you are the magnet which drew me. *Elsie, I love you!*"

They were alone in one of the many bay windows which adorned the house. She started back and gave him such a look of horror that he never forgot it. She was turning coldly away, when he hoarsely gasped:

"Forgive me!" and was gone.

No sooner was she alone than she fell weeping on a sofa.

Mark, meanwhile, was hurrying as rapidly as he could toward Cumings' Point. He saw wild-eyed men on every hand. There were no yells nor cheers; but a silent excitement, more awful than the loudest thunders of battle, seemed to prevail. Mark gained the island just as some one said:

"Time is up!"

The battery was lighted by brilliant torches, and he saw the wild, excited faces of men everywhere.

"There is old Ruffin at the gun," said one man. "Beauregard gave him permission to fire the first shot."

Mark looked and saw an old man with a face like a devil, his long, gray hair streaming in the night wind. This was the white-haired Virginian Ruffin, who begged the privilege of firing the first shot,—a deed of which he boasted as long as he lived.*

When the hour of four in the morning arrived, the fort had not surrendered. Then came an order from Beauregard to fire the shot. The old white-haired man could be seen dancing about like a man possessed. Suddenly he seized the lanyard and gave it a jerk. There was an earth-shaking

---

* In the summer of 1865, Ruffin, at the age of seventy years, committed suicide, declaring in a note left behind, "I cannot survive the liberties of my country."

A LARGE ROUND SHOT WENT HISSING THROUGH THE AIR AND
STRUCK AGAINST THE SOLID WALL OF FORT SUMTER.

report, and a large round shot went hissing through the air and struck against the solid wall of Fort Sumter with fearful force.

A few moments' silence,—then tremendous yells rose on the air, and a storm of cannon-balls and shells flew over Fort Sumter.

Not a shot was returned until after seven o'clock. Mark, in his anxiety, asked himself again and again:

"Can it be that they will surrender without firing a shot?"

Day dawned, and the thunder of guns went on.

"Hello, Mark, are you here?" suddenly cried a voice at his side, and, turning about, he saw Alec. "The terrible war has begun, and God only knows how it will end; but Sumter don't seem to be doing anything. The fight is all on one side. By the way, Mark, do you know that cuss of a nigger Eph has played me a mean trick. I bought him to send him to his old mother, before she died. I started him home with my fine team. Some of the infernal abolitionists persuaded him to escape, and he has gone North, horses and all. I say cuss a nigger, anyhow———"

At this moment, a puff of smoke was seen to issue from the top of Fort Sumter, and a shell came screeching through the air. The famous siege of Fort Sumter had begun.

10

CHAPTER VII.

THE ALABAMA.

THE first year of the war, Dick Stevens, whom we met in Florida, was in England. He had been travelling in Europe, and his father, having some interests in a Liverpool cotton house, ordered his son there to look after them. This was not unpleasant to Dick, especially as he had met with a Miss Lorena Lancaster, a Liverpool girl, while travelling on the continent, and had formed a warm attachment for her.

Dick had heard much of the war. He knew that his father was in the command of a regiment, had fought valiantly at Bull Run, and that his country was all in the wildest state of excitement; yet so wholly were his thoughts taken up with his love affair, that war, country and friends were of minor consideration. Of course the South would gain her independence. Such a thing as defeat had never entered his mind. He did not suppose that Yankees could fight. They had taken but little part in the war of 1812, and practically no part in the war with Mexico. The West and South had fought those battles, and the idea that the speculating, canting, psalm-singing Puritan could or would fight, was too ridiculous to be entertained. They could organize negro-stealing societies, and incite slaves to murder masters; but he never dreamed they would fight. In France and in England he found strong sympathizers with the South. He was assured again and again that Great Britain would declare war against the United States and assist the South to obtain her independence.

He reached Liverpool in May, and one day, as he was walking leisurely down the street, he was accosted by some one with:

" Hello, Dick Stevens, what are you doing here?"

Dick looked up and saw a young man coming toward him. His voice and face were familiar, and, recognizing him a moment later, he cried:

" Charley Cole, can it be possible this is you? Where have you been?"

" Cruising about, my fine fellow. I supposed you were at home in the army, winning battles for your country."

" No," Dick answered blushing. " I am looking after some of my father's interests here; though I am going to help the South. But Charley, why are you not in the service?"

" I am."

" And why are you here?"

With a smile, Charley Cole said:

" I am engaged in a service for the South, Dick."

" What is it?"

" Do you really wish to help your country?"

" Certainly."

" Then you can have an opportunity," Charley Cole remarked. " We are organizing a crew, and are building a vessel to drive the Yankee commerce from the seas. This ship will soon be completed and will want recruits."

" I am no sailor, Charley. You graduated at Annapolis and served in the United States Navy; —you have experience, and I have none."

" But we'll soon make a sailor of you. I am going to ship as a common seaman. You can also."

" What is to be the name of this ship?"

" *The 290.** The Lairds of Birkenhead, England, are building her for the Confederate States government. Captain James D. Bullock, as agent for the Confederacy, is superintending her construction."

" How will you get her out?"

" As a ruse, she is to be sent on a trial trip with a large party of ladies and gentlemen."

---

* The name by which the *Alabama* was first known.

After that, Dick met his cousin Charley Cole quite frequently; but although Charley often endeavored to persuade him to join the cruiser, his argument had little effect, until one day, while in company with Miss Lancaster, she asked:

"What are you doing for the South, Mr. Stevens?"

Stammering and blushing, he answered:

"I am superintending my father's business."

"And your State, your kindred, all struggling with an invader! Oh, Mr. Stevens, I thought you a brave man!"

Dick blushed to the tips of his ears and felt his blood tingling to the ends of his fingers. How he got through the evening he never exactly knew. To be called a coward by the woman he loved, and, what was worse, in his own heart to realize that he was a coward, was humiliating. In his bewilderment, he asked:

"Would you advise me to ship as a common sailor?"

"Certainly, if your country needs your services."

He thought of the new privateer and his cousin's desire to have him ship with him. He left the house like one in a daze. The street lights glimmered, and he saw as through a mist. He had been reproved by the only being for whose opinion he cared. Dick resolved to prove his courage.

Next day, July 3, 1862, he signed the articles which made him one of the " *290*," afterward the *Alabama.* The shipping agent, Mr. Campbell, warned him against Yankee spies, and assured him that in three months Great Britain would declare war against the United States.

Dick hurriedly arranged his father's affairs, wrote a letter to his mother informing her of what he had done, and called on Miss Lancaster. She was out riding, the servant said, but would return soon. Would Mr. Stevens wait? He would, and it seemed ages before she returned. He spent most of the time in the picture gallery and library, trying to entertain himself, but feeling decidedly miserable. At last her coupé dashed up to the door; the lady was assisted to alight, and entered the house. A few minutes later she was at his side, her great blue eyes smiling as she said:

"I know all about it, Mr. Stevens; you have enlisted."

"How did you learn it?"

"Mr. Campbell told me. I am going on the trial trip."

"I shall be pleased to see you aboard, Miss Lancaster, and I hope that I may prove to you that I can defend my country."

She smiled, and he, in a very serious tone, added, "You first inspired me with the thought, and I trust you will not think me bold when I say that you inspire me to do only what is right and noble." Her eyes drooped and a faint flush suffused her face. He said when his ship had cleared the seas of Yankee merchantmen, and the great and glorious Confederacy had been established, he would ask her hand in marriage. Dick was of a good family; his father was wealthy, and there was no obstacle to such a union.

With a naïve smile and an arch look from the corner of her pretty eyes, she intimated that when he had built up the great southern empire, she might say yes. Until then she preferred single blessedness.

The following day, Dick went aboard the vessel, and was very well pleased with it. To even an unpractised eye, everything indicated the character of the ship. There were no platforms, but the places for the pivot guns were plainly marked. Her magazines were finished, and shot boxes were lying about.

It was the 28th of July that the *290* went out of the Mersey, on what was supposed to be a trial trip, loaded with ladies and gentlemen. Among the former was Miss Lancaster, of course. Though Dick was trying to learn the mysteries of seamanship, he managed to snatch a few moments and hold a short conversation with her. He squeezed her hand at parting and received an assuring squeeze in return.

The vessel anchored in a bay on the Welsh coast, where the ladies and gentlemen left, and they were joined by most of the crew. They had about one hundred men aboard now, half of them sailors, the others being coal-passers and longshoremen, and, in fact, a more motley crowd perhaps was never seen. They represented every nationality and every type of vice. After a day's delay, they sailed around the northern coast of Ireland, and in thirteen days arrived at Terceira, one of the Azore Islands.

Charley Cole was one of the crew, and he and Dick were assigned to the same mess and quarters. But for Charley, who had some knowledge of sailor life, Dick would have fared hard. The *290* was by no means as fast as had been expected. During her first trip, she did not make over ten knots an hour, and had a most disagreeable habit, when driven to the top of her speed, of burying her head and setting everything afloat. This was decidedly unpleasant for the crew in the berth deck.

A few days later, they were joined by an English bark, loaded with guns and munitions of war, and went to work laying platforms for the heavy guns and mounting the pivot guns, one a very fine

Blakely hundred-pound rifle cannon, and the other an eight-inch sixty-eight-pounder smooth bore. The Portuguese governor having ordered them out of the harbor, they were compelled to do their work in a rolling sea, three miles from an anchorage. Before they had finished, the steamer *Bahama* came alongside, bringing Captain Semmes and the remainder of the crew, also more guns, munitions of war, and, it was whispered, a large sum of money.

Dick had heard much of Captain, or rather Rear-Admiral, Raphael Semmes, and he was a little disappointed on seeing him. He was a tall, rather spare built man, with a light mustache and dark brown hair. He wore no beard, and his face would indicate that he was more for reflection than action. He seemed to lack the firmness necessary for such an undertaking as was before him; but Dick was in a measure mistaken. Semmes was a bolder and more daring man than he seemed.

Shortly after the arrival of Semmes, the crew all got liberty to go on shore. Dick, unfamiliar with sailors' actions, was shocked at the conduct of his shipmates. In common parlance " they took the town." The few policemen of the place were powerless; they were seized and mounted on the men's backs. The authorities were defied, and although no serious outrage was committed, the Portuguese officials remonstrated with Semmes for letting loose such a party of ruffians on them. Dick Stevens was appalled at their acts; but his cousin Charley Cole only laughed, and remarked:

"You'll think nothing of this, Dick, after a six months' cruise." But few of the men had yet signed articles, and the officers of the *Alabama* had no legal control over them. When the time for signing came, they were told they could go or stay, but if they went they must "quit backing and filling, and come aboard at once."

They went on board to a man and signed the papers, and for two days worked hard cleaning the ship. The crew was divided into watches, and the routine life of a man-o'-war commenced. Dick was delighted to have his cousin Charles assigned to the same watch with himself.

One bright Sunday morning they left Angra in company with the *Bahama.* The officers came out in full uniform; the band played "Dixie;" all hands were mustered, and the flag under which they were to sail was unfurled for the first time, and they heard the first of Captain Semmes's exhortations, in which he expressed his hope that Providence would bless their efforts to free the South from a grasping and unreasonable North.

"Yass, Providence likely to bless this ere crew!"

growled a boatswain's mate behind Dick, and Dick thought he was right.

Sailors' pranks began early. During the night, some one, appreciating the piratical nature of the craft, ornamented a bread-bag with a skull and cross-bones and fastened it to one of the mizzen braces. In the morning the master-at-arms was hunting for the delinquent; but the sailors laughing declared that Chucks * the marine had been at his tricks.

Dick was not long in coming to the conclusion that never in his life had he seen such a bad lot. All were sailors,—not a haymaker, or landlubber among them,—but they were mostly of that class, found in seaport towns, which on lakes and rivers would be "roust-abouts," and on the whole were a rough and mutinous set. They cared little for the ship's officers, and, according to a sailor called "Shakings," on account of his bushy yellow hair, "they'd stand no man-o'-war dicky from 'em."

Such yarns as they spun when off watch would put both Gulliver and Munchausen to shame. Dick, having never been to sea and not possessing extraordinary inventive powers, kept out of the lying contest. A Scotchman named Gill, in Dick's watch, was perhaps the greatest character on board the ship. He was in his prime, about forty years

---

* A sort of a "Robin Goodfellow" on a man-of-war.

of age, and could hold two ordinary men at arm's
length, as if they were children.   He could quote
scripture and sermons, drink more whiskey and
tell more lies than any man on board the *Alabama*,
and that was saying a great deal.   He was a daring,
dangerous ruffian, who had been engaged in a score
of mutinies, and was even accused of murdering
the officers of one vessel and beaching her.

The first officer, John McIntosh Kell, was most
respected of any; but such a crew could not respect
Semmes, whom some one accused of having once
been a preacher.   Shakings indignantly sized him
up as follows:

"He's a d——d psalm-singer, an' jury captain."
The diversion on deck, when off duty, was chiefly
fencing with broadswords, wrestling and fighting.

September 3, 1862, the *Alabama* took the first
prize, a whaling schooner.   It was no difficult job
to capture the poor vessel.   A shot across her
bow,——she came to, and then boats were sent out
to bring in the prisoners and the booty, which was
not much.   Dick here witnessed the burning of
the first ship, and as he watched the flames ascending the tall, tapering masts, crackling and roaring,
he asked himself:

"Is this legitimate warfare?"
The prisoners were placed on deck under a spar-
rigged sail, and fared badly in stormy weather.

They soon began taking prizes quite rapidly, and were so crowded with prisoners, that the crew became discommoded. Their hammocks touched each other, and the roughs took advantage of this to annoy their more quiet shipmates. Dick's hammock was cut down by a fellow called "Spotty." He watched his chance and, pouncing on the offender, almost pounded the life out of him. He was made to do double duty for three days, but was dumped no more.

"You must be careful, Dick!" said Charles to his cousin. "Spotty is a chum of old Gills."

"I care as little for Gills as Spotty," Dick answered, and his boldness to a certain degree won the respect of the tough element of the crew.

They were now within four hundred miles of New York in the "rolling forties," and directly in the track of American commerce.

Save plundering the prisoners when captured, they were treated fairly well; but the boarding crews were veritable pirates and quite beyond the control of their officers. They looted a prize when captured, going through the chests of the sailors and taking from the persons of the prisoners, such things as they wished.

Among the many prizes captured and destroyed, there were many varieties of character. Some were so odd as to cause Dick and Charley to smile.

On one occasion they accompanied officer Kell to the deck of a prize. The captain of the captured vessel stood trembling aft the main gangway, as if he expected to lose his head. The executive officer of the *Alabama* said:

"Captain, you many bring away such of your personal effects as you desire."

"Thank you, sir, I have one request to make of you," said the captain.

"Name it," said officer Kell.

"I beg you will permit me to bring away a copy of Spurgeon's sermons and a keg of very fine whiskey."

With a smile, the officer answered:

"You can take your sermons,—they will be safe from molestation; but your keg of whiskey would be taken from you and make half the men furious. It must go overboard."

It is not our intention to give a detailed account of the cruises of the *Alabama*. That has been done by many other historians, and only so far as it relates to the characters of our story can the reader be interested. Dick had little sympathy with the lawless crew, for they were too coarse for his refined taste. He could not spin yarns; but he had a splendid baritone voice, and often amused them with songs. Some one composed a song reflecting on the supposed clerical character of their

"HOLD ON! STOP THAT!" . . . "IF YOU EVER SING AG'IN WE'LL FIRE YOU
THROUGH THE LEE PORT."

captain.   This was bawled out in tones loud
enough to be heard in the mess room aft:

> "Oh, our captain said, when my fortune's made,
>   I'll buy a church to preach in,
> And fill it full of toots and horns,
>   And have a jolly Methodee screechin'.

> "And I'll pray the Lord, from night to morn,
>   To weather old Yankee Doodle—
> And I'll run a hinfant Sunday-school
>   With a part of the Yankee boodle." *

Top-Robbin, as one sailor was called, was a
prolific story teller; but as yet had never taken
any part in the singing.   It was decreed one evening while the watch were amusing themselves,
that Top-Robbin should take his part in singing.

"Come now, Top-Robbin, pipe up an' spread
all canvas," said Shakings.   With a look of intense misery, Top-Robbin commenced in the most
terrible squeaky treble and hoarse voice one ever
heard:

> "How Jerry Lee was hung at sea,
>   For stabbing of his messmate true,
> And his body did swing, a horrible thing,
>   At the sport of the wild sea mew—"

"Hold on! stop that!" screamed one of the sailors, and his request was backed by a general pleading yell from all.

----

* Century Magazine.

"If you ever sing agin in this 'ere watch while we're off soundings, we'll fire you through the lee port," declared Shakings. "Such a voice as that would raise a hurrycane."

"I wan't a-doin' this for my own amusement," said Top-Robbin meekly.

"Well, you needn't do it for mine," responded Shakings.

They arrived at Martinique, and Charley and Dick, who had about all the patriotism of the crew, were pleased to see the enthusiasm of the French over their success in driving Yankee commerce from the seas. Dick got leave and went ashore, as he had acquaintances on the island. There he heard the brightest side of the war. The Confederate victories were made large, and their reverses small.

Next day, Charley came ashore and went to the house where his cousin was staying.

"You missed the biggest row of the cruise last night, Dick!"

"Why, Charley?"

"Old Gill was on the warpath. The French corvette gave a dinner to our officers. Gill licked two of the Frenchman's petty officers almost to death, as his part of the entertainment; and our liberties were stopped as a result. Forest eluded the lookouts, swam ashore and from some place, I know not where, stole five gallons of the worst fighting whiskey I ever saw. It set the whole watch crazy. Forest kept pretty straight; but old Gill 'bowsed up his jib,' until he could scarce stand. Then such an uproar I never heard; the lanterns were lit in defiance, and when the watch was called, the officer of the deck was saluted with all manner of 'skrim-shander.' The boatswain fell by a blow from a belaying pin and everything loose was fired aft. The officers and marines, with the sober part of the crew, charged, and such a fight you never saw. Gill knocked the jaw of the gunner's mate out of place, but was finally laid out by a capstan-bar, and the drunken men secured. All are now under double irons."

Dick bowed his head and said:

"Charley, this society may be all right in time of war; but it is not elevating."

Charley whistled and turned his eyes toward the ceiling.

"I have sailed with many a crew, Dick; but this is undoubtedly the toughest I ever knew."

They went aboard, and that evening a rumor reached them that a Yankee cruiser, the *San Jacinto*, was outside waiting for them. Nearly all the crew, worn out with the monotony of taking merchantmen, wanted to fight; but Captain Semmes and his officers were against it, and by

11

the open and undisguised assistance of the French naval officers they got out.

Sunday, January 11, 1863, they had their first conflict. Hitherto, nothing but prizes and easy captures had fallen to their lot; but on this day the men were ordered to their guns in a rather business-like manner. Dick felt his heart beating wildly as he stood by his gun. Old Gill, Top-Robbin and Shakings were swearing on his left, while Charley, as cool as a veteran, stood on his right. Through the dusk he saw the bows of a small steamer coming toward them. Her officers must have seen that the men were at their quarters, with guns manned. She came within one hundred yards before hailing. Captain Kell answered:

" This is Her Britannic Majesty's steamer *Petrel!* " The answer came back:

" This is the United States steamer *Hatteras!* " At the same moment Captain Kell cried:

" This is the Confederate steamer *Alabama!* "

" Fire—Fire!" rang throughout the ship, and the *Alabama* poured in a whole broadside from their starboard batteries. They were not more than fifty yards away, and Dick could plainly hear the awful crash of their shot tearing the hull and rigging of the enemy. Soon bright flashes came from the enemy's decks, and they heard the whiz of shots above their heads. For ten minutes the conflict was sharp and terrible. Dick was ramming home a charge, when he heard a voice forward cry out:

" The enemy is sinking."

" Cease firing!" cried Captain Kell. Captain Semmes came along a moment later, and the officers ordered boats to be lowered.

Dick was almost exhausted with the violent exercise and nervous strain. He sat on the gun carriage and laid his hand on the barrel of the cannon. It was so hot he took it away. Meanwhile, boats had been lowered and brought off the enemy, and then the *Hatteras* went down stern foremost.

As Captain Blake of the *Hatteras* came over the side of the *Alabama*, he seized the hand of Captain Kell, saying:

" Aye, Captain Kell, we have sailed together in other years."

" Yes, Captain Blake, and under other circumstances."

" Fortune favors the brave!"

" I trust, captain, you will have a pleasant voyage on the *Alabama*."

Only five of the *Hatteras*' crew had been killed and wounded. The others were paroled at Kingston. While they were lying at Jamaica one day, Charles came aboard and said:

"Dick, I believe that Gill and Forest have killed that Irishman King-post."

"Why?"

"They do not like him, because he has reported on them several times. P. D. Haywood, the Englishman, told me that he saw them going with King-post out of the town. The Irishman was drunk, and, suspecting foul play, Haywood tried to follow them; but they eluded him. They came back without him, and when Haywood asked Gill where King-post was, the old Scotchman gave him a significant glance and answered:

"'I dunna know, laddie; but he'll haud his tongue noo; and ye better say naithing, yir a wise fallou.' King-post has not shown up yet, and I doubt if he ever will." King-post was never seen afterward, and was no doubt murdered by those ruffians.

CHAPTER VIII.

THE RECRUIT.

THE border States, Virginia, Kentucky, and Missouri, felt in full the curse of civil war, which finally brought great distress upon the inhabitants. In these States many leaders professed to be *conditional* friends of the Union. They would be its friends so long as the national government did not interfere with slavery, nor "attempt to bring back the seceded States;" in other words, they were friends of the republic so long as it did not take steps injurious to the rights of States. When the president's call for troops to suppress the uprising appeared, the *Louisville Journal,* the organ of the professed unionists of Kentucky, made haste to declare:

"We are struck with mingled amazement and indignation. The policy announced in the proclamation deserves the unqualified condemnation of every American citizen. It is unworthy, not merely of a statesman, but a man. It is a policy utterly harebrained and ruinous. If Mr. Lincoln contemplated this policy in his inaugural address, he is a guilty dissembler. If he conceived it under the excitement aroused by the seizure of Fort Sumter, he is a guilty hotspur. In either case, he is miserably unfit for the exalted position in which the enemies of the country have placed him. Let the people instantly take him and his administration into their own hands, if they would rescue the land from bloodshed and the Union from sudden and irretrievable destruction."

At a large "union meeting" in Louisville, over which James Guthrie and other leading men in the State held control, it was resolved that "Kentucky reserves to herself the right to choose her own position; and that, while her natural sympathies are with those who have a common interest in the protection of slavery, she still acknowledges her loyalty and fealty to the government of the United States, which she will carefully render *until that government becomes aggressive, tyrannical and regardless of our rights in slave property.*" They furthermore declared that the States were peers of the national government; and gave the world to understand that the latter should not be allowed to use sanguinary or coercive measures to "bring back the seceded States." The "Kentucky State Guard," which the governor had organized for the benefit of the secessionists, were commended by this union meeting as "the bulwark and safety of the commonwealth," and its members were enjoined to remember that they were pledged equally to fidelity to the United States and Kentucky.

"The Guard" was placed under the command of Captain Simon B. Buckner of the national army, who was then probably in the regular service of the Confederacy, for he effectively used his influence to win over large numbers of the members of the Guard from their allegiance to the North, and sent them as recruits to the Confederate armies. It was not long before he led a large portion of them into the camp of the South, and he became a Confederate major-general. Then the *Louisville Journal,* that had so savagely condemned the president, more savagely assailed Buckner with criticism, saying, "Away with your pledges and assurances—with your protestations, apologies and proclamations—at once and altogether! Away, parricide, away, and do penance forever!—be shriven or slain—away! You have less palliation than Atilla,—less boldness, magnanimity and nobleness than Coriolanus. You are the Benedict Arnold of the day! You are the Catiline of Kentucky! Go, thou miscreant!" And when in February, 1862, Buckner and some of the State Guard were captured at Fort Donelson, and he was sent to Fort Warren, Boston, many of those who were deceived by the assertion that the Guard was the " bulwark of the commonwealth," demanded his delivery to the authorities of Kentucky, to be tried for offenses against the State. As a little leaven leavens the whole loaf, so had the spirit of the South impregnated the thoughts of those naturally inclined to maintain the government of the North.

The South treated with derision President Lincoln's first call for seventy-five thousand volunteers to put down the rebellion, and the *Mobile Advertiser* inserted an advertisement for seventy-five thousand coffins for Lincoln's soldiers.

While Virginia suffered for her hesitation, and Kentucky for her attempt at neutrality, Missouri also became a four years' battle-field by trying to follow their example. But for the prompt and energetic action of Captain, afterward General, Nathaniel Lyon, Missouri would have been forced into the Southern Confederacy. Lyon's prompt seizure of the Home Guards at Camp Jackson, his rapid descent on the governor, whom he obliged to depart from the capital, kept the State in the Union. Had Lyon lived, he undoubtedly would have been one of the Northern heroes of the war. No man displayed more courage or ability; but he fell at the battle of Wilson Creek, August 10, 1861.

Soon after the bombardment and evacuation at Fort Sumter, Mark Stevens returned to his home in Boone County, Kentucky. The dear old plantation with the blue hills in the distance, the white-haired father sitting beneath his favorite tree, the negro shanties, the merry laughter of slaves going to or returning from the fields, all made up a pleasant scene for the memory of the youth when away.

They knew he was coming, and John, a mulatto man, who had once tried to run away, but instead of gaining his liberty had been kidnapped and sent to the West Indies, was sent for him. Since John's terrible experience in trying to gain his freedom, it was thought he would never make the effort again, especially as he declared that he would not leave " moster Stevens," even if he gave him his freedom; but John, like the majority of his race, was fickle, and in 1862 accepted a fine opportunity to escape and went over into Ohio, afterward joined in a colored regiment, went to the war, and perished at Fort Pillow.

When Mark returned, he found the old farm but little changed. His aged father, whose venerable locks were white as snow, was sitting on the long piazza with the wife and mother at his side.

They rose and greeted the return of their son with smiles of joy. Other members of the family

had been summoned from the surrounding plantations to make the return pleasant. They talked
of almost everything save the coming struggle.

It was not until next day that Mark mentioned
it to his father.

"Well, my son," said the old major, shaking
his gray head, "I have long seen it coming.
When I first began reading the speeches of Calhoun, I knew it was not far off. It was dangerous
doctrine. In our institutions it was like a living
coal of fire in a powder-mill. Washington and
Hamilton saw this, and they tried to prevent it.
Had their words of wisdom been heeded, it might
have been averted."

"Father, I have made up my mind to enlist
under the president's call."

The gray-haired patriot was silent a few moments; then he said:

"It is no easy thing for one to give up his child;
but I will do it. Yes, you may go. I hope you
will be an honor to the name of Stevens. Remember that you can look back through twelve
generations to the ship in which Columbus sailed
and see your ancestor Hernando Estevan among
the first to touch the soil of the new world. Your
grandfather fought under Washington for this
country. Your father fought under General Scott
and Andrew Jackson to sustain its honor, and

your brother fought to humble the pride of the Mexicans. Now, if Heaven has decreed that you shall fight for the preservation of the Union, I shall not oppose it. Do as your convictions dictate; but don't forget you are a Stevens."

Volunteer companies in Kentucky at this time were scarce. There was not one at this time organized in Boone County, and Mark was compelled to pass over the river and enlist in an Indiana company.

Mark learned that Captain Hawk was recruiting a company in Indiana, just across the river near the village of Rising Sun. He determined to take the first opportunity that offered and enlist. Ascertaining the day of muster, he went across the river.

Rising Sun was not wholly northern. In fact, there were some of the most ardent sympathizers with the cause of the South in the southern part of Indiana anywhere to be found. Entering Rising Sun, he inquired of a man who kept a grocery store for Captain Hawk. The Rising Sun merchant gave him one or two fiery glances, and answered:

"I dun know where he is, an' I care less."

"Don't they muster in Rising Sun?"

"Not by a h——l of a sight! If they want their necks stretched, let 'em try it."

Mark turned away somewhat discouraged, when a stranger beckoned him aside.

"D'you want to find Captain Hawk?" he asked.

"Yes; I heard he had regular muster days, and that he organizes for the war."

"D'you want to enlist?"

"Yes."

"Well then, if you're all right, I will tell you something." Mark assured him he was all right, and the stranger said: "This part of the State is pretty nigh all secesh, and you've got to look out. Cap'in Hawk musters to-night at moonlight at the Kholmier School House."

"Where is that?"

He was informed it was in the forest about three miles away, but if he would meet him at the big bridge in the west part of town, he would show him to it. Mark made the appointment and went at nine o'clock.

The moon was shining brightly from a clear sky, and he found the stranger standing by the bridge, while two or three more were a short distance away. The men were armed with shot guns or rifles and looked more like a party of hunters than soldiers.

"So ye've come," said Mark's first acquaintance.

"Yes."

They started along a narrow, lonesome path, leading through the wood, and Mark at times entertained a fear that they might be enemies leading him into a snare. Such was not the case, however, for in due time the schoolhouse loomed up before them, and they saw fully a score of men sitting or standing about it. They were mostly farmers. Each man had brought a gun of some kind, the rifle prevailing. Two or three survivors of the Mexican war had brought their old-fashioned yagers, which were a curiosity to those unacquainted with military arms.

Bill Simms, who had never seen a day's service in his life, was holding the crowd spellbound with hair-raising stories of the trying times he had seen under old " Gineral Percy."

" It's a fact," said Bill, " we marched for a hull week on only three meals a day, and had nothin' but bread, beef and potatoes, cabbage and beans at that."

" It's a wonder ye hadn't a starved to death, Bill," remarked Nick Marks.

" I tell ye, boys, I never want ter see sich days as them agin."

" What war ye fightin'?"

" Injuns."

The appearance of the group to which Mark belonged put an end to the discussion. A man who looked much more like a farmer than a soldier came forward, and was introduced as Captain Hawk. He asked Mark if he came to enlist, and Mark answered in the affirmative.

"Well, we're trying to get up a company here, but hain't got it full yet. Hope we will soon. You make sixty-five. If they'll take us, we'll go right off. Some say Lincoln's got his seventy-five thousand men; but they won't be enough."

Mark signed a paper, and Captain Hawk went through the formality of swearing him into service, though his authority was so questionable that afterward they were again "mustered in." The men were ordered into line, and stood very straight while Captain Hawk harangued them for a few moments on loyalty, and the necessity of securing thirty-five more volunteers in order to make up the company. Almost everybody knew of some one else who ought to join, and Captain Hawk disbanded them, sending each man as a "recruiting officer on his own hook."

There lived in Boone County, Kentucky, not far from Major Stevens, a man named Abe Bolton. Abe was not far from twenty-five, and a loud-blowing Unionist. Mark went to see him and at the next muster brought Abe along.

To the surprise of all, the company was filled up, and everything ready to move. The first move was on Rising Sun, where they rendezvoused at midnight, formed in something like order, and marched away to Dearborn, where they went into camp.

By reading general history, one can have little knowledge of how soldiers are made. They seemed to spring up from the ground as it were, at the order or proclamation of the president, already armed, equipped, drilled, and ready to perform prodigies of valor. Such was not the case in 1861. The South had most of the experienced officers. The American regular army never amounts to much in either peace or war, and when the volunteers were mustered into service they had to be educated in the art of war.

At Dearborn the company was organized and the men drilled in platoons and squads. The long months of drilling three and four hours per day, the inability of some of the "tangle feet" to get the step, the mysteries of the manual of arms, all engaged the attention of the company. Some had drill books showing the various positions of the soldier, and these were read and discussed with avidity by the men.

They were quartered in old houses, but at night built camp fires to look as much like soldiers as possible. Among the many curious specimens of the genus *homo* belonging to the company was a tall youth about seventeen or eighteen years of age, who answered, when the roll was called, to the name of George F. Ellis; but the sobriquet by which he was known in camp was "Sis." This had probably been given him on account of his beardless face, though his features were too coarse to be feminine. At first Sis was remarkably bashful. He was a tall, slender, awkward youth dressed in a striped linsey roundabout, a pair of blue jeans trousers and a low cap, the peak of which did not protect over half of his prominent nose.

Sis soon became the butt of half the jokes in the company; but he had the good sense to preserve his humor, and possessing some native wit, he retaliated on his persecutors, until they came to respect him.

Bill Simms was the most persistent persecutor of Sis. Bill claimed to have all the knowledge of military matters there was to learn, and the stories he told were calculated to raise him in the estimation of the volunteers. At last after long waiting the uniforms and blankets came. Every volunteer in 1861 knows what a scramble there was for uniforms. They could hardly wait until the boxes were open. Blue coats, trousers and vests with brass buttons and caps, were jerked out at a lively rate. The misfits were laughable. Sis had a pair of pants which came little below the knees, and Bill Simms bawled out:

"Hello, Sis, yer must think yer a revolutionary soldier wearin' knee breeches."

"These pants are a leetle short," returned Sis good humoredly; "but they're wide enough to let out the slack."

"Well, may be ye could piece 'em."

Mark had a coat large enough for a two hundred-pounder; but Abe Bolton had a coat and pair of pants too small, so that by trading around, Mark managed to get something like a fit. When he was presentable he went out on the street and roared with laughter to see at least fifty recruits in the most ill-fitting uniforms he ever beheld filing away to the picture gallery to have their pictures taken. Many of those tin-types are still in existence. The reader may have met them. They represent the recruit, in a coat much too big, holding a cocked revolver in one hand and a musket in the other, and trying to look very fierce. They were sent to wives and sweethearts to let them know how "he" looked in his new soldier clothes.

HOW "HE" LOOKED.

"I wonder when we are goin' to git out o' here and be givin' the secesh a race," said Nick, one evening.

"Wall now, Nick, ye may soon git more o'

fightin' than ye want. I remember durin' the five years I was with Percy o' sayin' once just what you did. Next day we jumped up fifty thousand Crows an' fit the whole week."

"What war the Crows doin', Bill?" Sis asked.

"Waitin' to grab us by the hair."

"Oh, I thought they were a-pullin' up corn."

The roar of laughter which followed this sally of wit Bill Simms did not relish. In a voice of thunder, he responded:

"I mean Crow Injuns, you igiot! Did ye think I meant birds?"

"Yes."

"So did we, Bill."

"You're all as big fools as John Barnhart. We called him Knuckle Bone Johnny. I met him durin' the ten years I war out in Pike's Peak, and he couldn't tell the difference between a Injun and a stump."

"How long were you at Pike's Peak?" asked Sis.

"Igiot! didn't ye just hear me say ten years?"

"How long war ye with Gineral Percy?"

"Five."

"How long on Red River?"

"Eleven."

"You must be purty old, Bill," said Sis.

"Why?"

" Your ten years at Pike's Peak and five years
with Gineral Percy makes fifteen. Eleven on
Red River twenty-six; and four on White River,
thirty," Sis went on, marking on the ground
with his finger. " Then the ten on Black River,
twenty on the plains, thirty on the sea and all the
other places ye've been, makes ye about two hundred and thirty years old, Bill."

There was a roar of laughter at this, and Bill,
puffing away at his pipe, coolly remarked:

" I guess ye've made some mistake there, Sis."

The company were getting fairly well drilled.
Sis was perhaps the most awkward. He could not
keep step. His long legs rebelled against the
regulation twenty-eight inches. He was fully as
awkward in the manual of arms, in wheeling and
facing for awhile, and the drill sergeant who took
him in hand to give him some private lessons was
almost in despair.

" Now look here, Sis. This is yer right foot."

" Is it?" Sis asked innocently.

" Yes, and when I say 'right,' put the hollow
o' yer left foot behind yer right heel. When I
saw 'face,' raise yourself on both toes, turn half
way round to the right, raise yer left foot, bring
it down by the right, and there you are!"

The movement looked very simple; but for Sis
to perform it exactly and neatly seemed impossible.

"Heavens! did ever anybody see such tangle legs as you have? Why, I'd as soon try to teach a daddy-long-legs to waltz as to give you the movements of a squad."

Mark learned very rapidly, for he had the advantages of an excellent education and a retentive mind, which received and comprehended the orders. He had not been appointed to any of the non-commissioned offices; but he sought no such appointment. He had gone into the service fully imbued with the idea of fighting for his country, and he believed that the best way to do it was with a musket.

While lying in the camp, he heard of the bloody fight and northern defeat at Bull Run. Then came still later the news of the disaster at Wilson Creek, with the loss of General Lyon, a loss that was sadly felt, as he could not be replaced.

The fiery, impetuous General John C. Fremont, a good explorer, but too impetuous and hot-headed for a general, was placed in command of the western army with his headquarters at St. Louis. For a while, it had been feared that this city would be seized by the South; but Fremont soon had it too well fortified for them to do that. Meanwhile, Captain Hawk's company had been placed in a regiment and ordered back to Rising Sun. The southern sympathizers in this part of the State were very bold and outspoken, and it was said that men were coming over from Kentucky to attack the Yankees.

Colonel Belcher, who had been a volunteer officer in the Mexican war, was a man of more military ability than many of his superiors. Though they were expected to stay but a short time at the place, their colonel ordered them to entrench and prepare against an attack. He laid out a line of earthworks, and pick and shovel were plied until the work was completed.

"I tell ye, ye needn't fear the secesh," declared Abe Bolton. "They'd never git us out o' here."

This recalled to Bill Simms' mind some reminiscences of his experiences with General Percy, and he set about telling a new recruit in company A a story that almost raised his hair on end.

It was reported after the work was completed that the enemy were contemplating crossing the river at Grummet's landing from Kentucky and attacking them. Mark was sent with Sis and Nick to the river to reconnoitre, with orders to remain all night, unless the enemy appeared sooner. It was no pleasant situation with two raw recruits, one of whom (Nick) was especially nervous, waiting for an enemy reported to be ten thousand strong, to come over and cut their throats.

Nick started at every sound, the falling of a

leaf, or dropping of a clod of earth in the water, and exclaimed:

"What is that?"

On the other hand, Sis lay down at the root of a tree and snored. Between keeping one awake and the other from running away, Mark had his hands full, and he welcomed the approach of dawn with delight. Shortly after daylight a boat was seen to put out from the opposite shore, and Nick wanted to open fire on it, then run to town and tell the Colonel they were coming.

"Say, Nick, I believe you're a blamed coward," said Sis, rubbing his eyes and yawning.

"No, I'm not; I'm as brave a body as any in the regiment."

"Yes; but you've got a pair o' cowardly legs, that runs away at first sign of fight."

The skiff landed, and it proved to contain some loyal Kentuckians, whom Mark knew, and who came to inform them that there was not an armed Confederate within a week's march.

CHAPTER IX.

LOVE AND EXCITEMENT.

It was certainly a cause for congratulation that from the first to the last the war had its humorous side, and that in the southern as well as those northern and border States, even in the midst of greatest trials, their spirits were never so crushed as to not appreciate the reflex view of their misfortunes. From their very necessities the most absurd dilemmas and exigencies arose which would have been annihilating mortifications had they not had the presence of mind to treat them as capital jokes. No doubt this, and this only, enabled them to endure to the end trials and disasters which otherwise would have been overwhelming. In looking back now to the vicissitudes of the struggle, they confess the fact that they never neglected a single opportunity for amusement which the situation admitted. Being a child during the struggle, the author visited the armies of the Confederates and Federals without fear or hindrance, and he never saw a jollier set. Such practical jokes, such singing and dancing, such laughter——it seemed more play than war. The author once watched a Confederate army retreating from a lost battle-field, and most of the soldiers seemed merry, jesting over their own defeat. Even some of the slightly wounded were laughing at the drollery of others.

Early in the war Colonel Cole's regiment was removed to Richmond, Virginia, where it was thought the seat of the Confederate government would be established. The colonel's wife and daughter accompanied him, and thither came Alec, who, after Mark's desertion of the fair prize, began to woo Elsie in earnest.

Elsie seemed glad to have the young Floridian with her. She treated him sometimes like a dear friend, but most of the time as a trusted servant, a real good fellow whom she could trust, and who was absolutely indispensable to her happiness; but she never looked on him in the light of a lover. She told him her plans, sent him on errands, had him for a companion; but when he began to mention love, she laughed outright.

"Elsie, you are the most singular person I ever saw. You must be a new and unclassified speci-men of the female order——"

"Oh, hush, Alec! I want you to come with me to the lecture room at St. Paul's this evening.

There is to be a meeting of southern girls to do what they can for the army."

He looked at her strangely and, giving utterance to a prolonged whistle, rose to his feet, saying:

" Well, of all the girls I ever saw, you do beat them. I'll go and join the army and let the Yankees shoot me——"

" If it is such an irksome undertaking, I will excuse you."

" Now, Elsie, why do you say that, when you know that I am never so happy as when I am your slave?"

" But I don't blame you if you join the army. Every loyal son of the South should fight for his country."

" I intend to serve my country. Just give me time, Elsie, and I will be a full-fledged soldier."

" Well, run along now, Alec, like a good boy, and play soldier with a broomstick until I want you," and she gave him a push toward the door, laughing in a way that vexed poor Alec.

" I never saw any one who could so completely get away with me as she can," he said as he strolled out into the street. " I declare I feel just like a fool. I wish I was a thousand miles from here. Sometimes I am tempted to go and join the Yankees just for spite. Why didn't I go to England with Dick? Now that Mark's gone, I don't

seem to be any nearer to the prize than I was before. I've a notion to never see her again."

All the same Alec was on time to escort Elsie to
the lecture-room. It was a little odd for a young
lady to ask a gentleman to be her escort, and it
would have been highly improper in any other person than the pretty, saucy, jolly Elsie Cole. Alec
was quite sure she would ask no one but himself.

They went together to the lecture-room at St.
Paul's Church, where, after a short patriotic address, the ladies were asked to aid in making
trousers for the soldiers. When all who would
sew were called upon to rise, Elsie Cole was among
the first to spring to her feet.

"Elsie, Elsie, haven't you made a mistake?"
asked Alec. "Why, girl, you never threaded a
needle in your life."

"I will take you along to thread my needles."

"No you won't, by ginger! You may lead me
around by the ear like a poodle dog; I'll drive
your coach, make your bouquets, sharpen your
lead pencils, give you my coat to walk upon, run
your errands, make your fires, carry you across
muddy brooks, fight for you, lie for you, steal for
you; but may I be teetotally thunderstruck, dragged
through a crab-apple thicket, and squeezed to death
in a cider-press, if I am going to any female sewing society."

She asserted that he would go just wherever she wanted him; but in this Alec was firm. He vowed his intention to enlist at once, and next day volunteered in a company of infantry; while Elsie, who had scarcely ever had a needle in her hands, went to show her patriotism by making soldiers' trousers. War is a great leveller. There were scarcely any grades in society then. Rich and poor labored alike, and the wife of a poor blacksmith, who had enlisted in Alec's company, gave Elsie her first lesson in sewing. She bravely threaded her needle and set to work upon a pair of trousers. Never did woman have a more difficult task. Nothing but the lovely creature's patriotism for a cause that she believed just, could have induced her to sew away for hours. She finally presented the trousers to the directress, as she thought nearly finished, for further instructions. The directress looked at them rather gravely for a second, turned them round with a furtive smile, and then, to Elsie's horror and mortification, held them up to the general view. A shout of laughter went up from the busy women and girls. Elsie had carefully sewed the front of one leg to the back of the other, and so joined the parts in a most discordant unity. But for the directress, she would doubtless have faced them down, put on the buttons and sent them off to camp, when, alas! the poor fellow to whom they fell must evidently have marched two ways at once in order to wear them, for as they hung in mid-air, the legs seemed to step out in opposite directions, and if the wearer had gone persistently forward, one leg of those trousers would have stayed behind. Amid the peals of laughter which overwhelmed Elsie with confusion, a voice from the window cried:

" I pity the fellow who wears those pants, Elsie; he'd have to advance and retreat at the same time, which would be a little inconvenient." Turning her eyes toward the window, Elsie saw Alec, leaning his elbows on the window-sill with a triumphant smile on his face. She "flashed up" in a moment and declared:

" Alec Stevens, I warrant that I know as much about sewing as you do about soldiering."

" I don't know, little girl; I would not try to march two ways at once."

She ordered him away, and he, like a willing slave, obeyed. That evening he went to see Elsie and found her with her hand tied up. She had pricked her fingers until they were quite sore, and declared that she was among the first martyrs to the southern cause. Alec stuck his hands very deep into his pockets, and tried to look very brave and dignified in his new uniform; but he didn't.

" I declare I feel just like a fool," he thought.

"I PITY THE FELLOW WHO WEARS THOSE PANTS, ELSIE; HE'LL HAVE TO ADVANCE
AND RETREAT AT THE SAME TIME."

At last he managed to recall a part of the pretty speech he had been all day making up, and began: "Elsie, I have something that I want to say to you."

"I know what it is," she interrupted. "You want to pity me, Mr. Alec, for having pricked my fingers with the needle. You may suggest that if I had learned to sew before I came to Richmond, I would not be wounded and in pain now. Very well, Mr. Alec, it is none of your business."

"Oh, Elsie, don't fly to flinders that way. Who in the name of Tom Walker's ghost is saying anything about sewing? I suspect that you do as well as a good many others, who never tried to work before; but what I wanted to say was— was——"

"Was what? Can't you speak?"

"Not when you keep interrupting me. I want to say something of importance, of great importance, and I don't want you to say 'no.'"

"Then don't say it."

"Oh, Elsie!"

"It will be safest not to say anything."

"Don't talk that way. Mark is gone now——"

"Well, what can that have to do with what you are going to say, Alec?" she asked, turning her pretty face on him.

"Why, you see, Elsie," said Alec with his gaze

riveted on the floor, "I liked Mark; he was more than a brother to me; and when he came, and I saw that he loved you, I said nothing. I left the whole field to him. It almost killed me; but I did. He was a dear, noble, good fellow, and I knew he was more worthy of you than a wild, harum-scarum, good-for-nothing scamp like me. So I gave him a free field; but he went away without telling you how he loved you. He has joined the Yankees, and we will never see him again, and now that the field is clear, I want to tell you how I love you, Elsie; but you must know it———"

"Hush!" she cried, so sharply that he started back in alarm. "Alec Stevens, you should be above such nonsense. This is no time to talk of love. If you are a soldier, you belong to your country, and to none other."

She had risen to her feet, her face had suddenly become white as marble, while her breath came in fitful labored gasps. For a moment she gazed on him in silence, and then, turning coldly about, she glided silently from the room. Alec gazed after her retreating form and scratching his puzzled head, dashed on his cap and left the house, declaring:

"That woman beats thunder. She makes me feel just like a fool."

When next they met, she was the same superior but kind being of yore. So long as he did not approach that most vital of all subjects to him, love, she seemed to like him as a lady of fashion does her pet poodle, or a trusty faithful servant. All this was gall and bitterness to the proud Alec.

The first movement of the military in Virginia, momentous as it then appeared, was the most absurd fiasco of the war. It was on a memorable Sabbath, April 21, 1861, that the alarm bell at the capitol sounded at mid-day its first call to arms. The churches were crowded, and the communion was about to be administered, when the dread sounds smote upon the air. In an instant all was confusion; congregations rose *en masse* and ran into the streets; delicate women shrieked and fainted; children were knocked down and trampled on; while one and all in breathless excitement demanded an explanation. It was quickly given. Dispatches had been received by the governor of Virginia (Mr. John Letcher) that the United States warship *Pawnee* was moving up the river to shell the city. Hundreds of soldiers, who might be compared to Falstaff's band of warriors, were marched down to Rockets to meet this terrifying vanguard of the United States navy. Two old bronze cannon that had done service in no telling how many Fourth-of-July celebrations were started down Main Street at a run. One broke down in front of the Post Office, and was abandoned, while they hurried on with the other; and every man and boy in Richmond, clergy and all, indiscriminately armed with pistols, shotguns, rifles, swords, and even clubs, were hurrying to the seat of war. Alec, with a double-barrelled shotgun in one hand and a pitchfork in the other, joined the rabble.

Left to themselves, the women and children next took up the line of march and flocked by thousands to the brow of Church Hill, immediately overlooking the river, in which position they must inevitably have received the full force of the bombardment, had there been one. The city was in a tumult, and the wildest confusion prevailed until twilight, when it was ascertained that the alarm was wholly unfounded.

Alec Stevens was slowly making his way back to the city, his gun on his shoulder and his hayfork in his hand, when a voice called out from the stream of women and children pouring into town:

" Alec, Alec, what have you been doing with that hayfork?"

The merry voice was familiar, and through the gathering shades of twilight he saw the lovely face of Elsie Cole, gleaming like a ray of sunlight in the sombre shadows.

" I was going to fight the Yankees," he answered. A scream of laughter went up from a dozen girls, and Elsie, finally getting control of her merriment, said :

" So, you propose to fight men-of-war with a hayfork !"

" Oh, confound it, Elsie, why do you make sport of everything I do?" cried Alec, throwing his fork into the river, and walking home at her side, quarrelling all the way.

The *Pawnee* did, at some time during her operations in Virginia, ascend the James River to a point some fifty or sixty miles below Richmond; but at the moment the citizens of the Confederate capital were rushing *en masse* to fight her she was lying harmlessly at rest, and the telegram sent from Norfolk was said to refer to Elizabeth River.

The retreat of the valiant army from the bloodless battle-field was very droll, and those whose patriotic eyes had actually descried the dread man-of-war, and had been able through their glasses to detect her movements, were naturally a little " touchy" on the subject, which, however, did not exempt them from the merciless raillery of their companions.   Neither Burnside, McClellan, nor Grant, with their " grand armies," ever occasioned so great a panic in the Confederate capital.

13

Later on, the inhabitants of Richmond grew more accustomed to war's alarms, and could lie down and sleep with the cannon of the enemy thundering at their gates.

Those were the gala days of the war. The ladies were full of ardor, and spent their time sewing on the clothes of the soldiers. Love affairs were plentiful; but the girls postponed all engagements until their lovers had fought the Yankees. Their influence was very great. Day after day they went in crowds to the fair grounds, where the First South Carolina volunteers were encamped, showering upon them smiles and such delicacies as the city could afford. There were young men worth from one hundred thousand to half a million dollars in that regiment, serving as privates.

The camps of instruction were crowded with soldiers. The cadets from the Virginia military institute, rendered good service as drill-masters. The Maryland boys began to gather into companies in Richmond and to form the Maryland line. South Carolina sent her braves, Louisiana her magnificent "Washington artillery," superbly equipped. From the Lone Star State came her rangers, and as the different banners floated in the air at the head of their columns, they cheered to the echo. In all the excitement attending the marshalling of the clans from the sunny land, Mars and Cupid clasped hands, and many a bud of love was then first blown, which, ere it proved a beauteous flower, was twined in a funeral wreath.

There was no more ardent lover among those southern soldiers than honest, good-hearted, but reckless Alec; whose ill-starred fate is only another exemplification of the proverb that the course of true love does not always run smooth. Alec, temporarily offended at some slight on the part of Elsie, strolled off to camp, and sat down at the root of a tree, heartily wishing that the Yankees would come up and put him out of his misery. A group of Kentucky soldiers who had been quartered near attracted his attention by their peculiar quarrel. It was quite evident that prior to enlistment they had been farmers in the bottom regions of Kentucky, where ignorance and poverty prevailed. Of the four principals in the animated discussion he soon learned that one was named Long, one Brown, one Jones and another Smith. The conversation seemed to grow out of some remarks about the drought which prevailed in the month of May in Virginia.

"Don't rain putty soon, everything'll be burnt bodaciously up," remarked Brown, as he fingered a deck of greasy cards. "Hain't had 'nuff rain fur three weeks ter lay the dust."

"Hain't had nuff ter lay an egg," put in Long.

At this there was a roar of laughter, and Jones remarked:

"Ef I could say as many funny things as Long, ye wouldn't ketch me in the army; dinged ef I didn't go to town an' practise law.   Bet I'd win every case.   Why didn't you do it, Long?"

"Feered I mought hatter whup somebody. Never did like ter fight.   It's too much like hard work ter suit me."

"Sensible, thar, dinged ef you ain't.   I had a fight once, an' afo' I got through, wush I may die ef I didn't think I wuz breakin' a yoke ov steers," remarked private Brown.

"Ur that tother feller war a-whuppin' a calf," put in Long, which produced another roar.

"Jes' so; but I give him a mighty good tussle. Who's got that canteen?"

"Here she is," said Smith.

"Wall, send her on th' warmin' rounds of charity agin," returned Brown.

"Calls it charity, I reckin, 'cause it didn't cost him nuthin'," the witty Long remarked.

"Reckin it cost me about ez much ez it did you.   Wall here's at you, dod rot you, had never seed you, would never a toch you," and after a drink Brown added, "Boys, that's poetry."

"'Tain't as strong as the licker," asserted Smith.

"Nur as good," said Long.

" But jist as free," declared Brown.

" Things that are bad are ginerally free. Flat terbacker costs money, but you can git the chills for nothin'."

" An' ter git well is good. You've got ter pay for that."

" Er man pays mighty dear fur bein' sick. Last fall I tuk sick standin' at the 'lection poles, an' it cost me five dollars."

" Guess it was th' result of th' 'lection made ye sick."

" Let's all licker!" They did so, and the contents of the canteen began to show its effects on them.

" Bet thar ain't a mess in th' regiment whar th' soldiers are so good humored," said Smith.

" Bet so too," added Brown. " Hain't had a fight since I enlisted."

" That's cause everybody knows ye. Brown, I reckin you air about th' best man in th' company," suggested Long, ironically.

" Reckin not. Don't think I am ez good a man ez you are."

" Didn't you outlift me at Fergurson's log rollin'?" asked Long.

" No, don't think I did."

" I hearn you did."

" I don't know who told it."

" I hearn you did. "

" You hearn somethin' that ain't so.   I don't go round blowin' my own ho'n. "

" Wall, somebody's been blowin' it. "

" 'Twarn't me. "

" Guess you furnished a good deal uv th' wind. "

" Come, boys, let's licker an' then sing a song, " interposed Jones to prevent trouble.   They all drank, and Smith, who was a tall man, said :

" A leetle o' that goes a long way. "

" Does when you swaller it, cause it hez a long ways to go, " remarked Brown.

" That remark was about ez sharp ez a cabbage, " Long declared.

" All remarks in shape of cabbages should come from your head. "

" I'd ruther be a fresh cabbage, than an old bellows. "

" Who's a old bellows? "

" A man what goes round tellin' how much he can lift. "

" There ain't no ill wind in the truth, " Brown declared.

" But thar ain't no truth in th' wind you blow, " Long, quite exasperated, replied.

" Wall, now, ef you are still harpin' on that log-rollin', I want to say right here, afore all these gentlemen, that I did outlift you.   When you an' me was under the same handspike, at the end of th' old sycamore log, you come mighty nigh cavin'."

"Here, boys, this has gone fur enough. Let's licker," interposed Smith, and again the canteen was passed as a peace offering. But Brown was by no means satisfied, and after smacking his lips, he mopped his florid brow, and ironically remarked:

"It ain't agin the army regulations to tell the truth."

"Ef it was, you'd not be court martialled for violation of th' rules," growled Long.

"An' ef every coward was drummed out o' th' service, you'd be hoin' co'n in Kentucky."

"You're a liar."

At this the angry Kentuckians flew at each other, and the blows were flying fast and reckless, when their two half-tipsy companions, aided by Sergeant Bragg of the same company, tore them asunder.

"What air you'uns quarrellin' about?" the sergeant asked.

The malefactors stood panting and silent with downcast eyes, while Smith explained that the *casus belli* was over which had outlifted the other at the Fergurson log-rolling last fall.

"Why, you dinged fools, you warn't neither of you at the log-rollin'," declared the sergeant.

Brown and Long exchanged glances, and the former remarked:

"Come to think of it, I war at town that day, and got drunk afo' noon. Guess I didn't go."

"An' now I come to think, I had the chills, an' never left the house," returned Long. The belligerents shook hands, all took a drink, and next moment all were singing the "Old Folks at Home."

On the 20th of May, the Confederate government was removed to Richmond, and a few days after that, there was an immense popular furore over the arrival of the president. The presidential mansion, at the corner of Twelfth and Clay streets, now a public-school building, had not been procured, and the president and his family were temporarily provided for at the Spotswood Hotel. An immense concourse of people assembled at the depot and thronged the streets leading to the hotel. On the way numbers of bouquets were thrown or handed into the carriage. One thrown by a pretty little child fell just a short distance from it, and Mr. Davis stopped the carriage, got out and picked it up amid tremendous applause. That night there was a serenade, and Mr. Davis spoke briefly from the window of the hotel. Alec, who had come from the camp to escort Elsie to the scene, managed to get himself and his fair companion near enough to see and hear the president.

Mr. Davis was at that time a man of very striking appearance, tall, lithe and graceful, straight as an Indian, dignified and reposed in manner, but without hauteur. His address was scarce more than an acknowledgment of the enthusiastic welcome and a word of encouragement. He was followed by Senator Wigfall of Texas, General Henry A. Wise and others.

During the speaking, Mrs. Davis was discovered near the parlor window, and was vociferously and persistently cheered, until she advanced to the window and acknowledged the compliment by bow-

PRESIDENT DAVIS.

ing to the immense concourse assembled to welcome her. She was of commanding height, with dark hair, eyes and complexion, with strongly marked and expressive mouth. It was a fine face, indicative of intellect, energy, and strength of character, yet beautifully softened by the gentle expression of her dark, earnest eyes. Her manners were kind, graceful and affable, her conversational powers brilliant, and her receptions, which Elsie attended, were characterized by a dignity very properly belonging to the drawing-room

entertainments of the chief magistrate of a republic.

As Alec was conducting Elsie home that evening, he overheard a voice near him in the crowd
saying:

"Yaas, we war 'bout ter fight, Long an' me,
'bout liftin' at th' log-rollin' at Fergurson's last
fall, an' then come ter find 'at neither one o' us
war there at all, huh, huh, huh, huh!"

In the speaker, Alec recognized one of the Kentuckians whose humorous quarrel he had overheard
a short time before.

Military discipline soon put a stop to the frequent visits of Alec to the home of Elsie. Leave
of absence was hard to obtain, and he began to see
much less of the fair damsel than was agreeable to
the lovesick swain. Alec soon realized his mistake in not starting into the service as a commissioned officer. It is a long and hard road to climb
from a knapsack to shoulder-straps.

His regiment was ordered to the front. By
June 1, 1861, there had been some skirmishing,
and the two armies were preparing for the great
struggle which was soon to commence. West
Virginia had refused to secede, and there was
already talk of forming a new State out of the territory west of the mountains. General Robert E.
Lee was made commander of the Confederate army

of Virginia, while General George B. McClellan was placed in command of the department of the Ohio.

Alec's regiment left Richmond, May 26th, and the young soldier, unaccustomed to such hardships, gloomily trudged along the dusty road with his gun on his shoulder.

They camped on the banks of a stream. He never knew the name of it nor did he ever know why the regiment halted there for almost two weeks. Thousands of rumors were floating in the air and more than two-thirds of them were believed. Steel-clothed Yankees, with bristling horns, were said to be just beyond the hills, advancing to cut them to pieces. Alec took his first turn on picket duty. Perhaps there is nothing more trying on the nerves of a raw recruit, than midnight duty on a solitary picket post. But Alec had left Elsie in a huff, and declared he hoped the Yankees would kill him, so it did not make much difference whether he was killed on picket, or in line of battle; but when the captain called him to his tent and gave him his final instructions before going to his post, Alec felt his blood congeal. The captain sought to impress on his mind that the post was important, the danger imminent, and the foe near. If attacked he was to fire and fall back on the reserves. He was to be on the alert for an ambuscade or some trick of the enemy. Above all things, he was to remember that the safety of the regiment, the army, and the Southern Confederacy depended on his vigilance.

Although Alec thought the officer overdoing the matter a little, the great responsibility made him exceedingly nervous. A more drear, wilder or lonelier place, could not have been found, and Alec declared:

"Hang me if I could find my way back to camp, if I was attacked."

Alec never realized what it was to be alone on picket before, until he found himself alone on this dreary post, with the blackest of nights gathered all about him. A melancholy breeze was abroad, and the rustling leaves seemed moved by the wings of ghosts. Black clouds thickened in the sky, shutting out the faint light of the stars and leaving all plutonian darkness. Alec seemed all of a sudden to feel that he was alone, and helpless, with an enemy in front who was probably at that very moment creeping forward to stab him dead at his post. Retreat was utterly impossible, and for the first time in his life, he began to feel all the pangs of fear. Naturally Alec was brave; but he was unacquainted with war and danger, and this new experience had been thrust on him so suddenly, and with such little preparation, that he was seized with the strange and unknown sensation of dread.

Alone with the dark night, the forest all about him, not a companion to whom he might whisper a word of consolation, or hope,—no wonder he began to quake with fear. At times the silence was so deafening, and the darkness so appalling that he felt as if he must cry out in his agony. Not even a night bird fluttered by, not an owl uttered its thrilling hoot, nor the mournful cry of the coon reached his ears. All was silence, deep, awful silence. It seemed as if an icy blast from off some frozen river had suddenly struck him, causing his form to tremble with an unknown sensation, while he grasped his musket with an energy of despair.

He stood near a small oak, and at last leaning against it, tried to hum a tune in order to convince himself that he was not scared. His own voice seemed to sound hoarse and unnatural, and though he did not hum above his breath, it went out on the air, like the boom of a cannon, as if its reverberations would never cease.

At last he heard an awful tread. It was a stealthy, terrible, tramping sound, moving slowly and cautiously through the bushes, like some giant rifleman creeping forward to slay him. At first he thought his ears were deceiving him; but at last he became convinced that there could be no mistake. He could hear the bushes parting carefully, as if a man were pushing them aside with his hands to thrust the barrel of his gun forward, in order to make a sure shot at the guard.

In the first transports of his dread, Alec thought to fly, but having forgotten the direction to the camp, he knew that he was as liable to run right into the arms of the enemy. Then his heart began to palpitate, his hair stood on end, and his knees tottered; his thoughts teemed with presages of death and destruction; his conscience rose up in judgment against him, and he underwent a severe paroxysm of dismay and distraction.

In that awful moment, poor Alec remembered his misspent life, his many sins, and fully realized how unfit such a wild, harum-scarum fellow as he was to appear at the bar of eternal justice, and yet here was a whole army of Yankees creeping forward to blow him into eternity. Appreciating the uncertainty of life, and the certainty of death, he for the first time entertained serious thoughts of preparation for the latter. He sank on his knees and tried to pray, but " Now I lay me down to sleep" was all that he could think of at that moment, which in the least resembled a prayer. From one extreme of fear he rushed to another. His last desperate idea was to fire and run. He knew not where he would run, nor what would be the result of the flight; but he determined to run.

At this moment the clouds parted, and the pale lambent glow of a star, dimly lighting the scene, fell upon a spot in the bushes where they had been separated and he saw a pair of slender objects, which to his heightened imagination, might be either swords or bayonets, pointed directly at his breast, ready to slay him. Nerved with an energy of despair, he took a hasty aim and

"Now I lay me down to sleep," was all he could think of.

pulled the trigger. There was a stunning report, and Alec was sent heels over head by the recoil of the musket, into a thorn bush.

Scratched, torn and bleeding, he crawled out

from his uncomfortable position, and ran as fast as his legs could carry him, shouting:

"To arms! to arms! the foe! the foe!"

More by good luck than judgment, his mad flight took him in the direction of the camp, where he found the long roll beating, and men falling into ranks. Guards came hurrying in from other points, and the brass six-pound cannon was loaded.

Alec was running up and down the line, wildly yelling "To arms!" when his captain seized him, shook him, and demanded:

"What's the matter? Who fired that shot?"

"I did."

"What did you shoot at?"

"The Yankees."

"How many are they?"

"I saw fifty at least, and I am sure there are ten thousand behind them."

A reconnoitring party, one hundred strong, was finally sent forward to see what had become of the enemy, who were making no noise. Alec was chosen to guide them to the spot.

"Where is your musket?" the officer in command asked.

"I don't know," he answered. In fact he had not thought of his musket since he fired.

Slowly, carefully, yet boldly, they advanced through the bushes to the outpost. Not a word was spoken, save when the commanding officer issued some order.

The place was at last reached, and the captain, with drawn sword, led the way to the thicket where Alec had seen the phalanx of bayonets. The spot was reached, and the commanding officer flashed a light over a dark object lying on the ground, and burst into a roar of laughter.

"What is the matter?" asked Alec, fearing that he had made some miserable blunder.

"Why, you idiot, you have killed a cow!" was the answer, and then the forest rang with a hundred peals of laughter.

14

CHAPTER X.

FIRST FIRE.

MARK STEVENS had been two months at Rising Sun before his regiment moved. Then they went down the river to Cairo, where General Benjamin M. Prentiss, a brave Illinois brigadier of volunteers, was in command. General Prentiss, not having been a regular-army officer, was not in favor with the war department. Shortly after Mark's arrival, he was superseded by General Grant. Soon after taking command, Grant sent a force to seize Paducah, Kentucky. This was done just in time to prevent the Confederates from making a like effort. This was of course in violation of the disloyal Kentucky governor's ideas of armed neutrality.

Mark took no part in the capture of Paducah, and in fact had not yet seen an armed Confederate, nor heard a gun fired in conflict. He had learned that General Fremont was in the field. On August 31st, Fremont had proclaimed the freedom of the slaves, and confiscated the property of the disunionists of Missouri. This was a dangerous

210

proclamation, but in keeping with a man whose ideas are based on the force of the army, instead of statesmanship. No one yet thought of the freedom of the slaves, and not one soldier in ten had enlisted with that object in view, and the proclamation, had it been enforced, would have driven thousands of soldiers out of the army. Lincoln seeing the folly, checked the wild career of Fremont before he had gone far enough to do any great mischief.

Fremont moved against Price. Fearing that the Confederate troops at Columbus might reinforce Price, General Grant, who with twenty thousand men was at Cairo, was ordered to make a demonstration on both sides of the Mississippi, in order to engage the attention of the forces at Columbus. Colonel Richard Oglesby was dispatched with troops to meet about three thousand of the enemy on the St. Francois River, fifty miles south of Cairo. On the 5th, Grant dispatched Colonel W. H. L. Wallace from Bird's Point to overtake and reinforce Oglesby, with orders to march to New Madrid, a point some distance on the Missouri side. General Smith was ordered, at the same time, to make a direct demonstration against Columbus with what troops he could spare from Paducah. He was ordered to make only a demonstration, and to halt a few miles from town.

Some of these orders reached the ears of the privates, and Mark felt that an attack was not very far off; but where or how the bolt would strike he could not tell. On the evening of November 5, 1861, the soldiers were sitting about their camp fires smoking and telling stories.

Bill Simms was lying on a bundle of straw, his hands clasped behind his head and a pipe in his mouth. It was already conceded that Bill was the chief liar in the regiment.

" Boys, we're goin' to have some hot work before three days," said Bill.

" How d'ye know, Bill?" Abe Bolton asked, while Sis rubbed his smooth chin in silence. Bill, giving an extra puff or two at his pipe, went on:

" I see them ginerals puttin' their heads together. Then they hurry Oglesby off one way, and send Wallace after him with a thousand men. I tell ye, boys, there's goin' to be trouble. I remember one time when I was with Gineral Percy!"

" Say, Bill, let up on your Percy experience," interrupted one of the soldiers.

" Well, lemme tell this story———"

" Don't do it, Bill; it'll only add one more lie to the long list you'll have to answer fur, when the rebels fill you full o' lead."

" Now, boys, there ain't no need to be makin'

light o' this, for we're goin' to have trouble. What do you say about it, Sis?"

Sis pressed his finger to his beardless chin, and asked :

" What did we come for?"

Mark joined the group, and a moment later a corporal came and detailed the guard.   Bill Simms was put on that duty, and it freed his mess from any further Percy reminiscences.   Next day the men were ordered to provide themselves with three days' rations and forty rounds of cartridges.   That sounded very much like business, and the soldiers began to ask each other where they were going. Large steamboats at the landing, sending forth volumes of black smoke, were strongly suggestive of an expedition on the water.

Mark's regiment was ordered aboard one of the boats.   The vessels were partially provided against bullets, their sides being guarded by thick boards which might turn an ordinary musket-ball.   The firemen were shovelling in coal, the steam escaping in deafening hisses, so that the vessel seemed to actu-ally tremble beneath the struggles of the confined monster.   The soldiers were silent, all realizing that they were about to embark on an expedition from which many would never return.

Mark gazed at the shore and camp, which had for weeks been his home, and asked himself, would he ever see it again? He knew not whither he was going. All was surmise. Columbus was down the river, and yet Mark did not believe that General Grant would be foolish enough to attack it. Grant had " gathered up all the troops at Cairo and Fort Holt, except suitable guards," and took them aboard the steamers convoyed by two gun-boats. The forces of General Grant were between four and five thousand men, embracing five regiments of infantry, two guns, and two companies of cavalry.

General Grant had no idea of making an attack at the outstart, and the glory of the fight at Belmont belongs to the troops. The conflict was forced on the general by the volunteers. They had enlisted to fight, and were heartily tired of the inactivity of camp life. Nothing is so calculated to discourage and demoralize a soldier as inactivity. When General Grant saw how elated his officers and soldiers were at the prospect of the long-promised engagement with the enemy, he realized that, in order to retain their respect, he must make some effort before returning to Cairo. Grant, in a great measure, owed his success to his having the good sense to take advice from others; to his ability to appreciate the situation and to act accordingly. He knew that it would be folly to attack Columbus; but about two o'clock, he learned that the enemy was crossing troops from Columbus to the west bank, to be dispatched, presumably, after Oglesby. There was a small camp of Confederates at Belmont immediately opposite Columbus, and at this point he resolved to make the attack.

The great steamers at last began to move. As they cast off from the shore, and glided out into the stream, Bill Simms, who stood on the forward deck smoking his pipe, said:

" Now, boys, look at Cairo. Some o' you may never come back."

Mark felt the full force of this idle speech. He was no coward; but any reflecting man who comes face to face with danger, experiences a sensation called fear. The man who says that he goes into battle without any of the pangs of dread either does not possess the good sense requisite to self-protection, or is an unmitigated liar. The man whose fears are subordinate to pride and patriotism makes the best soldier. The brave man dreads going into battle, but when he feels the touch of his comrade's elbow, it seems to inspire confidence, and he looks forward, not backward.

As Mark stood in the stern of the boat, his mind went back over the past. The sun set, and darkness gathered over the scene as the steamers sped on their way, trailing showers of sparks and volumes of black smoke in their wake. Mark glanced at the stars, asking himself if he would ever see them again. He realized that a broadside of artillery, or the explosion of a torpedo might, at any moment, send them to the bottom. His aged parents, in their Kentucky home, might pass many anxious days ere they learned his fate. Then his mind wandered to another. That one was the peerless Elsie in her far off southern home. No wonder that Mark thought of her on this occasion, for she was scarce ever out of his mind. Months of excitement had failed to efface the image of the beautiful maid of the South from his memory, and he realized that time would never do so.

"O life! what a mystery," soliloquized Mark. "Men are born, enter on the stage of action, perform their little part and pass away. The past has been dark and stormy, while the future is darker than this starless night. We may talk of happiness, but where is it found?" Then his mind reverted to that dark shadow blighting his own life, and he said: "But for that, I might have been happy. A cruel fate is mine. Why was it decreed that I should meet her, when such a meeting was only productive of misery? Is it Providence, or is it fate, that makes puppets of men, plays with them for awhile and then casts them aside? There seems no ease from this strain called life, save the grave; then how foolish to fear death."

Mark Stevens felt bitter against the capricious fortune which had seemed to play with him as a cat does with the mouse. Misery had claimed him at his birth, for he had ever been unfortunate, and he might reasonably presume that he would fall in the coming struggle. What was death that he need fear it? When the sickly dream of life was over, then he would be at peace from the warring elements of outrageous fortune.

Thinking was painful, and Mark rose and went toward the pilot house. A score of soldiers wrapped in blankets lay snoring on the deck.

"Happy fellows!" sighed Mark. "Care sits so lightly on your brows that you sleep in peace, even while rushing to what may be your eternal doom. Perhaps it is wisest after all. Why take thought for the morrow, when the morrow is beyond control, and we know not what it may bring forth—sunshine or shadow?"

It was two o'clock on the morning of the 7th before Mark Stevens had even attempted to sleep. He was only dozing when the boats came to, and the officers on each met in general consultation. Then all pushed boldly down the river again. When day dawned they were tied up under the banks; but the pickets above Columbus were drawn in, and about daylight the boats moved out from the shore. Mark, who had been in a fitful slumber, awoke as the boats started from the shore.

"Where are we going?" he asked Bill Simms, who was filling his pipe.

"We seem to be goin' over to the Missouri side."

"Have you heard nothing of our destination?"

"No, old Grant and all the rest keep a close mouth."

The soldiers were gathered about the deck in groups, either silent, or talking in whispers. Mark saw Sis, a little apart from the others, sitting on a coil of rope, yawning, and only half awake.

"Sis, we'll be in Missouri soon," said Mark.

"Tho't we were goin' to Columbus," Sis growled.

"We will probably have some fighting any way," Mark returned, gazing at the shore they were approaching. The land was low and in places cut up with sloughs. Sis, who had followed the direction of his glance, with another careless yawn remarked:

"Good place fur ducks."

The soil on the west side was rich, and the timber large and heavy. There were some small clearings between Belmont and the point for which they were heading, but most of the country was covered with native forests.

" We are goin' to land right in front of them corn fields," growled Bill Simms, puffing away at his pipe. " Now it's bad policy. Gineral Percy would know better than that."

" Perhaps there is no other place to land," Mark ventured to answer; " and then, this may be only a feint."

" Wall, a feller'd faint afore he'd take Columbus from this side o' the river."

" There's one boat rounding to," put in Abe Bolton, pointing to one of the boats. " She's goin' to land."

" Yes, there goes the line. See the niggers jump ashore!"

" And the gang plank is run out."

In an incredible short time orders could be heard from the landed boat.

" Attention! Right face. By fours—forward—march!" and a long line of blue coats, with glittering muskets and bayonets were seen leaving the boat.

" There goes the gineral's hoss," said Sis. " Wonder if he run at the fair last fall?"

General Grant went ashore, formed the first regiment that landed, and marched it down the river a short distance, to guard against surprise. In the woods, a short distance below the landing, was a depression, where the men were stationed with orders to remain until properly relieved. These troops with the gunboats were left to protect the transports.

"Wonder if they've gone off to do all the fightin' themselves?" asked Sis with another yawn.

"No, our boat is goin' ashore," some one said.

"Fall in!" cried the lion-like voice of the colonel, then the captains took command of their companies, and in a moment every man was behind the stacked muskets.

Here they waited until the boat ran in to shore, and lay alongside the muddy bank. Mark watched a negro leap ashore and seize the cable which he wound about an old stump. The boat was soon secured, and then came the command:

"Take—arms!"

In two seconds' time a thousand muskets were seized as one, and brought to an order.

"Carry—arms!"

They brought their muskets to their sides.

"Right—face!"

That pretty movement was executed, and they received the command to march. They stepped off as one man, and walked down the stage plank to the shore.

"I believe they kin see us from Columbus," said Nick timidly.

"What if they do? We ain't hurtin' 'em over

there," growled Bill Simms, who still clung to his pipe. They marched a few hundred paces away, and the regiment came to a halt.

All the transports had landed, and the men were rapidly coming ashore. A long line of blue coats was seen forming. Up to this time, Mark and his companions were in utter ignorance of the intention of the officers; but when they had been formed and stood waiting the order to advance, a whisper ran down the line:

"There's Johnny rebs over there?"

"Where?" asked Nick.

"Just over the hill."

Then came the order to march by the left flank, and they advanced a mile and a half, and halted in a low, flat, marshy place covered with a heavy growth of timber in front. Then came a requisition on each captain to detail ten men from his company for skirmishers.

Mark, Sis, Bill Simms and Abe Bolton were detailed as four of the ten from their company. They deployed at the distance of about four rods apart at first, and began to advance carefully into the heavy timber. Mark could see no one, yet his heart was beating wildly, his face was very pale, though he was not trembling.

Sis was on his left, and Bill Simms on his right. They had not gone far when a hare started up before the former, and went bounding away.

"There goes a rabbit!" cried Sis, cocking his gun.

"You dern fool, don't you shoot!" cautioned Bill Simms.   "Don't you see there is bigger game ahead?"

It was hard for Sis to resist his natural desire for sport, but he did so, and let the hammer of his musket down.   The officers in charge of the skirmishers were passing quickly up and down the line, giving commands and words of encouragement.

As yet, not a shot had been fired, and Mark had not seen a sign of an enemy; but it became quite evident from the caution exercised, that they were nearing danger.   Mark saw some of his fellow soldiers crawling among the trees and bushes.

" Bang!"

The shot was fired two or three hundred yards on his left.   Whether it was a Union or Confederate shot, he never learned.   A moment later he heard two or three more in quick succession, and then he thought he saw something moving in the bushes directly before him.   It might have been a man, or some domestic animal.   Once or twice he raised his gun, intending to shoot it, but not being quite certain lowered his piece.

Suddenly there came a burst of flame and smoke from the bushes on the hill above, and the woods were filled with echoing shots. Bill Simms blazed away into the woods, and Mark did likewise, though he could see nothing to shoot at. All along the entire skirmish line, everybody was firing, save Sis, who stood in plain view erect and undaunted.

" Sis, why don't you shoot?" cried Bill Simms.

" Shoot, thunder! I don't see nuthin' t' shoot at. " Sis answered.

Mark Stevens had fired twice before he was quite sure he saw a man. Then he distinctly saw one, not two hundred paces away, running obliquely to his right carrying a gun in his hand. The man had no coat, and wore a red shirt and white hat. Before Mark could put a cap on his musket, the fellow was out of sight. But a moment later he saw another two hundred paces directly in front of him. This one had fired at some of the Federal skirmishers, and pausing in a cleared spot was deliberately reloading his gun. Mark blazed away at him, and was amazed to discover that he had missed. The ball evidently went close, for the fellow sought shelter behind a tree. The enemy now appeared in front in large numbers, but were falling back.

The skirmishers cheered and pressed on, gradually closing up as they did so. A man, named Jack Flint, in Company H, was a little to the right, and in the advance of Mark, loading his gun. He had rammed home the charge, returned the ramrod to its thimbles, when he dropped his piece, yelling:

"Oh, mercy!" Clapping his left arm with his right hand, he danced about very much like a boy who has been stung by a hornet.

"What is the matter?" Mark asked.

He made no answer, but dashed back toward the rear slinging his arm, from which the blood was trickling, back and forth, and screaming: "Oh, mercy!"

The first person Mark saw slain was a red-headed boy belonging to Company E. He had pressed forward ahead of the others, and was almost fifty paces in front, and a little to the right, when he fell among some under bushes. Mark did not see him fall, nor was he aware of his fate until, pressing on through the thicket, he suddenly came upon an object that caused him to start. Lying among the grass and bushes was the red-headed boy, shot through the heart. His cap and his gun lay at his side, his eyes wide open, staring, and glassy, and his face had about it something truly appalling. He had large front teeth which protruded, and the lips being slightly drawn revealed them in a terrifying grin. Mark had seen the boy in camp, but did not know his name. There was something so terrible in the spectacle, that he shuddered, and for a moment was seized with something bordering on a panic. He was recalled to the present situation by the shouting and firing ahead, and with a vow of vengeance, he leaped over the body, and hurried forward to join his companions.

The firing was continuous, and the whiz of enemy's balls constant. They cut the bark from the trees at Mark's side, clipped the leaves from off the branches overhead, and dug up the earth at his feet. It was a veritable baptism of fire. Again and again had they been reinforced by skirmishers, until Mark thought their whole force must be in the field. Suddenly the colonel cried:

" Rally on the centre!"

Then they came elbow to elbow, met by a solid phalanx of the enemy. The sharp crack of musketry had been growing more incessant, until it became a steady roar.

" Thunder and lightnin'! that ain't no skirmish line," cried Bill Simms. " We're fightin' a line o' battle."

Mark discovered a Confederate officer riding a short distance in front of him, and determined to give him a shot as soon as he had got his gun loaded; but while he was ramming home the cartridge, Sis raised his musket and fired, and when next Mark looked, a riderless horse was galloping through the woods. Reinforcements came to the Federals, and they drove the Confederates back through their own camp, following them and yelling like demons.

The mania for plunder seized both men and officers, and General Grant was unable to control them. Regimental organizations were lost, and the army became a mob.

The men had retreated over the hill, and but few had shown any inclination to follow them. General Grant's original design was only to break up their camp, and he made no particular effort at pursuit.

There was one, however, who had little thought of plunder. It was Sis. As Mark entered the camp of Confederates, and heard the cry to halt, he saw the beardless youth giving chase to the flying enemy.

" Run down the hellions ! Shoot 'em ! Bannet 'em ! Don't let a single gray back git away!" roared the angry Bill Simms, who instead of setting the example himself, fell to plundering the camp.

Sis, hearing his command, supposed that it came from headquarters. There is an excitement about a man chase, which exceeds any other specimen of hunting, and Sis was fairly intoxicated with it. He soon overtook two or three of the slower-paced Confederates, who surrendered quietly, and were turned over to the other boys, as they came up, and were conducted to the rear.

But Sis was not satisfied with the glory he had already won. A hundred yards ahead of him was a tall, gaunt Kentuckian, clad in butternut-colored jeans of a queer cut and pattern, and a great bell-crowned hat of rough, gray beaver. Though his gait was shambling, and his huge, splay feet rose and fell in a most awkward way, he went over the ground with a speed that seemed to defy even Sis's long legs to overhaul him. But ere long, the boy pursuer was encouraged by signs of distress; first the bell-crowned hat was thrown aside, then he flung off his haversack, and this was followed by a canteen of Kentucky whiskey. Next followed the fugitive's belt, loaded down with an antique cartridge box, a savage looking knife made from a rasp, and handled with buckhorn, and a fierce looking horse-pistol, ornamented with a flint-lock.

"Jerusalem, guess I'm bustin' up a moosyum o' revolutionary relics," cried Sis. "That feller drops his forefathers' keepsakes like a bird a moultin' on a windy day in May. 'Spect he'll shed Continental money and three-cornered hats next."

Sis did not look to see if the whole Federal force was at his back or not. The fugitive turned off to the right and he followed. The youth's gun was empty, but he had his bayonet fixed, and expected every moment to be within lunging distance. He had foreshortened his gun for the plunge, when three or four Confederates suddenly started up from behind a stone and some trees, crying:

"Stop, you Yankee cuss, or we'll let some streaks o' daylight through you."

Sis halted with his breast almost against four dark muzzles. Panting he said:

"Look here, boys, this is all infernal nonsense. Our fellers are comin'; they've got ye sure."

"Yaas, you think they hev," growled one. "Don't ye see our fellers comin' over from Columbus by the million? Look at them boats!"

Sis glanced in the direction indicated by the Confederate's hand, and saw two steamers coming over the river black with Confederate soldiers.

"Now, honey, you'uns'll git away from that camp faster than ye come."

All the while there could be heard from the camp, the loud cheering of the foolish Federals, who were congratulating themselves over their victory. Sis saw he was trapped; but he did not lose his wits. Coolly seating himself on a stump, he said:

"Boys, let's talk it over."

"Give us that gun first."

"No, it's my gun; you wouldn't rob me, would ye? Besides, I saw a rabbit down under the hill, and I want to go back and shoot it."

"Look here, Yank, we don't intend to stand

"Boys, let's talk it over."

any o' your tom-foolery,—give up that gun or I'll blow yer head off."

In a moment Sis was an unarmed prisoner.

"Have ye any flat terbacker about ye?" one of his captors asked. He had, and they took it.

He was then marched down under the hill, and shortly afterward volumes of smoke and flames told that the Confederate camp was burning. Immediately after that came the boom of cannon from Columbus. The prisoner was marched a mile down toward the transports, for the Confederate troops were moving in that direction.

Mark Stevens had noted the continued absence of Sis and had reported the matter to his captain, who sent a lieutenant with twenty men, among whom was Mark, in search of him. By accident they came on the guard just as the advancing Confederates began exchanging shots with the Union troops. The tables were turned and Sis was liberated, his captors made prisoners, and all set out toward the transports.

"Now see here, sir," said Sis to the man who had taken his tobacco, "I want my flat terbacker agin. It was blamed mean o' you t' take it from a feller that way. Ef ye'd a wanted a chaw, I'd a gin it to you, 'cause I ain't one bit stingy."

"Boys, we've got to make a run for it," said Lieutenant Tull, when they came to the cornfield on the river banks above the transports. "Our fellows are all aboard, and they are about to shove off."

Already the enemy had appeared, and opened a brisk fire on the boats.

"Git!" cried Sis to the prisoners. "Run, consarn yer picturs, ur I'll jab ye with my bannit."

They all ran, and when within a few hundred paces of the transports, they discovered that they were pushing off from shore. A horseman was seen riding toward the boat frantically waving his hat, and ordering them to return for him. The captain of the boat ordered it back, and the horseman dismounted and went down the bank and entered the boat by the gang plank. The horse taking in the situation, determined to follow his master. There was no path down the bank, and every one acquainted with the Mississippi River knows its banks, in a natural state, are not far from perpendicular. The horse put his fore-feet over the edge of the bank and with his hind feet well under him, slid down the bank, and trotted on board the boat, twelve or fifteen feet away, over a single gang plank. They afterward learned that the horseman who preceded them on the boat, was General Grant. Mark and the party that had rescued Sis came up at this moment.

"Hold just a minute, captain," cried Lieutenant Tull.

"I can't, run and jump aboard."

It was a risky business to force the prisoners to jump on the boat, as it was pushing off, and the gang plank was dragging along the muddy bank, but they got three of them on the boat, while the fourth ran away. Mark slipped on the stage plank as it was being drawn in, and fell in the water; A rope was tossed to him, and by the aid of Sis and Abe Bolton he was pulled on board, where he sank, almost exhausted, on the boiler deck.

CHAPTER XI.

SHILOH.[*]

A FEW days after the fight at Belmont, Mark Stevens was seized with a lingering fever and, for months, lay in the hospital at Cairo. Then he went to his home in Boone County, Kentucky, on a sick furlough, where he remained through the months of January and February, and until the middle of March, 1862. He kept posted on army movements, and read in the newspapers how Commodore Foote, on February 6, 1862, captured Fort Henry on the Tennessee. On the 8th, Burnside captured some forts and valuable supplies on Roanoke Island. On the 12th, General Grant and some gunboats invested Fort Donelson. On 13th, General Curtis advanced to Springfield, Missouri. The Confederates lost Nashville, Tennessee, on the 23d of February, and, on the 27th, abandoned Columbus. March also proved a memorable

[*] For the personal adventures of Mark Stevens in this chapter the author is indebted to O. C. Snider, late of Company H, 6th Iowa Infantry Volunteers.

month. On the 2d, the Union gunboats captured a battery at a place called Pittsburg Landing on the Tennessee. On the 6th and 8th, Curtis fought the combined forces of Price and McCullough at Pea Ridge, defeating them. McCullough was among the Confederate slain. On the 9th, the *Monitor* defeated the Confederate ram, *Merrimac,* silencing that powerful instrument of the southern cause. On the 13th, the Confederates evacuated New Madrid, Mo.; on the 14th, General Burnside captured New Berne, North Carolina. On the 23d a battle was fought at Winchester, Virginia, in which the southern forces were defeated. On the 28th, three thousand Union troops had an unsuccessful engagement with about eleven hundred Texans at Union Branch, New Mexico.

These were the chief stirring events that had transpired while Mark was away from camp. When he started, March 15th, to his regiment, he could not at first locate them. On the restoration of General Grant to the immediate command of the troops, and his arrival at Savannah, March 17, 1862, he converted an expeditionary encampment, at Pittsburg Landing, into rendezvous of the armies of the Cumberland and Ohio, by placing his whole force on the west side of the river, where Sherman with his division already was. No rule of military art or common expediency could justify such an arrangement. In fact it was General Grant's greatest blunder, and proves that, great military hero as he became, his education was not complete. A militia captain of this day who should be guilty of such a blunder would be court-martialled for incompetency. An invading army may, as a preliminary step, throw an inferior force in advance upon the enemy's coast, or across an intervening river, to secure a harbor or other necessary foothold; but, in such a case, a good general would see that his advanced force was securely entrenched. Pittsburg Landing was in no sense a point of such necessity or desirability as to require any risk, or any great expenditure of means for its occupation. General Grant, for some unknown reason, had his headquarters at Savannah, leaving Sherman with some sort of control at Pittsburg Landing.

The official reports of the battle of Shiloh are so conflicting that, from the commander-in-chief down to the lowest officer who has made a report, one can hardly find two that agree. General Grant's own report shows that he was at Savannah, about ten or twelve miles away, when the battle began. The conflict must have raged three or four hours before he was within hearing of it. General Grant censures General Lew Wallace for not obeying his orders to join him, and belittles the services of Buell. General Buell, on the other hand, in an article in the March, 1886, number of the *Century Magazine*, shows how the arrival of General Nelson with the head of his division, saved the army from being crushed. General Grant, in his memoirs, volume I., page 347, infers that it was night that saved his army from suffering defeat, and that Buell and Wallace had little to do with it. Some one made a blunder at Shiloh; and, but for the gunboats, Buell, Wallace and night, General Grant's whole army would have been utterly destroyed. In fact, the first day's fight must be regarded as a Union defeat. When victories are won, it is common to give all credit to the commander of the army, although he might not have been near enough to see an enemy, or hear the whistle of a bullet; and where mistakes are made, the commanding officer should be made to bear the blame.

The disposition of troops would be a discredit to a three months' volunteer colonel. General Benjamin M. Prentiss, with a brigade of raw troops, but few of whom had ever been under fire, was placed on the frontier. There they lay almost two weeks, while Johnson and Beauregard were carefully advancing on them. Not a ditch was dug, not a tree felled for protection. If they were surprised at Shiloh, neither General Grant nor his friends can offer any excuse for such surprise.

They should have sent scouting and reconnoitring parties out; and known that an army was advancing. If they were not surprised, if General Grant knew of the near proximity of a large Confederate army, why was he ten or twelve miles away when his forces were attacked? Why did he not have his troops entrenched, and so distributed that they should not be compelled to fall back every time their cartridge boxes were empty? The general's only possible excuse was that he was not certain whether the attack would be made at Pittsburg, or Crump's Landing. In such a dilemma he would, in later years, have entrenched at both places.

Instead of admitting his mistake, as Washington would have done, General Grant falls to scolding Wallace and Buell, the men who ultimately saved his army from ruin.

The northern hero at Shiloh was the man who carried the knapsack and not him who wore the shoulder straps. The private deserved the glory, the officers none, or little. The officer most worthy of praise has always received least. That man was Brigadier-General Benjamin M. Prentiss of volunteers. General Prentiss being a volunteer, as is usual, the regular army officers sought to make him the scapegoat for all the blunders. He was on the left of Sherman, and on the morning of the 6th, in the advance. General Prentiss believed that there was a large force in their advance, and recommended the necessity of entrenching; but as Braddock replied to Washington, that a Provincial Colonel could not teach one of His Majesty's officers the art of war, so the West·Pointers thought the opinions of " Ben Prentiss" not worth considering. After the battle was fought and he and his brigade, with a part of W. H. L. Wallace's, became sacrifices for the army, they sought to malign him, by circulating the report that he was captured early in the morning. He was the only general officer that was not surprised. Whoever may have been expecting a fight, General Grant was not; for on the 5th, he was at Nelson's camp, and said he would send the boats for his division, " Monday or Tuesday, or some time early in the week." He added: " There will be no fight at Pittsburg Landing; we will have to go to Corinth· where the enemy are fortified."

General Prentiss,· volunteer as he was, believed there was danger, and his vigilance gave first warning of it. The two or three days' skirmishing told him something, even if it did not a West Pointers. On Sunday morning, April 6, 1862, at about three o'clock, he sent Colonel David H. Moore, of the 21st Missouri Infantry volunteers, with five companies to strengthen the picket guard. On the way, Colonel Moore met the picket guard as it was being driven in by the enemy; and, forming his regiment, he advanced and began to open fire on the enemy. The steadily increasing roar of musketry and artillery swelled in volume: but the little band of steady Missourians held their ground, until Colonel Moore's leg was shattered by a grapeshot, his horse killed under him, and his brave little band flanked on both sides. Then they began to fall back, fighting as they ran.

General Prentiss' brigade was under arms and waiting when the remnant of Colonel Moore's brave band came in. According to the accounts of both Grant and Buell, General Prentiss' raw troops fought like veterans. They would not run to the river as many of the veterans did. General Buell says: "General Prentiss promptly formed his division (doubtless meaning brigade) at the first news from the front, and moved a quarter of a mile in advance of his camp, where he was attacked before Sherman was under arms."

But enough of wrangling and dispute among men thirsting for glory. We find it difficult to believe all that either side has said, and think it best to listen for once to men who fought the battle, the "rank and file." "Old Rank-and-File" is seldom allowed to speak. It is supposed that he knows little about battles, and has less to do with fighting them; and it is only when the "big bugs" fall out, and cannot agree in the division of glory and spoils, that " Rank-and-File" gets a hearing. As he fought the battle of Shiloh, we will listen to his account of it. Some critics suggested a few years ago, when the *Century Magazine* was publishing its excellent series of war-sketches, that the private soldiers should not be permitted to give their views, that battles were fought at headquarters, and not in the ranks. Headquarters were at Savannah on this day, and there was no battle fought there; so we can be excused for giving the battle as a private saw it.

Mark Stevens reached Shiloh on March 29th, and went at once to his regiment, which was in Sherman's division in the front, two or three miles out from the river. On the way from the river to the camp, he noticed that the land was nearly level, or slightly undulating, covered with forests, with an occasional cleared field. He passed the log house known as Shiloh Church, from which the conflict took its name.

Reaching his company, Mark was warmly welcomed by his companions. Bill Simms, lighting his pipe, declared that he was as proud to see him as a comrade who once served with him under " Gineral Percy." Sis rubbed his smooth chin and grinned, while Abe Bolton began to narrate their service at Donelson, frequently interrupted by Bill, who had had a similar experience while under " Gineral Percy."

Mark was not yet strong, and was exempted from picket duty. All day long occasional shots had been fired, and sometimes a volley was heard in the distance.

" I wonder why them infernal pickets air fightin'?" Nick nervously asked.

" Jist for the fun of it," Bill answered, lighting his pipe.

Sis came in from the picket line, and showed a musket ball half buried in the stock of his gun.

" Who did that?" asked Nick.

" A Johnny reb," answered Sis. " Two o' th' boys were playin' keards and blamed if they didn't shoot one's fingers off."

" And spiled his hand," put in Bill.

Shortly after this, Mark and Sis went down to the sutler's tent to make some purchases. The sutler's name was L. M. Blakeley. He had grown a trifle nervous, and when he and his assistant, a negro called Dock, were alone, he cursed the officers from Grant to corporal for incompetency.

" I'll bet, Dock, we git licked like thunder right here," Blakeley declared. When Sis and Mark approached the sutler's tent, he asked:

" Wall, boys, what news in front? Have ye been on picket, Sis?"

16

"Yes."

"Will there be a fight?"

"Yes; ye kin look for it right soon."

"Why, I heard Gineral Grant say they wouldn't dare fight us."

"He'll find he is mistaken before this time to-morrow," Sis answered.

As they returned to their quarters, Mark asked:

"Sis, do you really think there is going to be a fight?"

"I do; I tell you we'll have it before two days."

Mark spent the day in lying about camp, reading a novel. At taps he turned in and went to sleep. He remembered that just before closing his eyes, he heard distant firing a mile or two away, and he entertained a vague suspicion that the pickets were shooting at somebody, or being shot, he was not certain which. Then he closed his eyes and went to sleep.

Mark never had sweeter sleep. His dreams were clear, distinct and pleasant. He was once more with Elsie Cole, roaming through the flowery plains of Florida. They walked hand in hand with the confidence of children and the affection of lovers. That great load which had been bowing him down, had rolled away,—that skeleton in the closet was forever gone, and he was free to love, woo and win.

At two, he was partially roused by one of the pickets coming in off duty. As he unbuckled his belt and laid his accoutrements away, he casually remarked in answer to some question which Mark did not hear:

" We'll have h——l afore mornin'!"

The tired soldiers paid such little heed to the remark, that nearly all sunk into profound slumber a moment later. Mark had been asleep about two hours longer, when he was awakened by some one shaking his shoulder, and heard the voice of the orderly sergeant saying:

" Hurry up, boys, dress and fall in!"

Some one had lighted a candle in the tent, and Mark, glancing at his watch, saw that it was four o'clock. With the aid of Sis, he found his gun and accoutrements.

" Is your box full of cartridges?" Sis asked.

" Yes, I have forty rounds."

" That'll be more'n we need," some one boastingly put in. " They will run after the third round."

The men were hurriedly buckling on belts and adjusting straps over their shoulders. When Mark left the tent, he found Captain Hawk and his lieutenants forming their line directly in front of their tents, about a hundred paces from them. Mark took his place in the line, and then they stood at a parade rest, listening for some sound of the enemy. Only the wailing of the night wind, like some lost spirit as it sighed through the tree tops, could be heard. Mark found his imagination grown active, and the effect it had on his nerves no one can understand, save those who have gone through similar experiences. He imagined every snapping of a twig an enemy. He could not determine whether there were skirmishers or a picket line in front, and sometimes was quite sure he heard a line of battle advancing. At times he shivered with mingled dread and cold. The hours wore on, daylight came, and they were ordered to stack arms and get breakfast.

"Keep your accoutrements on," said Captain Hawk. "You may have to jump to your line at any moment." Mark went to the rear of the tent where there was a barrel of water, filled his canteen and, dipping out a basin full, washed his hands and face. By the time he had completed his toilet, breakfast was ready, and he sat down with his mess to eat it.

During the meal, they heard a steady noise, left in front, which gradually drew nearer and swelled into a continuous roar. This was the attack on General Prentiss' advance. Mark had just finished his breakfast and was wiping his mouth with his handkerchief, when the drums sounded the long roll.

" Fall in!   Fall in!"

The terrible command rang out along the entire
line.   He who has never heard the long roll on
the battle field, can form but slight conception of
the sensations it produces.   It is the dread alarm
which summons men forth to die.

In three or four seconds, the entire division was
in line and, taking arms, stood ready and waiting.
By this time the roar of battle was growing heavier
and heavier, and the thunder of cannon was shaking the earth.   Mark heard one of the file closers
say:

" Old Ben Prentiss is havin' it hot and heavy
over there. "

The officers were hurrying up and down the
ranks, trying to conceal their own anxieties by
saying:

" Keep cool, boys,—keep cool,—take it easy,
and wait until they are near enough to see them,
and make your shots sure. "

How long the line stood thus with the wild
storm of battle raging over where Prentiss' brigade
was fighting forty thousand Confederates, Mark
never knew; but it seemed hours.

So ill formed were the troops, that there were
wide gaps between the divisions.   As they stood
in front of their tents listening to the trembling
thunder, the rolling storm sweeping down on Pren-

tiss, a horseman suddenly appeared from their left, spurring at full speed toward a group of officers already in consultation. It proved to be an orderly with dispatches from some one.

A few moments later, the command rang along the line.

" Carry arms!—left face!"

In a moment the entire line had faced to the left. " Trail arms! Forward, double quick—march!"

Away they went at full speed, running in a southeast direction, toward the storm. All the while the battle was approaching, and from the woods on their right, Confederate skirmishers were firing through their ranks. Lieutenant Guinn suddenly uttered a groan and grasped his leg in his hands. It had been shattered by a bullet. He was the first man Mark Stevens saw struck that day. Three of his comrades took him up and hurried him from the field.

By this time, all was wild confusion. The uproar was tremendous. On every side came the peals of cannon, the crack of musketry, while the earth trembled beneath the explosion of shells.

The sutler, L. M. Blakeley, took fright at first shock of battle and ran, leaving all his stores. His negro assistant " Dock" harnessed the mules amid the flying bullets, loaded the wagon to its fullest capacity, and drove off at a gallop toward the river amid the screaming shells and whizzing bullets.

As the regiment was running left oblique, double quick, Mark heard a crashing, tearing and snorting of horses, and oaths of drivers, and turning his eyes in that direction, saw a battery hopelessly tangled up in the bushes and trees.

During the time they were changing position, they paid no attention to the shots of the enemy, which whistled like hail through their ranks.

" Halt !"

They had run about a mile when this command came. They obeyed, and changed front, marching by the right flank forward, and formed a line of battle. Through the opening in the wood, Mark now saw the enemy not over two or three hundred yards distant. The crashing of cannon and falling of branches, cut off by the iron balls, mingled with the roar of small arms, and continuous yelling, made it seem as if pandemonium reigned.

Some one gave the command to charge; and companies B and H, of the Sixth Iowa infantry, with fixed bayonets charged the enemy. Ere they had run a hundred paces, half of their number had been shot down. In Company B, John Uphard fell with a leg shattered by a musket ball. His brother " Billy," who was a favorite in the regiment, ran to his assistance, and was standing over him to lift him up, when two bullets passed through his body, and he fell dead on his wounded brother. Companies H and B fell back to their regimental line, and then there rang out along the line, the command:

"Lie down,—down all!"

In a moment the men fell upon the ground, firing and turning over on their backs to load. The oft repeated command given by the petty officers, "Give 'em h—l!" rang along the line.

When they commenced shooting, the enemy's fire slackened. On Mark's right, Captain White, of an Iowa regiment, was killed by a shell.

As Mark could not shoot very well from the ground, he crept to a tree near, and kneeling by it, loaded and fired as rapidly as he could. In the hurried formation or rapid march, Mark's company had become partially mixed with some Iowa troops. One of these, named Bill Spain, belonging to Company H, 6th Iowa Infantry volunteers, was shot through the body and fell within a few feet of Mark. He begged some one to cut off his cartridge box, as it was hurting him.

"I will do it, as soon as I am out of cartridges," said another of the same company, named Orcinas Snider, who standing behind a tree not ten feet away, was loading and firing with marvellous rapidity. Mark, moved by the cries of the fallen Spain, went and got his cartridge box, and again hugged the tree.

Soon the bullets began flying all about him, and he discovered that they were knocking the bark up in his face. Glancing off to the left, he saw that the enemy had flanked him and that but few of his comrades could be seen. Orders had been given to fall back, which he had not heard.

At the rear was an open field of a few acres. Most of the army had retired beyond that. Grape-shot, canister and musket balls were raking the open field, and he dreaded to attempt to cross it.

Biting cartridges soon filled his mouth with powder, and provoked a thirst that was maddening. There was a pile of logs at his right, where they had been carried off the field to make a review ground. He saw Dick Mattern, a musician, Sis, and two or three others, behind the logs, and halted with them to load and shoot a few more rounds. He was reloading his gun when Sis looking up cried:

" Great Scott, look at the rebels !" They were flanking them on both sides, and the only show now was to cross the open field, which was continually swept with grape, canister and musket balls. Mark was already reeking with perspiration, and the constant wiping his face with his powder covered hands had smeared it until he was black as a negro.

Half a dozen or more started to run across the field, and Mark saw two go down. A grapeshot cut off the stock of his gun, and he threw the useless barrel away. A soldier was lying dead about forty yards before him, his gun at his side. Mark discovered that their guns were of the same calibre, and he picked up the dead man's musket as he ran.

He saw a tall man just in front of him, seemingly outstripping the wind. Mark envied him his long legs, yet they were not sufficient to save him. The tall man suddenly tumbled head foremost on the ground, face downward.

"He stumbled, and is stunned by the fall," Mark thought.

His course took him past the fallen man, and he was about to call to him to get up, when he discovered that the top of his head had been shot away.

Mark felt a slight sting at his side, and something trickling down. At first he thought himself wounded, but it proved to be that a bullet had gone through his canteen. The same shot had cut the string of his haversack, and he lost his rations.

Dick Mattern * got across safe, though a bullet cut off the mouth-piece of his cornet, and Sis reached the woods beyond, unhurt. By this time Mark was suffering so from thirst that he resolved to drink at the first pool of water he came to, regardless of danger. He soon discovered a pool twenty feet long by five wide, and dropping on his hands and knees, thrust his face into the water, until it almost came in at his ears and drank. Having slaked his thirst, he raised his head and saw a dead man lying near the edge of the pool. He had been shot in the head, and the blood was trickling down to the water's edge.

About one hundred yards from the pool, he found the regiment. They had fallen back for two reasons; first, they were out-flanked, and, second, they were out of ammunition. So poorly was the army managed, that they were out of ammunition half the time. The want of cohesion and concert of action in the Union ranks that day is conspicuously indicated in the official reports. A regiment was rarely ever ·overcome in front, but fell back because the regiment or division on the right or left had done so, and thus left its flank exposed. It then continued its backward movement until it was well under shelter, thus exposing

---

* Two or three years ago Dick Mattern was still living. He was then a musical director in Chicago.

the flanks of its neighbor, who in turn also fell back. Once in operation, the process repeats itself indefinitely, sometimes step by step and again by flight and rout. The out-flanking, so common at Shiloh, could not be excused on the plea that they had inferior commanders; but it was the practical consequence of the absence of a common head, and the want of judicious use of reserves to counteract partial reverses, and preserve the front of the battle.

In a short time after the regiment had made a stand, it was again out of ammunition. Again they were out-flanked and fell back. They hugged the swamp on their right, and had only their left to fear. Another stand was made, and they fought until after the sun had passed the meridian. By this time their prospects of success seemed poor. Again they were compelled to fall back. A branch, cut from a tree by a cannon ball, fell upon Mark, knocked him senseless and broke his gun. He recovered in time to join the regiment. He had no trouble now to find another gun, for the field was strewn with arms of all kinds.

It was late in the day when the regiment made its last stand. By this time regimental organizations were almost wholly lost, and Mark found himself mixed up with Iowa, Illinois, and Ohio soldiers. The enemy could be seen on the hill above them, bringing up batteries and siege guns. Cannon roared, and storms of grapeshot and canister swept through their ranks; but the soldiers held their ground. Few commands were given, and for a long time there seemed to be no one to command. The men acted on impulse in concert. Three times they repelled the fierce charges of the enemy; but the day was well nigh spent, and so was the fury of the attack. Far on their left could be heard the roar of Webster's artillery, and the cannon from the gunboats, *Tyler* and *Lexington.* Bugles sounded, wild cheers rose on the air. Buell had come, and they were saved. Nelson, leading Buell's advance, had crossed the Tennessee, and regiment after regiment quickly formed and hurried to the front. The roar of battle was momentarily renewed and the Confederates fell back, relieving the exhausted soldiers who had fought since early morning. The storm of battle retired, leaving the officers and men huddled together in an indiscriminate mass. It was some hours before they began to re-form and re-organize.

Darkness came quickly over the scene, and the woods having been fired by the explosion of shells, a terrible conflagration threatened to add to the other horrors. About ten o'clock that night, a merciful Providence drenched the field with pouring rain, which lightened the suffering of many a wounded hero, and extinguished the fire which threatened him with a terrible death. Mark thought it the darkest night he had ever seen. The air was filled with groans and cries of the wounded. Part of the time he stood up, and a part of the time lay down in the mud and rain; but he could not sleep.

About two o'clock in the morning, General Grant came to within a few rods of him and lay down on a board to sleep or rest. By this time the rain had ceased falling in torrents, though all night long it came in a fine mist.

Mark spent the night wandering up and down the line for food. He was hungry after the long hard fight, and had lost his rations. It was broad day before he found Sis, who had some "soft bread" and raw bacon, which he divided with him, and which they ate without cooking. It was still drizzling when morning came.

The bugle sounded, they fell in, and the roll was called. Many a gallant fellow failed to answer to his name. Abe Bolton was dead, Nick Marks and Chris Creps both mortally wounded. But Bill Simms answered while he filled his pipe, and muttered, "I swear this beats anything I ever saw with Gineral Percy."

Shortly after roll call, they began to advance. But Buell's army was now doing the work. The roar of guns told that the battle was still stubborn. The Confederates, who were overwhelmed only by superior numbers, retreated from the field, leaving Buell in possession. Blakeley came back and set up his sutler's shop, and Mark and Sis bought some food; then helped gather up the dead and wounded, after which came a short season of rest.

CHAPTER XII.

ALEC AND MARK.

FOR some time after the battle of Shiloh, General Grant was under a cloud. Various unjust charges were laid at his door. Under all the abuse heaped upon him, General Grant had a firm friend in President Lincoln, and though for awhile he remained under the cloud, in time he came out into the sunshine of almost unparalleled popularity. General Halleck superseded Grant, and, on May 10th, captured Island Number Ten, a Confederate stronghold, which greatly encouraged people in the North.

The summer passed with alternating success and disaster to the Union cause. At times the lamp seemed burning low, and northern hearts were almost ready to despair.

One afternoon, just before the battle of Iuka, Mississippi, Mark Stevens was on one of the extreme outposts. It began to rain. There was a lull in hostilities just then, and there was a sort of tacit understanding between opposing pickets that there should be no firing. Mark's post was under a dead, leafless tree, with a screen of bushes in front. Having no poncho to keep him dry, and knowing it would be over an hour before he would be relieved, he advanced at "left oblique" about forty paces to a large tree which promised shelter. He had stood with his back to the trunk for ten or fifteen minutes listening to the rain pattering on the leafy roof above him, when he thought he heard a noise on the other side. Pigs were often met with in the woods on their front, and as Mark turned and carefully poked his head out from behind the trunk he fully expected to see one. What he did see was a man, who poked his head out to look around on Mark's side. It was a sun-browned face covered with a scraggy beard, surmounted by an old, drab-colored hat, with a narrow rim and peaked crown. Below the face was the collar of the gray coat of a Confederate. The tree was only about three feet through, and their faces were within a foot of each other. Mark knew at a glance that he was a Confederate, and the other seemed to realize that he was a northern soldier. They gazed at each other for half a minute, and then the man in gray clothes, in a hoarse, unnatural voice, asked:

"That you, Yank?"

"Yes; that you, Johnny?" asked Mark in a voice made husky by surprise.

17

"Thought you was hogs."

"So did I."

"What you going to do about it?"

"Nothing."

"That suits me. Come round here on my dry spot."

Without any hesitation, Mark Stevens complied. There was something frank and honest in that sunbrowned bearded face and the voice, which, like his own, was hoarse from sleeping on the ground, exposed to all sorts of weather. There was something strangely familiar in both voice and face.

He came round to where the soldier was, and for a moment they stood gazing at each other in amazement. Then, dropping muskets to the earth, they cried:

"Mark!"

"Alec!"

Next moment they were clasped in each other's arms, tears streaming down their cheeks. It might seem foolish and unmanly for those great, bearded men to cry like children; but the heart of the bravest soldier is tender, if his trade is cruel. After the first tempest of emotion had passed away, they sat down side by side alternately laughing and crying. Alec was first to speak. He said:

"Mark, are you a soldier or an officer?"

"Only a private, Alec."

"THAT YOU, YANK?"

"So am I."

"I enlisted as a private."

"So did I, and I have not gone back any, nor have I gone forward. I have been at a standstill. Promotions from the ranks come precious slow. They have flown all around me, and sometimes I can't see why they missed me. I tell you, Mark, it is in the army just like in everything else; if a fellow gets caught in the current, he goes flying on to success. If he don't, he has a hard time of it. Why, there are some fellows who went right up from captain to general, who don't know any more than I do; but they were in the swim, and I was left out. I think that fate has put her thumb on me to hold me down. Then I don't care. I am not fighting for glory or fame, and the fact is I am sometimes so infernally befuddled that I don't know what I am fighting for. Mark, you may not believe it, but the other night as I lay on picket line, and heard your bands playing the old 'Star Spangled Banner,' some kind of a weakness came over me, and I cried like a baby; I couldn't help it. Once, when I saw the head of your column marching, and caught sight of those glorious old Stars and Stripes, under which I was born and used to make so many Fourth of July speeches, I took off my hat and began to cheer. My lieutenant grabbed me by the shoulders and asked:

" ' What the d—l are you cheering for ? '

" ' It's the old flag. See, it's the old flag ! ' I cried, pointing to your banner. The officer did not like it one bit, and he shoved me down the road saying :

" ' You fool, if you don't want to be killed or captured, you had better turn your back and skeedaddle ! '

" Then I remembered, Mark, that that old banner, that pretty banner under which my great-grandfather fought with Washington, and my grandfather fought under at Lundy's Lane, was my flag no longer, and I shed tears. Oh, Mark ! this cussed war is just killing all of us. It makes brothers hate brothers."

" It is an unfortunate war, Alec."

" I believe the South was wrong to secede. The North couldn't have got their niggers. Now they'll have 'em as sure as guns made of iron. The impudent black cusses are already getting unbearable. I wish they were all in Africa."

Alec ran on in his usual strain for some time, and Mark was unable to get in a word, while there was so much he wished to talk about. He wanted to know when Alec was transferred from the eastern to the western army.

" Oh, yes ; well, you see it was when General Beauregard was sent over to this country that I came.   They sent several of his old regiments with him, and mine among the others.   Say, Mark, do you have any coffee in your camp?"

" Yes."

" Great guns!   I wish you had brought some."

" Alec, if I had known that I was going to meet you, I would have filled my pockets.   You poor boys must fare badly."

" Fare badly is no name for it, Mark.   Why, I tell you, we live on corn pone and sorghum half the time.   We marched to Shiloh and fought two days on less than half rations.   Great goodness, it is no wonder that we were overcome.   A spoonful of rice often makes a meal, and I have lived two days on an ear of raw corn.   We have no money, except Confederate shinplasters, so depreciated in value that it takes twenty-five dollars to buy the commonest kind of a pair of shoes."

" Don't   your   government   furnish   you   with clothes?"

" Sometimes, and sometimes we are compelled to go barefooted."

" Do you have no hard money?"

" No."

Mark drew from his pocket ten dollars in gold, and some silver coin.   Gold and silver were scarce in both armies; but Mark had managed to get some, and he gave all he had freely to Alec.

"What! what! Mark, do you intend giving me this money?" he asked, quite overcome.

"Yes."

"Gold and silver! where did you get it?"

"From home; father sent it to me."

"Why, Mark, a handful of that would buy our entire camp. No one there has seen as much gold as this in a year."

"Alec, I want to ask you about home."

"Well, Mark, last I heard from home, mother and father were well and still living on the old farm. My brother George was killed at Pensacola."

"And your relatives in Charleston?"

"Dick Stevens went to England, and I heard was on board the Confederate cruiser *Alabama*, with Charles Cole, a cousin of his, and a brother of Elsie Cole."

Mark was silent for a few moments. The vital question had not been asked. How dared he approach a subject so much and yet so little to him?

"Alec, are you married?"

"Married? No. Why, do you think I look like a married man? These times are too hard to marry or think of giving in marriage. A country that's a military camp from one end to the other; —a land that has for its chief diet rice and cottonseed; where the masters are begging their niggers to let them share their quarters with them, is too poor to think of marrying."

"Where is Elsie Cole?"

"I don't know, Mark. I last saw her in Richmond."

"Is she the same determined little rebel?"

"Yes, yes, Elsie is Secesh through and through. I never saw such a girl, Mark. She was raised in ease and luxury like most of the girls of the South. Life with them was a pleasant summer picnic, and they never had a care; but the southern girls have spirit, Mark, and when the war broke out all went to work doing something for the southern cause."

"Elsie, too?"

"Yes; those pretty white fingers learned to handle the needle. They were awkward at first, but they soon came to manage it."

"Alec, why did you not marry Elsie?"

"A good reason. I could never get her in the notion. Whenever I began to mention the subject, or even approach it, she would just laugh at me, and then I felt just like a fool. Why didn't you marry her, Mark?"

Mark, shuddering, answered:

"Alec, I am a consummate villain."

"No, you are not. Why do you say you are? You loved Elsie, and she loved you, and yet you never proposed?"

"No, no, thank Heaven I never did. I tried never to talk of love to her; but in some of my insane moments, I might have said something approximating the subject."

Alec was silent a moment, as he punched the point of his bayonet into a bit of rotten wood.

"And it was all on my account, Mark," he said. "You did it all on my account; but you needn't. Elsie don't care for me only as a sort of a convenience to run errands and such like."

"Alec, it was not on your account. No, you make me too good, too noble to accredit such action to your account, or any regard I may have for any one. I am miserably selfish. I am wretched."

"Well, Mark, on whose account was it? Why didn't you propose?"

"I cannot tell."

"You loved Elsie?"

"Loved her, Heaven! yes, I did; I love her yet. I would give every moment of life, every drop of blood to make her happy; yet I was too foolish,— too selfish to permit you to woo and win her."

Shaking his head gravely, Alec answered:

"'Twouldn't a done any good, Mark, not a bit. She didn't care one bit for me, and she was never happy unless she was making me feel just like a fool."

"Yet, but for me, she might have learned to love you, Alec."

Alec sighed, and after giving two or three more punches at the rotten wood with his bayonet, answered:

"No, it wouldn't have done any good, Mark, not a bit. Some other fellow would have taken her from me. But, Mark, when I saw that she loved you, and only liked me as an easy, good-natured kind of a cuss, who would run errands for her and be her nigger, I said, 'Let Mark go in and win her, I won't interpose.' It was only right."

Alec Stevens, careless and jolly as he was, had some excellent qualities. He was one of the few who are willing to make martyrs of themselves for their friends. The class to which he belonged is very nearly extinct at this day. He was kindness, gentleness and simplicity itself. Poor Alec was never designed for a soldier; for there was nothing cruel in his nature. He could not hurt a worm, and though a harum-scarum fellow, with but little apparent refinement, he was almost effeminate on some subjects and had a great respect for the rights of others. No child loved birds and flowers more than he. To him they were emblems of innocence, happiness and beauty, and he was in love with nature.

" You don't know where Elsie is now?" Mark
asked.

" I heard about six months ago that she had
gone back to Charleston, though I have not seen
her for over a year."

" Alec, did you ever hear her speak reproach-
fully of me?"

" No."

" She knew I had gone to the Federal army?"

" Yes."

" And never even reproached me for it?"

" No."

Mark sighed and murmured:

" Oh! would to God it had been different, or
that I had never seen her."

" Well, Mark, you are the greatest mystery I
ever met. Why, you are worse than a quadratic
equation to solve. You love Elsie Cole, and I am
dead certain that she loves you. Now, why in the
name of Tom Walker's ghost don't you say so,
and marry her?"

" Alec, you don't know all."

" No; I've all along been impressed with the
notion that there are several things I am incapable
of comprehending, and you and Elsie are among
them."

" You don't know after all, Alec, that my love
is returned. You have never heard her say so."

"No, and I wouldn't know it was so, even if I had heard her say so; but, Mark, there are some things that speak louder than words."

"Actions?"

"Yes, and eyes, cheeks, faces, which turn red and pale by turns. These tell a great deal more than words do."

Mark was silent, while Alec continued to thrust his bayonet into the rotten wood. After a few moments, he asked:

"Mark, how is all this going to end?"

"I don't know."

"Blamed if I know either."

"I wish it was over."

"Well, Mark, there are thousands of people in the same fix on our side. You don't know much of the South now; it is changed;—oh, there is an awful change. The great snow-banks of cotton have disappeared, giving place to blackened ruins. The good, old-fashioned country mansions are no more. They have been burned down, or converted into hospitals or stables. Why, few of the towns throughout the South can boast of a church suitable to worship in. Even these sacred places have been made into barracks, hospitals and stables. I entered a church in Richmond a few months ago, and what a change war had made of it! Nearly all the pews had been split up for wood. The

"EVEN THESE SACRED PLACES HAVE BEEN MADE INTO BARRACKS."

doors of the vestibule were wide open. A company of cavalry was quartered there, and in one corner was a pile of saddles, bridles and halters. In another were carbines and swords; while soldiers were sitting or standing about in groups, profaning the house of God with vulgar stories and oaths. On the right, to the rear, was a man kneading dough to bake bread for his mess in a large cook stove, which had been set up in the church, while in the gallery was a great black-haired fellow, combing his head.

"All ornamentation had disappeared, and that church, once the beauty and pride of the people who worshipped there, was little more than a dilapidated ruin."

"Alec, terrible as this war is, I fear that it is not half over."

"Not half over! Oh, heaven, Mark, I hope it is! We cannot stand this much longer,—I won't!"

"What are you going to do, Alec?"

"I don't know."

Mark rose to his feet and said:

"Alec, it is about time for my relief to come."

"Must you go, Mark?"

"Yes. When are you relieved?"

"It'll be an hour."

"I must not be found here when the corporal of the guard comes with the relief."

"Mark, it's blamed hard to have you go away. Say, Mark, if we meet in a fight, I believe I will know you now; but I would not before."

"Nor would I have known you."

"I'll shoot high, if you are in front."

"Alec, I would rather shoot myself than you."

"Same with me. If you never fall until by my bullet, you'll die with old age or sickness."

Mark had risen to his feet, and grasped Alec's hand. It had almost ceased drizzling, and the sun which had been hidden by the clouds promised to soon burst forth in all its glory and splendor. As Alec saw it, he squeezed his cousin's hand and, with strong emotion, said:

"Mark, maybe it will be so with our troubles. The sun may break through, and our sorrows pass away like a storm cloud, and leave the sun of happiness shining upon us."

"Let us hope so, Alec. I am going now. In less than ten minutes I will be relieved. Stay by this tree and don't let the picket who takes my place see you. I know not who he may be, and some of them are unscrupulous enough to shoot you."

"I'll lie low, Mark."

"If it should be a friend of mine on picket, I shall tell him of you, and then you will be safe. In that case I will tie a white handkerchief on the point of my bayonet."

"All right, and I will let him alone."

The man sent to relieve Mark was Sis. Mark knew he could trust him, and before he returned to camp he said:

"Sis, do you see that large oak tree?"

"Yes."

"On the other side of that tree I have a friend with whom I have been talking for an hour. He is a noble fellow, whom I love as a brother. You must not know that he is there."

"Is he a Johnny reb?"

"Yes; but my relative, my friend, my more than brother. He will not harm you, and, whatever happens, do him no harm."

"I won't."

Mark tied a white handkerchief to the end of his bayonet and went back to camp. Alec saw him from behind the tree and knew that he was safe from molestation.

CHAPTER XIII.

IT is not the intention to make this volume a history of marches and battles. Such a narrative would consume too much space and destroy the unity of the story. The author aims to narrate only such phases of the war as directly relate to the characters in the story, and are essential to the development of the plot. We must step aside to note some very patent facts of the period, which have a greater bearing on the story than may at present seem.

It is a singular fact that, though England had been sneering at the United States for half a century because of the toleration of slavery, yet when the South went to war, she secretly, and, one might almost say, openly espoused her cause. It was not so much England's wish to perpetuate slavery, as it was her great desire to witness the disruption of a country whose example is a standing menace to monarchy. The Confederate government early in the struggle sent diplomatic agents to Europe; but these proving ineffective, they dispatched John M. Mason, author of the Fugitive Slave act, and John Slidell. They were captured on board a British vessel, the *Trent*, by an American war-ship, the *San Jacinto*; commanded by Captain Wilkes, and taken to Boston; but, after some diplomatic correspondence of a threatening nature, the United States government was forced to give them up.

Early in 1862, the Confederate government was changed from a " provisional" to a permanent one. The war had been going on almost two years, before the thinking men of the Republican party began to seriously consider the idea of the abolition of slavery. Perhaps it would not have been carried out then, had not Mr. Lincoln and his advisers discovered that slavery gave the Confederate cause its sinews of strength. It nurtured a producing class that fed, by its labor, the armies arrayed against the Republic; and only a very small proportion of that class were drawn from the pursuits of agriculture to the camps.

It was not until this had become verified, that the president of the United States and his supporters resolved to destroy the system. Mr. Lincoln proposed to give pecuniary aid to any State government which might provide for the abolition of slavery; but the interested friends of the insti-

18

tution refused to listen to any sort of compromise. Congress proceeded to abolish slavery in the District of Columbia, over which that body had direct control; and gave the president discretionary powers to declare the emancipation of the slaves in States wherein insurrection existed. Finally, late in September, 1862, President Lincoln issued a proclamation in which he gave public notice that it was his purpose to declare such emancipation on the first day of January, 1863, to take effect immediately wherever a state of insurrection might then exist, *unless the offenders should lay down their arms.*

This friendly warning, this forbearance to strike the blow that was to free millions of bondsmen, was treated by the slave-holders with scorn; treated by them as an act of sheer impuissance. It was compared to the " Pope's bull against the comet; " and because of this menace, resistance to the government was more bitter than ever. It was evident that this warning would not be effectual, and the President prepared a proclamation of emancipation. It was submitted to his cabinet and approved; and on the first of January, 1863, it was promulgated with the whole force of the North—its army, its navy, and its judiciary, its executive and legislative powers—back of it, to enforce its provisions. The moral force of that proclamation was very great. By its act, nearly four million slaves of African descent were set free. From the hour of the promulgation of the proclamation of emancipation, the power of the Confederate government began to wane. The South has hardly recovered her former prosperity since, and will never again outstrip the North in wealth and power. Slave labor made cotton king, and the loss of slave labor dethroned the monarch.

But enough of philosophizing; let us return to our story. In the fierce battle of Iuka, won by General Rosecrans, Mark Stevens, by personal bravery, saved the regimental colors and the life of his colonel, who mentioned him in his official report. The second lieutenant, who had been accused of cowardice and dishonesty, resigned, to save a trial by court-martial, and Mark, upon a petition by the entire company, was promoted over all of the non-commissioned officers to fill the vacancy.

Never did man feel prouder of his shoulder straps. He determined, now that he had entered that mysterious and aristocratic circle, " commissioned officers," to retain his position if honesty, industry and courage would do it.

The battle of Iuka was fought September 20, 1862, and General Rosecrans, who commanded the army, fell back shortly after, to Corinth, to give his army a little rest and be prepared to meet the greater storm that was to come early in October.

Shortly after Rosecrans' army entered Corinth, there appeared a young woman, scarce more than a girl, very beautiful, refined and accomplished. She played the piano, sang well, and soon became a general favorite. She expressed much interest in military movements and asked a great many questions of the officers. She gave her name as Miss Estella Mott from Tennessee, declared that she was thoroughly loyal, and dared any one to prove she was not.

This lovely creature, who was a mystery to all, seemed to have no particular acquaintances in the town. She excused her presence by saying she had come to look for a brother, who belonged to a loyal Tennessee regiment, and had been captured by the Confederates. She thought that he might have been exchanged and sent to Corinth.

This very interesting young creature boarded at the Corinth Hotel, the proprietor of which held flexible views on politics. She became a great favorite with many Union officers, and proved to be an untiring coquette.

Major Micks, a gay bachelor of thirty-five or forty, was thought to be the favorite of the blonde. The Major discovered that she was well educated and did not talk, look, or act like a Tennessee girl. She was bright and cheerful, all smiles and animation, winning her way to every heart by her subtle charms. When she asked Major Micks to show her about the works, he of course assented.

"When can we go?" she asked.

"This very after-noon I shall be off duty," the major de-clared.

"Oh, major, I shall be so happy. I am so interested in mili-tary matters."

Major Micks never felt so happy as when, with the beautiful Estella Mott on his

"To fool the Johnny Rebs!"

arm, he started to go the rounds. Having the password, he was admitted to every part of the works, and took particular pains to explain every-thing to her, and her interest in the matters seemed only equalled by her admiration of the major.

"And those outworks, major, are your troops going to occupy them?" she asked, glancing at the outside rows of trenches, inside of which smaller works were being constructed by the engineers.

"Oh, no, those are only a sham," the major answered.

"To fool the Johnny Rebs?" she asked, with an arch smile.

"Yes."

She laughed a merry peal at the proposed trick, and the major joined her.

"When do you expect an attack, major?"

"Almost any time. We are prepared for Price and Van Dorn whenever they come."

"Oh, are you?"

"Yes."

"I suppose, if they knew it, they would not come."

"No doubt they already know it, but there are some things they don't know."

"What are they?"

"They don't know our weak points."

Then, with a girl's inquisitiveness, she asked:

"What are your weakest points?"

"Forts Robinette and Williams," answered the major. "But we have no fears of their attacking at these points."

"Haven't you, really?"

"Oh, no."

So simple, so guileless, and so girlishly inquisitive was the fair Estella, that the major never once dreamed she was aught than she seemed, a beautiful Tennessee girl, loyal to the core. Next day, Colonel Grafton, of an Illinois regiment, seemed the favorite of the fickle coquette. She was in the colonel's society most of the time, asking him as many questions as she had asked the major, and gaining very much valuable information from personal observation. They were returning to the hotel, when she espied a man across the street in the uniform of a lieutenant. The girl shrank back, clinging nervously to the colonel's arm, while she gasped:

" Who is he, colonel?"

" The lieutenant?"

" Yes."

" That is Lieutenant Stevens of an Indiana regiment, recently promoted from the ranks."

She made no response. The colonel thought her conduct rather peculiar, but gave it no thought at the time, and a moment later, when they passed out of sight of the lieutenant, she became the same gay, prattling, charming, vivacious little creature she had been before.

That night Mark Stevens was in his tent writing some letters, when an officer entered and asked:

" Lieutenant Stevens, have you heard the latest?"

" No; are Price and Van Dorn coming?"

"Worse than that."

"What?"

"A spy has been captured to-night."

"A spy? Where?"

"At the Corinth Hotel. It seems she has been there for several days, flirting with the officers; and one of Baker's secret service men, having his suspicions roused, got on the trail and followed her for two or three days, and to-night, caught her."

"Is she really a spy?"

"Yes,—no doubt of it. She was turned over to our colonel."

Mark taking an indifferent interest in the matter asked:

"Is the proof clear?"

"Not a doubt of it. She had made out a complete map of the fort; had even written down some of the information she had gained from some of the officers; and, besides, Joe Putnam, of Company B, saw her in Van Dorn's camp when he was there a prisoner. He says she is related to Van Dorn, a niece, cousin or something of the sort. He recognized her the moment he set eyes on her, and set Trotter at once on her trail. He caught her just as she was about to skip with all her information."

"Surely, she has played her part well!"

"You are right she has. She is as pretty as a picture, and I don't blame those officers one bit for falling in love with her. She is in a bad fix now though; for, pretty as she is, she will hang for this."

With a momentary shudder, Mark dismissed the pretty spy from his mind, and turning into his bunk, was soon sleeping soundly. Next morning, shortly after roll call, an orderly summoned Lieutenant Stevens before the colonel. He found the colonel, a stout, bald gentleman with a very large face, and his hands in his pockets, looking very much perplexed.

"Lieutenant," he said, "I have detailed you to take four men and guard the new captive, the spy. Confound this business! We can't confine her with the men, for, spy though she is, she is, beyond question, a lady."

Guarding a woman was not a duty congenial to an ambitious young officer, like Mark Stevens; but he made no complaint. He was longing for an opportunity to win honors, and what honors could be won guarding a female?

"I want to impress on you, lieutenant, the necessity of guarding the prisoner with the utmost care," said the colonel. "I hope that you fully appreciate the importance of this prisoner, at the same time remembering that she is a lady, who is so full of secession, that she has forfeited her life for what she calls patriotism."

Mark went from the headquarters of the colonel, to the hotel where the spy was to remain. Mr. Trotter, the secret service agent, was at the door of the prisoner. Mark handed him his order to relieve the detective.

"Thank you, lieutenant, I am pleased to know you." Through the door, which was partially ajar, Mark saw a slender, graceful girl reclining on a sofa, gazing from an open window. Her face was from him, and he could only see that she had golden hair, and a faultless form. But when he spoke to Mr. Trotter, she suddenly turned so he had a full view of her face.

It was well for Mark that he had his hand on the door; had he not, he would have staggered and betrayed his emotion. Stunned, confused and bewildered as he was, he realized that he must conceal everything from the keen eyes of the detective. He averted his face for a moment to gain strength. Mark still retained his presence of mind, though in a bewildered sort of a way. In five or six seconds, each of which was an age to him, he had regained his composure, and turning his back upon the prisoner said:

"Mr. Trotter, will you be kind enough to keep watch until I select my guard? It is not every one that can be entrusted with such a delicate matter, you know."

" Certainly, lieutenant; go and select your men, and select those on whom you can rely."

Mark hurried away. He felt that to remain longer he would betray himself. No clearly defined plan had yet been formed in his mind. It required time and careful deliberation to form a plan. On reaching the street he hoped that fresh air would revive him, but he staggered, and the sun seemed to glimmer as if there were an eclipse. He was forced to recall himself constantly to the terrible present, to convince himself that it was not all a horrible dream.

Nevertheless, his mind was active and intuitively planning. He knew that he must have four men whom he could trust, and going to his company, he selected Bill Simms, Sis, and two others, named Collins and Bradford.

" Report at the Corinth Hotel in an hour," said Mark.

" Are we to be quartered at th' hotel?" asked Collins.

" Yes."

" Wall, that's jolly good luck for us."

" You bet it is. I remember once when with Gineral Percy——" Mark did not wait to hear Bill Simms' reminiscences, but hurried back to relieve the secret service agent. Mr. Trotter was sitting near the door of the room in which he kept his fair prisoner, reading a newspaper, and at the same time keeping a lookout for her. By a great effort, Mark had wholly regained his self-possession, and there was not the quiver of a muscle when he reported ready to relieve the detective.

"I am very glad you came, lieutenant, for I have some very important matters on hand," said the detective, as he hurried away.

Mark remained at the door listening to his retreating footsteps until he was well below; then, closing the door, he turned to the prisoner and said:

"Elsie!"

Coldly, proudly, and with supreme hauteur, she raised her queenly head and gave him a stare.

"Elsie, what does this mean? Why are you here a prisoner on such a charge?"

Though much of the sunlight in her face had been obscured by the clouds of sorrow which had hovered over her, she was still beautiful.

"I suppose you are my jailer?" she remarked, coldly.

"Not of my own choice. God knows, when detailed for this service, I never dreamed who my prisoner was to be."

"It is all the same. You consented to guard a woman, and it may as well be me as any other."

" Elsie,—you surely do not know the duties of a soldier. "

" I do, Lieutenant Stevens. Do your duty !" She turned coldly away to the window. Had she rebuked him sharply, had she melted into tears and sobs, she would not have wounded his feelings half so much as by her indifference.

He closed the door and, sinking in a chair, buried his head in his hands, and trembled as if in an ague fit. Elsie Cole could be haughty, cold and indifferent, so long as her captors were stern ; but when she witnessed the mental agony of Mark Stevens, she was amazed, dismayed, humiliated and crushed. Rising, she hastened to his side, and gently laying her hand on his shoulder said:

" Mark,—Mark—why this emotion? Surely it is not on my account—I am not worth it !"

" Elsie !" he gasped in a hoarse whisper, " don't you realize your situation?"

" I do. I understand it fully !" she answered in a voice that was strangely calm. " I have been captured as a spy in the enemy's camp. The rule of war is that a spy suffers death. I knew it when I undertook the dangerous task. I was only as patriotic to the poor, losing South as you have been to the arrogant, haughty North. You staked your life for your principles, and I staked my life for mine. I lost. Am I any better than the countless thousands of other brave men and women, who are dying all over the South, for their native land?"

Her voice was firm and calm, but had nothing arrogant about it. She offered no censure, and asked no favor. She had never seemed more beautiful and angelic than now.

Mark went to the door, glanced out into the hall to assure himself no one was listening, then returned to the room, gently closing the door and bolted it to secure them against intrusion. She stood with her back to the window. Her face was calm, unmoved, with all the sweet confidence of innocence, which a consciousness of right gives. With Mark it was different. When he returned, she noticed his cheeks were wet with tears. A look of pain swept over her fair face.

"Mark, don't give way like that. Remember you are a man, and should be strong. If I can bear it, you should."

"Elsie, Elsie!" he groaned, "may God have mercy on the man who prompted you to this step."

"Blame no one; I came of my own free will," she answered.

"Did you not come at the request of General Van Dorn?"

"No," she quickly answered. "General Van Dorn seriously objected to my coming at first, but, when he found me determined to serve my country in the only manner I could, he assented."

"Why did you leave the East?"

"My father's regiment was sent to Atlanta, and I came with him. When I reached this country, I could not remain inactive when the South needed my services. I could not fight in the ranks like a man; but I could do good service as a spy, and, dangerous as the undertaking was, I resolved to make the risk. I failed, and—" her voice faltered a little—"I am willing to suffer."

"Do you know the fate of a spy, Elsie?"

"It is death. Not even the death of a soldier, but a criminal; but so many have suffered this ignominious death, they have made it honorable."

"Elsie, you shall not!" Mark said with spirit.

"What do you mean?"

"You shall not die."

"Mark, remember that you are a soldier fighting for your country."

"I will remember nothing of the sort. What is country, what is principle, what is honor, or even the soul's salvation, compared to your life? Elsie, you know I would give them all for you."

"Mark, do you mean——?" she began.

"Hush—your fate is in my hands, and I can and will save you."

"You forget, I am a spy."

" I remember only that your life is in danger, and that you shall be saved."

" Would you betray your country?"

" To save you I would. If they wish to hang me for a traitor they can do so. I have never shirked duty. I have slept on the frozen ground, faced storms of iron and leaden hail for my country; I would do more for her,—I would give my limbs one by one, my life inch by inch; but I cannot, I will not give you. You shall be saved."

It was her turn to become weak now, and she trembled, while great tears stole down her cheeks.

" Mark, Mark! I am not worth this!" she said. " Don't place yourself in danger for me."

" I will! Listen, Elsie," he went on hurriedly. " I enlisted because I loved the Union. I did not enter the army as an officer, though I might have organized a company, but enlisted as a private soldier. There I soon learned the weight of the iron heel of military despotism, which makes the rank and file underlings and machines. I longed to get above a private, and by risking my life a dozen times to almost certain death, I did so. No man was ever prouder of his honors than I; but I will lose them all—will suffer court-martial and an ignominious death—rather than you shall suffer the fate of a spy."

" No, no," she sobbed; " please don't, Mark. I

might accept such a sacrifice from any other, but from you, I cannot!"

"You must, Elsie. Hush, don't interpose any objection to my plan, or I shall go mad. Listen! My men are coming. I can trust them. There is not one of the four who would not lay down his life for me. They will aid me, and you shall escape."

Quite overcome, she fell down upon the sofa and wept. Elsie would not have shed a tear to have saved herself from death at the stake, but the thought of bringing all this woe on one so devoted to her, was overwhelming.

The four guards came, and though they kept a strict surveillance over her, she could not have been treated with greater respect had they been her own brothers. Only one was on guard, just outside the door, at a time. The others had a room set apart for them in the hotel.

"I am going away, Sis," said Mark to the smooth-faced boy-soldier. "I leave you in charge of the prisoner, see that she is not disturbed."

"I'll do et, leftenant," Sis answered, "cos I know she's a leddy. I told Bill Simms thet she wuz a leddy from 'way back."

Had Mark been severe, had he even confessed his love for her, she would have remained defiant and would have died scorning his proffered aid.

19

But when his actions revealed his solicitude, when she witnessed his agony of spirit, when she realized his determination to give position, honor, country, and life itself, her proud spirit broke down. Hatred, patriotism, mistaken principle, all gave way before a storm of overpowering emotion, which she was unable to explain, and with her face buried in her hands, she wept bitterly.

Meanwhile, Mark Stevens was hurrying to the headquarters of his colonel. Having saved his life on two occasions, Mark had special claims on his friendship. The young officer did a very manly, yet a very dangerous thing. He told the colonel all, and that officer listened in open-mouthed amazement. Two hours were spent pleading, with tears on bearded cheeks, for a life,—the life of the being he loved. The colonel's duty made him stubborn. His honor, his official pride, his patriotism, his country's interest, were all arrayed against this girl. She was a spy, a most dangerous spy, and must be treated as such. What mattered it if she did come of the best family in the South, and if Mark was in love with her? She was still a spy.

At last, Mark, growing desperate in his appeal, sublime in his oratory, and supreme in his agony, declared:

" Colonel, forgive me,—I admire your ideas of

duty, but I love that woman, and I will live or die with her!" The colonel was stunned by the declaration, and Mark continued: "My life has been offered on more than one battle-field. I

"MY COMMISSION, MY HONOR, MY LIFE YOU CAN TAKE, BUT YOU SHALL NOT HAVE HER!"

never shrank from duty before, but so help me high heaven, I will save that girl or die with her. My commission, my honor, my life you can take, but you *shall* not have her!"

The colonel bowed his head in his hands for moment, and when he looked up his cheeks were wet. After several efforts he finally said:

"Lieutenant, hang me if I wouldn't do the same thing, and so would any other man, who had a spark of manhood in his soul. Go now—I can't help you —God may, and I believe he will, but I cannot."

Mark left the headquarters of the colonel, feeling that he had, at least, one sympathetic friend. That evening, while Sis was on duty in the hall, two horses, ready saddled and bridled, might have been seen tied in an alley, at the rear of the hotel. Over each saddle a blanket was thrown, so that the passer-by might not notice that one was a lady's saddle. Sis had had his suspicions roused, and when Mark came to send him on an errand, he hesitated.

"Leftenant, I am afraid you are going to do wrong," he said.

"It is for me to command, and you to obey."

Sis did not think he was in duty bound to obey a superior whom he doubted as true to the cause for which he was fighting, and he asked:

"What air them hosses doin' in the alley?"

"Ask no questions."

"Leftenant, I promised I would treat the prisoner ez a leddy, an' I'll do it; but I swear she shan't escape."

"Sis, I am your superior officer, and you must obey; and if any wrong is done you will not be responsible for it."

Sis hesitated. He realized that the army would be ruined by the escape of the spy, and his quick perceptions had penetrated Mark's secret. For a moment Mark Stevens was perplexed. Then he wrote a message to the colonel which he folded and gave to Sis, ordering him to deliver it at once.

Sis was too good a soldier to disobey. Placing his gun against the wall, he hurried off, and when he was gone, Mark took from under his coat a long, dark cloak and veil, and entering the room of the prisoner gave them to her, with instructions to don them at once. When she had done so, he told her to walk boldly down the stairs and out into the street. At a certain corner, she was to wait until he came with the horses, for Sis' stubbornness and suspicions had, to a certain extent, disarranged his plans. She returned not a word, but obeyed his instructions. When she was gone, Mark locked her door, and called to Bill Simms, who was in the room where the guard was quartered, at the upper end of the hall, and bade him guard the prisoner's door for two hours, and to allow no one enter her room under any circumstances. Then Mark went leisurely downstairs, to the alley where the horses were. He mounted one and, leading the other, rode quickly to the dark corner where she was to meet him. He suffered much apprehension until he came in sight of the spot, and found her waiting.

"We have not a moment to lose," he whispered, as he sprang from the saddle, and lifted her to her seat.

Not a word was spoken as they galloped out of town. Mark had the password, and they passed the guards without any trouble. He suffered the greatest anxiety and dread until the last picket post was passed. They might not even yet be safe, for, at any time, a pursuing party might be sent to bring them back. Often they paused, listening for some sounds of pursuit, and then pressed on.

"Elsie, have you any friend near?"

"Mr. Myers lives only twelve miles away. His wife is my father's cousin; but Mr. Myers is in the Confederate army."

"Can you trust his wife?"

"Yes."

"We must go there." They rode on for a few moments, and Mark added: "I have a request to make of you. It may do neither of us any good, yet it would relieve my conscience if you granted it."

"What is it?"

"Promise me not to use any information, you may have gained this time, against the Union army."

"If I should promise, your officers would not believe me."

"Promise me, and I will believe you."

"Then, to you, I promise."

"I ask no better assurance, for I know you will keep your word."

They reached the home of Mrs. Myers, and, leaving Elsie safe with friends, Mark bade her adieu and, wheeling his horse about, started back to meet his fate.

CHAPTER XIV.

THE ALABAMA AND KEARSARGE.

IN Chapter VII. of this story, we told how Dick Stevens with Charley Cole, Elsie's brother, shipped on board the Confederate cruiser, the *Alabama;* and it will be necessary at this point to return to them, as their exploits form a part of the warp and woof of the romance. Dick Stevens was heartily not at home with the crew of the *Alabama;* but he was in for it, and must either serve his time out, or desert. The crew broke all bounds, and nearly all the petty officers were unlike his kind of folks; they were unable to secure any respect from the crew and yet were responsible for them to their superior officers. Dick was offered the position of quartermaster, but declined.

Off the coast of San Domingo, the crew of the *Alabama* had a little fright over fire; but the flames were easily extinguished, and no damage done. They had been taking prizes very rapidly and burning them; but on July 2d, they fell in with a sailing vessel which fairly outstripped them. It was near sunset when the look-out at the masthead descried her, and the *Alabama* as usual hoisted the English ensign; but the Yankee captain was wide awake, and piling on all canvas, he kept the weather-gage. It was quite apparent that he was using every device known to a good sailor to beat them. Dick asked their boatswain, an old clipper sailor, if they were gaining.

"Not an inch, and we are doin' our best," the old man answered. The wind freshened, and they tried a long shot with their rifle gun, but it was no use. The escaping ship was a cloud of canvas, and well handled, and in his heart Dick could not but wish her success.

It soon grew dark, and they espied a light on the water which made the men cheer, as they were quite sure they were overhauling the prize. They headed the vessel for the light, and when within two or three hundred yards of it, the look-out cried:

"That's a floating light."

The Yankee had deceived them by an old ruse. The light proved to be only a lantern tied to a spar fastened in the centre of a raft.

The Yankee escaped, and when Dick and Charley were alone, the former said:

"I am almost glad of it, Charley."

"So am I."

"I feel that this life is decidedly demoralizing."

" It is."

" If Captain Semmes would give his crew an occasional opportunity to fight, it might reconcile them to this sort of thing, and they would not be compelled to resort to other work for amusement."

Dick and Charley, who were often together on the watch, made each other confidants in many personal and family secrets. On one dark night, as they were bowling along through the troubled waters, Charley Cole narrated a part of his family history, that was sad, mysterious and romantic. It was, as yet, an unfinished story, and little did they dream that they were to be living witnesses to the sequel. The strange, dark, sad story made an impression on Dick Stevens that he never forgot.

They sailed for the eastern seas and made many captures on the way. They had a long chase after a fine clipper ship called the *Contest*. She was a swift sailor, and but for the Blakely rifle might have escaped. Her mate was an Englishman and resisted to the last. He knocked one of the officers down, and offered to fight any man aboard the ship. Dick took part in the stand-up fight with a gang of large baboons on a small island near the Straits of Sunda. He had his jacket ripped off at one clutch, and came very nearly being torn to pieces. The baboons threw stones and clubs like men.

Shortly after leaving Singapore, Dick was apprised of an effort on the part of some of the rough members of the crew to take the ship. "Shakings," a crony of Gill, told Dick that if he would stand in with them, they would make a rush aft on the next night, and could easily capture the ship; that the American consul would guarantee them one hundred thousand dollars, and see that no harm would come to them.

"Who are with you?" Dick asked.

"Four of the petty officers and about twenty men," Shakings answered. Dick did not like this man, for he had a bad countenance. He did not dare openly refuse, for he remembered the fate of Kingpost, so he said:

"I will think about it."

Next day Dick was accosted by Gill, who was strongly in favor of the mutiny. He assured him they would not be opposed by the petty officers, and one determined rush would do it! Dick listened attentively to his plan, and then interposed a carefully worded objection.

"I am afraid the officers are on the alert," he said. "And besides as we are going to England soon, it would scarce pay. And again, Gill, I have not much faith in the American consuls; they would repudiate the whole affair, and bring us within the grip of the English law, where we would be hung as pirates. If we could run her into a Yankee port it would be different."

Gill gazed hard at the young sailor, and Dick, understanding the man's dangerous character, assured him that he was one to keep his counsel under all circumstances.

The sailors were given to understand that their course was now for England, which news had a very wholesome effect on the men. The Stars and Stripes were seldom seen floating from the mastheads of any of the merchantmen, for the *Alabama* had almost swept the commerce of the United States from the seas, and after leaving the African coast they had dull times aboard the cruiser. They were off Lizard Point, June 8th, with England dimly visible from the port bow. Taking a pilot aboard they sailed for Cherbourg on June, the 13th. It was quite evident that the *Alabama* needed repairs. She forged through the waters in a way that told that her copper was stripping, and in sailors' parlance she had become a veritable "tub." Her engines being out of order produced a constant thumping and fizzing in the engine room. Charley Cole, who was a pretty fair seaman, told his cousin that her cruising would soon come to an end. It was thought that, if she went into an English port, that government would not permit her to come out again.

Dick was never so glad to get ashore in his life, as when they reached Cherbourg. He had not been long on land, when he met Charley Cole, who said:

"Dick, I heard the *Kearsarge* is coming into port."

"Who is the *Kearsarge?*" Dick carelessly asked.

"A Yankee man-of-war, by Jove! and you may get acquainted with her before we get out of port."

"Is that so?"

"Yes, and old Captain Winslow is said to be a fighter."

"Very well, we will have a chance at last to try our guns."

"I should not be surprised, for I heard that Captain Semmes has expressed his intention to fight the *Kearsarge.*"

The rumor was correct; for that same day, Captain R. Semmes had sent to Mr. Bonfils, the Confederate commercial agent, a message to be forwarded to the United States Consul, Mr. Liais, at Cherbourg. It read as follows:

"C. S. S. '*Alabama,*' CHERBOURG, June 14, 1864.*
"*To A. Bonfils, Esq., Cherbourg.*
"SIR:—I hear that you were informed by the United States Consul that the *Kearsarge* was come to this port solely for the prisoners landed by me, and that she was to depart in twenty-four hours. I desire to say to the United

---

* Century Magazine.

States Consul that it is my intention to fight the *Kear sarge,* as soon as I can make the necessary arrangements I hope these will not detain me longer than until to-morrow evening, or the morning after at the furthest. I beg that she will not depart before I am ready to go out.

"I have the honor to be very respectfully, your obedient servant, R. Semmes, *Captain.*"

On sending this communication, Captain Semmes requested that a copy would be furnished Captain Winslow for his guidance. Thus the giants of the ocean began to prepare for battle.

When Dick and Charley went on board at an early hour, June 15th, it was told through the ship that the *Kearsarge* was coming through the east end of the harbor. From the berthdeck ports they had a good look at her.

"What do you think of her, Charley?" Dick asked.

"She seems to rest rather low in the water; but there is no doubt that she is in fighting trim."

At the rate of nine knots she steamed past them, and out at the west opening. Through the wardroom servants, the report of Captain Semmes' challenge reached the ears of the crew, and most of them were eager for the conflict.

"I believe we shall have a fight, Charley," said Dick.

"Yes."

"What do you think of the chances?"

"The crew who work the guns have no confidence in any but the Blakely rifle."

Everything was in order by Sunday, June 19th, and early on that bright morning, the *Alabama* steamed out of Cherbourg for her last cruise, which was destined to be a short one. A beautiful English yacht called the *Deerhound* was discovered following in their wake. Dick did not dream who was aboard that yacht, until he heard the name Lancaster mentioned. Then he turned to Charles Cole and asked:

"Lancaster? Charley, did you hear the name? Was it Lancaster?"

"Yes."

"Perhaps Lorena Lancaster is aboard."

"Pshaw! why do you think so?"

"She lived with her uncle, John Lancaster, who was very fond of yachting."

"Well, if she did, does that signify that she is aboard that yacht?"

"It would be a little romantic, Charley, if she should be aboard that yacht. She sent me to the war. For her, I signed as one of the crew of the *Alabama*, and now she has come to see me win my victory."

Dick was in the highest spirits this morning. Charley had never seen him so confident, and having more knowledge of naval warfare than he, could scarce repress a sigh, for he knew that chances were against them. Walking slowly forward to the Blakely rifle, Charley said:

"You must do the work to-day, if it is done."

A full head of steam was on, and the *Alabama* was soon gliding boldly out of the harbor escorted by a French armored vessel. The crew were all at quarters, and every man ready and eager for the fight. Dick turned his eyes toward the harbor as they glided out, and clutching Charley's arm, said:

"She is following. She is going to witness the fight."

Charley turned his eyes in the direction indicated by Dick's finger, and saw the *Deerhound* following in their wake. When they got outside the harbor, Dick heard some one say:

"There she is!" and going forward saw the low dark hull and rigging of the *Kearsarge*, with the black smoke issuing from her great dark chimney.

Yes, there lay the enemy not over four or five miles away, waiting for them, and a sight of her sent a thrill to Dick's heart. He was not afraid to fight, in fact was rather eager for the conflict, yet he would have been more highly pleased had she run away or surrendered without exchanging a shot.

The report of their going out to fight the *Kear-*

sarge had been widely circulated, and many persons from Paris and the surrounding country had come down to witness the engagement. They, with a large number of inhabitants of Cherbourg, assembled on every point of the shore that would afford a view seaward. On discovering the *Kearsarge*, the *Alabama* immediately headed for her with all hands at the quarters, and the starboard battery cast loose. The men were neatly dressed and the officers in full uniform. Upon reporting to Captain Semmes that the ship was ready for action, he directed Captain Kell to send all hands aft, and mounting a gun-carriage, he made the following address:

"OFFICERS AND SEAMEN OF THE ALABAMA:

"You have at length another opportunity of meeting the enemy—the first that has been presented to you since you sunk the *Hatteras!* In the mean time you have been all over the world, and it is not too much to say that you have destroyed, and driven for protection under neutral flags, one-half of the enemy's commerce, which at the beginning of the war covered every sea. This is an achievement of which you may well feel proud, and a grateful country will not be unmindful of it. The name of your ship has become a household word, wherever civilization extends! Shall that name be tarnished by defeat? The

20

thing is impossible! Remember that you are in the English Channel, that theatre of so much of the naval glory of our race, and that the eyes of all Europe are at this moment upon you. The flag that floats over you is that of a young Republic, which bids defiance to her enemies, whenever and wherever found! Show the world that you know how to uphold it! Go to your quarters!"

The crew with a cheer hastened to their quarters, and the friendly French vessel, having done all she dared, left the *Alabama*, which steered straight for the *Kearsarge*, that, like a marine monster, awaited the assault. As the *Alabama* was steaming toward her enemy, Captain Semmes passed the quarters where Dick and Charley stood. Charley whispered to his cousin:

" Something is the matter with Captain Semmes; he seems flurried."

" What are they going to do, Charley?"

" Going to fire the Blakely."

" It is folly at this distance."

" The captain is anxious."

" See, there comes the *Kearsarge*. By Jove! she has got her bristles up, and coming right at us."

" Boom!" The sea seemed to tremble beneath the heavy report of the Blakely 100-pounder.

" The shot did not strike her, Charley," said Dick.

" Why did they waste the shot at that distance?"

" What is she doing?"

" Going to circle around us, so she can get us at a point that she may rake us fore and aft. "

All the while, the gunners at the Blakely were busy ramming home another charge.

" They are sighting her again, Dick."

" It's all nonsense, and I wonder Captains Semmes and Kell don't see it. "

" She is still circling about us and getting nearer. "

" We'll feel her iron soon. "

The two ships were caught in the current which set westward at the rate of about three knots per hour. Like two pugilists, they did an immense amount of sparring and circling about each other, all the while, in order to get in a position for a telling blow.

Dick saw old Gill, like a grim monster, at the eight-inch gun waiting for the time to come when he should make the attack. Shakings was near the port bulwarks, handling shot, swearing all the while and wishing that they could carry the enemy by the board.

As yet the enemy had not fired a shot. Suddenly Charley, who had been watching her, cried:

" She is in position; now look out!"

The *Kearsarge* was within seven or eight hundred

yards, when, suddenly gracefully rounding about, her entire broadside became a sheet of flame, and the *Alabama* seemed to reel and shake all over from the force of the shot.

Dick and Charley were serving on one of the thirty-twos, and they fired with the others, but could observe no visible effect from the discharge of their guns. Their sponger, an old man-of-war's man, remarked:

"We might as well fire batter puddens as these pop-guns; a few more biffs like that last, and we may turn turtle."

His speech was cut short by a tremendous crash. A shell had burst under the pivot gun, tilting it out of range and killing five of the crew.

"What is wrong with the rifle gun?" Charley asked. "We don't seem to be doing the enemy any harm."

Boom!—boom, boom! with slow precision came the crash of heavy shells from the Yankee. One missile, which to Dick seemed as large as a haystack, whizzed over their heads, tearing away a section of the port bulwarks, and missing Shakings, who was handling shot, by not more than two feet. That individual, glancing at the wreck made by the shot, coolly remarked:

"I believe the cussed Yankees are firin' steambilers at us."

Shot and shell were striking them thick and fast, and, to their amazement, even their Blakely rifle, on which they had put so much reliance, seemed to make little or no impression on the enemy. On finding that their shells failed to penetrate the enemy's sides, their captain ordered them to fire solid shot. These seemed to have as little effect as the shells, and from that to the end of the conflict, the Blakely alternated between solid shot and shell.

Captain Kell claimed that the *Kearsarge* was protected by chain armor, and that the powder of the *Alabama* was so defective that they failed to hurl projectiles with the force of the enemy's shot. Charley in an undertone to Dick said:

" We are going to get it this time."

" No, let us hope not. We may whip her yet."

" We are not doing it, fate is against us; our shot has no visible effect, while they are raking us fore and aft."

At this moment, a shell struck them amidships, exploding, and causing the ship to list to port, so that the gun of our friends raced in, pinning one poor fellow against the port-sill. They made frantic efforts to get him clear; but he was dead when rescued. The shell which caused the disaster was evidently the terrible eleven-inch shell that sank the *Alabama*, for a few seconds after it exploded, Dick heard the cry:

"She's going down!"

All was confusion and some of the men deserted the guns, though the officers ordered them back.

A moment later another shell struck about the water-line, and the vessel reeled like a drunken man. The dead and wounded now strewed the bloody deck.

"We are whipped, Dick. The ship is going down."

Grinding his teeth in rage, Dick answered:

"Let us send them down with us."

The officers did their duty and made every effort to get up the wounded men. The cutter and launch were in the water, and Dick heard Captain Semmes tell Officer Kell to go below and see how badly the vessel was injured.

All the while, the *Alabama's* crew was firing as rapidly as they could, receiving crash after crash from the enemy in return. In a few seconds Officer Kell came back, saluted Captain Semmes, and said:

"Captain, she cannot keep afloat ten minutes."

Captain Semmes replied:

"Then, sir, cease firing, shorten sail, and haul down the colors; it will never do in this nineteenth century for us to go down, and our decks covered with our gallant wounded."

"I felt it from the first!" sighed Charley as the

colors were hauled down, and orders given to cease firing. " I suppose now we will have to go to some infernal Yankee prison and rot. I would rather go to the bottom."

Though they had ceased firing and hauled down their colors, the enemy's guns still roared, and their shot still came tearing through the sinking ship.*

" Why, in thunder, are they firing at us yet?" cried Charley Cole. " Do they intend never to stop until they have murdered us outright?"

" Stand by your quarters and don't flinch from their shot," cried Captain Kell. " Quartermaster, show the white flag over the stern."

A few moments later the fire of the enemy ceased. A boat was dispatched to the *Kearsarge* to notify Captain Winslow of the surrender of the *Alabama*, to report the ship sinking, and to ask aid in rescuing the wounded. They began at once to get up the wounded. Every effort was made to keep the men back from the cutter and launch until the wounded were put in; but Dick was quite sure that many of the disabled were left behind, for he saw several on the berthdeck after they had pushed off.

---

* Captain Winslow of the *Kearsarge* gives his reason for firing on the *Alabama* after she had struck, that he supposed her colors shot away, or that it was a trick of Captain Semmes to get back into neutral waters, and thus escape.

When it was ascertained to a certainty that the ship was going down, all order was at an end, and men ran here and there in every direction.

Dick's few effects, with two or three valuable keepsakes, were in the locker between the decks, and he ran below to secure them. He had scarce done so when he heard the cry from the deck:

" All hands on deck——ship is going down!" He had just reached the upper step of the forward companion-way, when the water entering the berth-deck ports forced the air up, and almost carried him off his feet. He called for Charley and cast his eyes around on the horrible scene, the result of the conflict. Shakings lay near the main gang-way, his body torn open by the explosion of a shell. Old Gill, with his head crushed under the carriage of an eight-inch gun, was lying there, his brawny hands clutching the breast of his jumper.

" Charley!" Dick called.

For a moment he was appalled lest his companion, friend, and kinsman had met with an accident; but a moment later he received an answer, and saw Charley lashing two spars together to form a sort of a raft. Just as the water came over the stern, the two sailors launched their frail craft, and went over the port bulwarks. Both men were good swimmers, and were pushing their raft along, when the yacht, which they had seen watching the fight from a distance, bore down upon them, and picked them up.

This was Mr. Lancaster's yacht, the *Deerhound*. A few moments later Captain Semmes and his officers were also taken aboard the yacht. When Mr. Lancaster had rescued Captain Semmes, he said:

" I think every man has been picked up. Where shall I land you?"

" I am now under English colors, and the sooner you put me with my officers on English soil, the better," replied Captain Semmes.

" I will do it in a few hours," Mr. Lancaster answered, and at once steamed away to Southampton.

Everything had happened so rapidly that Dick's brain was in a whirl. But a short time before he was on the unconquerable *Alabama;* then the fight and sinking of the ship, all seemed like a vivid dream. When he closed his eyes, he could still see her going down stern foremost, and her head high in the air.

The sailors were given an opportunity to wash the powder and stains of battle off their faces. Dick was standing aft gazing on the fast disappearing coast and sighing at the terrible fate of his ship, when he heard a light step near him, and turning beheld Lorena Lancaster. He started and for a few moments was overwhelmed and unable to speak. At last he went boldly to her side and said:

"You saw it all?"

She nodded.

"Lorena, I enlisted for you. I failed. We are defeated. Will you forsake me in my distress?"

They were alone. Everybody was forward, and the cabins and rigging hid them from view. For a moment the beauty of England hung her head, then, blushing, answered:

"No."

It was all arranged in a few moments, and he was the accepted lover of the proud English beauty, who averred that she would marry him out of pity for his misfortunes; but it was determined to postpone the wedding until the war was over. After a few weeks' sojourn in England, Dick and Charley took passage for their own country to continue the battle on land which had come to an end on sea. We shall meet them again in the course of this story.

CHAPTER XV.

THE DESERTER.

THE very least Mark Stevens could expect for aiding the spy to escape was a trial and conviction by court-martial. His past good conduct might tend to mitigate the sentence; but disgrace and discharge must inevitably follow.

"I have saved Elsie, that is one consolation." There was a sweet, holy satisfaction in the thought. His love for the proud little rebel was of a purely unselfish sort, and surmounted every obstacle. For no other person would he have given so much. Glancing at the shoulder straps which he had won after so much hard work, he sighed: "It is all over now. I shall soon lose them; but I lose them for her."

It was noon on the 3d of October when he came in sight of Corinth. The air was suddenly filled with the sharp crack of musketry, and roll of artillery.

"They have come. Price and Van Dorn have come," cried Lieutenant Stevens, and forgetting all else, save the coming battle, he plunged his spurs into his horse's flanks and galloped down the road. Before he was aware of it, he actually rode over the enemy's skirmish line and, with bullets whistling like hail about him, dashed into his own lines, waving his sword and cheering the soldiers.

Rosecrans had not long been in Corinth after the battle of Iuka before he ascertained that the enemy was concentrating on that place, or some other point, which would cut off his communications and compel him to evacuate it. Price, Van Dorn and Lovell had united their entire forces for the purpose of crushing his comparatively small army, before he could receive reinforcements. Rosecrans, calling all his troops from adjacent posts, watched with deepest solicitude the development of the hostile plan. At length, discovering that the enemy had marched around him to the eastward, and were moving down on Corinth from the north and northeast, he formed his plan, and disposing his troops to the best possible advantage, calmly awaited the attack. He knew he was outnumbered two to one; but he relied on the strength of his position, and the indomitable character of his troops. McKean commanded the left, Davies the centre, and the gallant Hamilton the right, where Rosecrans supposed the weight of the struggle would fall. The old fortifications thrown up by Beauregard were too extensive for his little army to hold, and so he erected works within them.

The plan of Rosecrans was to advance on the enemy as he approached, make an attack, thus forcing him to develop his lines, and then retire behind his own works, so that the batteries could sweep the enemy as they emerged into the open ground in front.

This was the programme that the Union army was carrying out when Lieutenant Mark Stevens came on the scene, rode through the extending skirmish lines, and without fully realizing it, joined his own company. The skirmishing was hot and lasted all day, and night found the Union forces in a town which the enemy had closely invested. Much uneasiness was felt on the part of the soldiers because they had been so easily driven back into the place, where the enemy's shells could reach them; but they did not understand the motive of their able commander. All night long the tramp of marshalling hosts could be heard, and the planting of batteries within close range.

Not a word had been spoken to Mark since his arrival. In fact they had been too busily engaged with the enemy to give thought to aught else. When they were all finally drawn within their newly constructed works, and night was falling on the scene, the captain came to him and said:

"Well, lieutenant, you got off from that detailed service to help us in this fight, did you?"

"Yes," he mechanically answered, wondering if the captain was in earnest, or speaking ironically.

"I am glad you are here, for Lieutenant Grafton will never fight again."

Mark had missed the first lieutenant for some hours, but had not, up to this time, learned his fate.

"Is Lieutenant Grafton dead?"

"No, he is still living, I believe, but he has a bullet through his chest and will die before morning."

"It is sad."

"Yes, but it is your promotion. You may be captain before the setting of to-morrow's sun."

"I hope not, Captain Hawk. I don't want promotion that way."

They listened for awhile to the low rumbling of artillery wheels, and Lieutenant Stevens said:

"Captain, we are going to have a hard struggle in the morning."

"It will be two to one."

"But we can beat them off."

Shortly after this he felt some one touch his arm, and looking about saw Bill Simms.

"Leftenant, I wanter speak t' ye," said Simms. Mark suffered himself to be led aside, and Simms whispered: "D'ye know that blamed gal got away."

"How?" he asked evasively.

"Hang me ef I know. When I was relieved by Collins, he asked if she wanted anything, and she made no answer. He supposed she was asleep and did not disturb her. At breakfast time I rapped at her door, and when she made no answer, opened it and went in. She wasn't there. Collins and I kept the secret to ourselves, and went out to look for her, but she couldn't be found, though how in thunder she got away, I don't know."

"Have you reported the matter?"

"Yes."

"To whom?"

"The colonel."

"What did he say?"

"He said keep it still; not to say a word that would get out among the men, but he thought I might tell you."

Mark thanked the colonel from the bottom of his heart; yet he felt some misgivings about meeting him. He did not meet the colonel until after midnight; then, as he chanced to pass his quarters, he was summoned to his side.

"You were in the front to-day, lieutenant?" said the colonel.

"Yes, colonel," he answered with a salute.

"I wish you would take this dispatch to General Rosecrans."

He hurriedly wrote the dispatch and handed it to Mark. It contained some information concerning the front. General Rosecrans was busy that night. It was almost three o'clock before he wrapped his blanket about him, and lay down to catch a few moments' sleep before the coming dawn which was to usher in a scene of fire and death.

At last the long wished for, but much dreaded, dawn streaked the eastern sky, and the rolling of drum, and pealing of bugle awoke the morning echoes, and were answered by those of the enemy in the dark forests beyond.

The Confederates were massed in the angle formed by the Memphis and Columbus railroads. The left of the Union army rested on the batteries extending west from Fort Robinette, the centre on the slight ridge north of the houses, and the right on the high ground which covered the Pittsburg and Purdy roads, that led away to the old Shiloh battle-ground. The Confederate plan was to mass against the Union batteries and overwhelm them by their impetuous charge. This could be done only by a terrible sacrifice; for four redoubts covered all the approaches, while batteries were in every place where guns could be advantageously posted, so that the whole open space in front of the Union lines could be swept by a storm of fire and iron hail.

With daylight skirmishing began, and the heavy boom of cannon here and there shook the field long before the enemy's lines became visible. They were forming in the roads running through the forest, half a mile or more in front, and every eye was strained to catch the heads of the columns as they moved out for the final advance. The very mystery that shrouded the attacking host, hidden in those stirless woods, added to the impressiveness of the scene. At length, a little after nine o'clock, the fearful suspense was ended by the heads of the columns issuing from the leafy covering. In columns and divisions the whole host moved in splendid order up the Bolivar road, straight toward the mysterious batteries. Long lines of glittering steel crested the gray formation below, as, with steady step and closed ranks, they swept forward. Like a great wedge at first, but slowly unfolding two expanding wings, the enemy swept down on Corinth. It was a beautiful movement and well executed.

Price on the left and Van Dorn on the right moved on together; but the latter, meeting with

21

unexpected obstacles, lost a little time, and the division of General Price caught the first fury of the storm.   Right up the turfy slope, the steady columns pressed, swept by the whole line of batteries, sending shot and shell tearing through their ranks, and like clouds shattered by lightning, they wavered.   The ground was covered by a dense white smoke, the line of breastworks being marked only by a fierce angry light playing through the sulphurous vapor.   It was the constant flashing from thousands of muskets, and so continuous was the fusillade that the flame never entirely died away.

The entire field was a scene of terrible confusion. Ammunition wagons were being hurriedly unloaded in the centre, the boxes of cartridges were moving on men's shoulders in the direction of the engaged lines, while hundreds of wounded men were streaming to the rear, a long string of stretchers accompanying them.   The dead and dying darkened the ground; but the firing never faltered.   With bent heads and leaning forms like those who breast a driving sleet, they pressed sternly forward, making straight for Rosecrans' centre.   Onward and upward, through fire and death and tempests of bullets, grapeshot and crashing bombs, they pressed like the march of fate. At last they reached the crest of the hill, and Davies' division gave way in disorder.

The eye of Rosecrans never for a moment left the rolling mass, and when he saw this disaster, he dashed amid the broken ranks, heedless of the raining shot and shell and rallied them in person; but the enemy seeing their advantage, sprang forward with a shout, and the headquarters of Rosecrans was overrun with Confederate troops, and the next moment their fire was pouring into the public square of the town itself. Hamilton's division of veterans was compelled to fall back, and with a shout of victory the Southern troops rushed on to Fort Richardson, the key to the position.

A single sheet of flame burst from its sides, and when the smoke rose, the space where they stood was clear of living men; only the dead and bleeding were left. But those brave men had not trod death's highway so far to yield at the first withering blast of destruction, especially when they found victory almost in their grasp; and once more rallying, they reformed their shattered ranks, and precipitated themselves forward with the fury and clamor of demons. Richardson sank dying among his guns, and next moment the Confederates with wild cheers were running over them. But the gallant Fifty-sixth Illinois were hidden in a ravine near, and springing to their feet they poured in a close and deliberate volley, dashed across the plateau, and into the fort, almost lifting the Con-

federates bodily out of it, so sudden, desperate,
and wild was their charge.

"Forward!" cried Hamilton, and the command
ran along the glorious line. Sweeping forward
with a front of bristling steel, he completed the
overthrow. Price's host was at last shattered.
Human endurance had reached its limit; despair
took the place of courage, and, flinging away their
useless arms they broke wildly for the woods.
And then such a shout of victory went up as those
who heard it will never forget to their latest day.
It rolled down the line and Van Dorn, on the left,
heard it with a sinking heart. Struggling through
a ravine, thickets and abatis, he was a moment
too late to have his blow fall simultaneously with
that of Price, else the issue might have been different. He was now in front of Fort Robinette,
within a hundred and fifty yards of which stood
Fort Williams. These guns had poured a deadly
enfilading fire through his ranks as he advanced,
and now the former with the ten-pound Parrott
gun stood right in his path. Over these he must
go, or turn back over the field, gained at such
horrible sacrifice. The shouts of victory borne to
him from the left sounded like the knell of doom.
Price had failed at Fort Richardson, and now
alone and unaided, he must carry the works before
him, or all was lost. It was a terrible task and

one could not have blamed him, had he paused before undertaking it. Did he fălter? No! Did he shrink? No—but gathering up all his energies for one desperate effort, he rushed to the awful undertaking. Two brigades, led by Colonel Rogers of Texas, swiftly advanced on the fort. Instantly its guns and those of Fort Williams opened their fire, and shot and shell went tearing through the dense columns; but they braced themselves for the fearful work they knew was before them, and breasted the iron storm with sublime devotion.

Coming nearer they were mowed down by the infantry. Their solid formation caved before it, as the sand-bank before the torrent; but, closing up compact as iron, the diminished numbers, with their eyes bent sternly on the prize before them, kept on their terrible way.

"*Forward!*—FORWARD!" shouted Rogers, striding along at their head, and seeming to possess a charmed life. His voice was heard even above the din and roar of battle. Struggling through the fallen timber, they fell and were caught among the branches, presenting a ghastly spectacle. Still the living never faltered—with eyes fixed on their heroic leader, they let the volleys crash, and the devastating fires burn along their lines, with stoical indifference. At last they neared the ditch, and for one awful moment paused. Rogers, still tower-

ing in front unhurt, waved the Confederate flag
in his left hand, holding a revolver in his right,—
still shouting:

"*Forward!*"

With one bound he cleared the ditch. Leaping
up the slope, he planted his standard on the ram-
parts. The next moment he fell a corpse, and
rolled banner and all into the ditch. Five brave
Texans, who had never for a single moment left
their brave leader's side, pitched heavily forward
into the fort, sharing his fate.

The Ohio brigade commanded by Colonel Fuller
had lain flat on their faces just over the ridge, and
now in close range, rose and delivered six swift
volleys, and cleared the front of the enemy. The
supporting Confederate brigade now advanced into
the same volcano, bent on the same hopeless
errand. Taking the close and swift volleys into
their bosoms without shrinking, they kept on until
maddened into desperation, they made one wild
rush on the Sixty-third Ohio that crossed their
path; but the brave fellows stood like a rock in
their places, and, in a moment, friend and foe
were locked in a hand-to-hand death-struggle.
Bayonets, clubbed muskets and, when these failed,
clenched fists were used. The fight was brief but
terrible, and the shouts, yells and curses that
arose on the air seemed wrenched from the throats

of demons. At last the Confederate hosts gave way, when the Eleventh Missouri and Twenty-seventh Ohio sprang forward and chased them to cover.

The battle was over. No second charge could be made, for the victory was won, though at a fearful cost.

As Rosecrans rode along the whole line of battle, he was greeted with thundering cheers. Even the wounded, the faint and the dying lifted their feeble voices to cheer their favorite commander. He told his brave troops, that although they had been two days marching and preparing for battle, and had passed two sleepless nights, and endured two days' fighting, he wanted them to fill their cartridge boxes, haversacks and stomachs, take an early sleep, and at daylight press after the flying foe.

McPherson, having in the mean time arrived at Corinth with a fresh brigade, was immediately started in pursuit, and the roar of cannon died away in the distance, as he closely pressed the retiring columns of the enemy. The roads and fields were strewn with the wrecks of the fight, and the Confederates narrowly escaped destruction in the Forks of the Hatchie. The battle-fields about Corinth presented a frightful spectacle, and for weeks the stench was terrible. The great victory made Rosecrans almost invincible. Victory followed his standard wherever he went, and with that fondness for nicknaming beloved commanders so common to American soldiers, his troops christened him, " Old Rosy."

" Rosecrans believed that if Grant had supported him, as he requested him to do, he could easily have entered Vicksburg and saved the sacrifice of men and money." *

Lieutenant Mark Stevens' regiment had borne the brunt of the assault at Fort Robinette. Conspicuous at every point where danger was greatest was the brave lieutenant. When the Texans rushed pell-mell into the fort, he, with drawn sword, faced bayonets and clubbed guns. He rallied the few men who were about to fly; others came to their aid; and as they held in check the on-surging foe, who were appalled at their stubbornness, hundreds and thousands of bluecoats came to their aid, and they drove the enemy back.

Mark had faced death for an hour, and the fight was over, and he unhurt; though Captain Hawk lay dead in the trenches with a bullet in the centre of his forehead. Mark was now the only commissioned officer in the company. Next day after the battle, he reported to the colonel.

Collins and Bradford were killed in the fight,

---

* Headley, vol. ii., page 108.

Sis was badly wounded, and in the hospital, and Bill Simms was too stupid to suspect that his captain had had any hand in the escape of the spy. So Mark went with tolerable good grace to the presence of his colonel; though he felt some misgivings, for he believed that the colonel suspected that he had been guilty of aiding the spy to escape.

Of course in the heat of battle, there was no time to consider his case. A captaincy was in sight, and yet when he remembered what he had done, he thought the sergeant might have as good a showing as himself.

He consoled himself all along with the reflection, that whatever he might have lost, he had saved Elsie. The colonel greeted him with a fatherly smile, and grasping his hand said:

"My boy, I had my eye on you yesterday, and your gallantry shall not escape mention in my report."

"But, colonel——" began Mark, determined to confess everything.

"Oh, I know what you would say. It's your commission. Go on and take charge of the company, and it shall be sent you in due time."

Mark breathed easier. He thanked the colonel, and wrung his hand while his eyes grew dim. He felt in his heart that the colonel must know all, and must suspect him. He received some orders and was about to leave the headquarters, when his blood was suddenly frozen by the appearance of the secret service agent, Mr. Trotter.

"Well, Colonel Belcher, you had some rough work yesterday," said Mr. Trotter. "I was an eye-witness to part of it,—oh, I see here is Lieutenant Stevens, whom I have been looking for——"

"Captain Stevens now, Mr. Trotter," corrected the colonel.

"So, he is promoted. Well, Captain Stevens, how about the prisoner,—the pretty spy?"

Mark realized that the truth had to come at last; but before he could speak, the colonel put in:

"Why you see, Mr. Trotter, we had it so devilish close here yesterday, and all got so badly mixed up, that your prisoner, I am afraid, got away."

"You were not guarding her yesterday, then?" asked Mr. Trotter fixing his keen eyes on Mark.

"No, the captain was in the front. Now, captain, you can go to your quarters and make an early report of how many men you have fit for duty!"

Mark Stevens left the colonel, blessing his name. In due time Mark's commission came. Next day the regiment pushed on after the flying Confederates, and on the third night Mark's company held a picket post on the extreme front.

Every man not on actual duty was sleeping on his arms. The enemy were at times so near that they could distinctly hear them talking, and some averred that they could even distinguish their words.

The night was dark and gusty. A fine mist like rain was falling, and the soldiers drawing their capes about their ears sat in groups under the trees, some of them nodding, and some wide awake. Their young commander was ever watchful, ever on the alert. He stood with his back against a tree, his eyes fixed front, as if he would pierce the intense darkness. Half a dozen men had been thrown forward to reconnoitre, and one of these came back, shortly after, with the report that the enemy were retiring. Suddenly the sharp report of a musket rang out on the rainy night.

" Fall in!" commanded Mark. In a moment his company was in line.

They waited for several moments and then all became still. At last they heard voices approaching. Perhaps their advance was falling back or had sent some one to report. Mark stepped out in front of his company, and ordered the man who was advancing to halt.

" It's all right, captain. · It's Jack Weston. Friend with the countersign. "

" Who fired that shot?"

"Tom Hall."

"At whom?"

"We've got a prisoner, captain."

"Where did you get him?"

"He came to us, and says he is a deserter from the enemy."

"Bring him here!"

The soldier disappeared in the darkness, and a few moments later returned with two more men, leading a man in badly faded and much worn gray uniform. It was too dark to see his features.

"Capen, here's a chap who thinks Judgment Day's comin', and he's not saved," said Bill Simms with a hoarse laugh.

"Come here, sir, and tell me who you are!" said Mark to the prisoner.

"I am a rebel tired of the business, and, if there is a peaceful spot on all the broad green earth, I want to find it."

The voice was familiar, and Mark Stevens, with a gasp of surprise said:

"So you have surrendered, Alec———?"

"Mark, Mark! Great Noah's flood, it's Mark!" cried the prisoner embracing him. "Oh, this is too good to be true. Say Mark, I dreamed last night that I found you. Have you anything to eat over there? Have you any coffee, and good bread. I've lived on hard-tack and English sea biscuit, until my poor stomach almost rebels against it;" and the poor fellow rattled on

"I'M A REBEL, TIRED OF THE BUSINESS."

at this rate, alternately exciting his captors to laughter and tears for ten minutes.

Mark then got him quieted and leading him aside asked:

"Alec, did you really intend to desert."

"I did, Mark, for I tell you I am tired of this. Besides, I heard one of the Southern Independence Association agents, from England, tell my colonel they aided the South because they hated the United States, which had defeated them in two wars, and was a living menace to monarchical forms of government. Mark, our fathers and our grandfathers fought the British, and, by the Eternal, I won't fight for them. They are just making cat's paws of us, that's all, and I am going to pull no more of their chestnuts out of the fire. Henceforth I am for Uncle Sam, if Uncle Sam wants me."

"Do you intend to enlist?"

"I do."

"Let us think the matter over, Alec," suggested Captain Stevens. "Meanwhile, stay in our camp."

CHAPTER XVI.

THE CONFLICT IN THE CLOUDS.

TIME and trying circumstances make some changes in men; but characteristics so indelibly stamped on one as were the peculiarities of Alec Stevens could not be wholly changed. He was the same loquacious, jolly companion of old, and had more amusing stories to tell than any one in the regiment.

"So, Mark, you've got a pair of shoulder straps at last. I dare say you didn't get them before you earned them. I have come to the conclusion that in this world, poor fellows like you and me get nothing gratuitously. You look like a military man now, one of the solid stuff, too; no West Point martinet, fit only for dress parade or the ball room, 'bout you; no weak-minded, effeminate, pedantic, pedagogical, carpet-pantalooned, long-haired, goatee and sweet-scented *creatah* about you, I'll bet. No sir, you are here to knock the Johnnies on the head, and I am glad to know that you have climbed completely and teetotally over the sun-baked, clam-headed fools, the half-finished squirts, the verdant dandies, lions of codfish aristocracy, coxcombs and scapegraces, who are a disgrace to the nation."

In order to change the current of his thought, Mark asked:

" When did you see your parents, Alec?"

" It's been more than a year."

" But you have heard from them?"

" Well, yes, I have. I had a letter from home about three months ago."

" Have you heard from Charleston?"

" Not for four or five months."

Mark was silent. He knew it was useless to ask about Elsie, for the chances were that he had seen her last. Mark went with Alec to the colonel of the regiment and the matter was laid before him.

" So, young man, you have deserted the cause of the South and come back to the defence of your country," said the colonel kindly.

" Yes, sir. As Patrick Henry said, I am no longer a Virginian, but an American. I realize that we were all teetotally bamboozled, befuddled and befooled by the wiles, traps and snares of Calhounism. Others can do as they please about it, but, as for me, I am back under the old flag, and I have come to stay."

Colonel Belcher grasped the convert's hand and answered:

"You have chosen wisely. You should have made this choice in the beginning; but it is never too late to mend. I hope the same truth may dawn on the minds of all your deluded fellow Confederates, and bring them all back to the fold."

After the conference was over, the colonel took Captain Stevens aside and asked:

"Do you know him?"

"Yes."

"Is he sincere?"

"I would stake my life on it."

"Then I will parole him for a few days and give him an opportunity to enlist."

Mark Stevens impressed on his cousin the danger that would follow his enlistment should he be captured by his former friends; but he declared himself willing to risk it.

"I felt all along that I was not exactly in my element, Mark. That was one reason that I never sought to elevate myself in the ranks. I was only a private in an humble place, for I felt that the less the responsibility on me, the smaller would be my crime. The South has good officers, Mark. You must admit that Lee, Jackson, and Joe and Sidney Johnston are away ahead of your Grant, McClellan, Sherman, or any other officer you

22

have; but I tell you their hearts are not really in it. With all the enthusiasm they claim, they feel way down deep in their souls that they are not right. They won't admit even to themselves that they are in the wrong; but they feel a keen sense of doubt. If it was under the old flag that they were fighting it would be quite different. Why, I can hardly keep from throwing up my old slouch hat every time I see the old Stars and Stripes."

Although Mark Stevens often wished to speak to Alec of Elsie, he refrained from doing so, and Alec, from some cause, though he was a fluent talker on all other subjects, had not mentioned the name of the maiden whom they both loved.

In due time, Alec was enrolled in Mark's company, and made a trusty, brave soldier.

Meanwhile the great war went on. They heard the thunders of it all about them, and frequently saw the blinding flash, and were buried in the sulphurous smoke. The battle of Perryville, Kentucky, was fought on the 8th and 9th of October. Then quickly followed Stuart's raid on Chambersburg, Pennsylvania, on the 10th, with a battle near Richmond, Kentucky. The armies in the East were moving about Richmond and Washington, and in the West about Vicksburg. The combats were many and terrible; but as yet the Southern troops seemed on the whole to have an advantage, and they threatened to invade the Northern States. On November 5th, General Mc-Clellan was superseded by Burnside as commander in Virginia. The same day the Confederates were repulsed at Nashville, Tennessee. November was noted for its many conflicts especially in the South and West.

December, 1862, was even more noted for its series of bloody conflicts than the preceding month. It ended with the terrible battle of Stone River or Murfreesboro raging.

January, 1863, brought the emancipation of the slaves, and the end of the battle of Stone River in favor of the United States troops. The remainder of the month was taken up with fighting and blockading. In fact, the year of 1863 was a year of decisive battles, and the historian and reader becomes sick of the horrible details. The Fourth of July, 1863, may be regarded as the turning point in the war for the Union. On this day, Vicksburg surrendered to General Grant, after a siege of forty-one days. On the same day, Major-General Benjamin M. Prentiss, at Helena, Arkansas, set a trap for a Confederate army five times as large as his own and drew them into it. He gained a wonderful victory, and perhaps against greater odds than any Union general during the war. Four days later, Port Hudson with seven thousand men, surrendered to General Banks. On the 13th of this month, there was a great riot in New York city brought about by the threatened draft.

The greatest battle of the war was fought on July 3, 1863. This was the battle of Gettysburg,

Pennsylvania, where General Meade with a little over one h u n d r e d thousand men fought General Robert E. Lee with almost as many. This was the greatest battle of the war in many respects. It was fought in a Northern State. Lee had left his own territory and invaded the enemy's country. It was the battle in

GEN. GEORGE G. MEADE.

which there were the largest number of men engaged on either side, and the battle in which Lee was defeated when his own numbers were more nearly equal to those in the Union army. Lee was defeated at last and retreated from Pennsylvania.

In August, General Gillmore, having invested Charleston, South Carolina, bombarded Fort Sumter most of the month. On the 19th and 20th of September was fought the terrible battle of Chickamauga, in which the Union forces, some fifty or sixty thousand strong, were defeated by Bragg with forty-five thousand men. The Federal loss was about fifteen thousand, yet they prevented Bragg from capturing Chattanooga. On October 16th General Grant took command of the Western armies.

Shortly after the battle of Corinth, Colonel Belcher's regiment was assigned to Sherman's division and served under that general to the end of the war. As soon as Grant heard of Rosecrans' disaster at Chickamauga, he ordered Sherman on the Black River, twenty miles east of Vicksburg, to send a division to his aid. Sherman received this dispatch on the 22d of September, and at four o'clock that day, Osterhaus with his division was on his way to Vicksburg, and the next day was steaming toward Memphis. On the 23d, Sherman was ordered to follow with his whole army, and he pushed forward in the manner which his judgment approved.

In the mean time, Grant was getting everything ready for his arrival, when he designed to make a general assault on the enemy's strong position.

Both troops and animals were suffering for want of provisions, which the obstruction of transportation rendered extremely scarce. Missionary Ridge drops like a pendant in a southwesterly direction from the Tennessee River above Chattanooga, and Lookout Mountain in the same direction from the river below. Chattanooga, lying in a bend of the river between the two mountains, was overlooked and commanded by both heights, and hence both must be taken. Hooker was selected to operate against Lookout Mountain; but in order to make a lodgement on the south side of the river, it was necessary to occupy Brown's Ferry, which was three miles below it by the river, and six miles from Chattanooga, yet, owing to the sharp bend of the stream that here runs back almost parallel to its course, was only half a mile from the latter place by land. The possession of this ferry must also lessen the distance of transportation to Bridge-port.

The chief-engineer, General W. F. Smith, proposed a plan for seizing it, which was adopted. Four thousand men were at once placed under his command. Fifty pontoons, capable of holding twenty-five men each, besides oarsmen, and also two flatboats for carrying about a hundred more, were built, in which fifteen hundred picked men, under General Hazen, were placed. It was six miles by the tortuous river to the ferry, three miles of which were picketed by the enemy. On the night of the 27th of October, these pontoons, mere boxes, were quietly pushed off and floated noiselessly down the current. It was very dark, and the current rendering oars unnecessary, they silently glided past the pickets on the shore, unheard and unseen. Down, around Moccasin Point, in front of Lookout Mountain, they rapidly floated, without being observed.

While landing, they were discovered, and soon the flash of musketry lit up the darkness. This roused the neighboring camps of the enemy; but the Union troops landed and quickly formed to repel an attack, while the empty boats were swiftly propelled across the river to transfer the remainder of the four thousand, who had secretly marched thither by land. These having been ferried over, a strong position was immediately secured, and entrenchments were thrown up. The enemy, taken somewhat by surprise, after a brief resistance retreated up the valley. The materials for a pontoon bridge, which had also been brought by land, and concealed, were now brought forth, and by noon a bridge, nine hundred feet long, spanned the river, by which supplies and reinforcements could be forwarded to the troops. On the following day, the whole of the Eleventh Corps was across, and encamped in Lookout Valley. The enemy, alarmed at this demonstration, made an attempt to drive them back by a night attack. This conflict was by moonlight, after midnight, amid those hills, that blazed the while with musketry and exploding shells,—presenting a strange spectacle. "Fighting Joe Hooker," as he was termed, was in the thickest of the conflict encouraging his men.

The Union forces maintained their ground, and being firmly established, steamboats could come up to Brown's Ferry, from which it was but a mile and a half to the upper bridge opposite Chattanooga. Unless the bridge should be carried away by rafts sent down the stream by the enemy from above, the army was now relieved from starvation.

Though this was a great improvement in the condition of affairs, Grant felt too weak to assume the offensive, until Sherman should arrive. Though Sherman crossed the Tennessee on the 1st of November, there was no way to get his army over, and it had to take the long march by Fayetteville to Bridgeport. On the 15th, Sherman rode into Chattanooga. General Grant was never more pleased to see a man. He had received a summons from Bragg to remove the non-combatants from Chattanooga, as he was about to bombard the town, to which he had made no reply; but he now felt that with his strong lieutenant he would be able to meet General Bragg beyond the walls of the city. Sherman's troops, after their long and wearisome march, were sadly in need of rest, and expected it, before entering on one of the most hazardous undertakings of the war.

With a part of his command, he was directed to make a demonstration on Lookout Mountain, while with the main army he crossed the river, and marched up above Chattanooga, opposite Missionary Ridge. Returning to Bridgeport, Sherman took a rowboat and passed down the river to hurry forward his weary, foot-sore divisions. Ewing's division was the force left to make the demonstration on Lookout Mountain. The rest were hurried forward along almost impassable roads. Though foot-sore, weary and hungry, the troops toiled cheerfully on in obedience to the orders of their commander, and by the 23d were well up, and lay concealed behind the hills opposite Chickamauga Creek, which, skirting the extremity of Missionary Ridge, here emptied into the Tennessee. One division, however, was left behind—a delay caused by the breaking of a pontoon bridge at Brown's Ferry—and it was compelled to join Hooker's Corps, and operate with him in the battle that followed.

By a skilful manœuvre the same night, a small force was silently moved along the river, capturing every guard of the enemy's pickets but one. Next thing was to get the army across the Tennessee, which at this point was nearly thirteen hundred feet wide. About three miles above Sherman's army was a stream emptying into the

Tennessee. Thither one hundred and sixteen boats were conveyed by a concealed road and launched; while three thousand men lay ready to embark in them. An hour after midnight, on the 24th, these boats floated silently down into the Tennessee, and passing within three miles of the enemy's pickets, landed the troops on both sides of Chickamauga Creek, which emptied into the river opposite Sherman's army. Two divisions with artillery were soon ferried over, and a *tête-de-pont* established. In a few hours, a bridge fourteen hundred feet long was completed, and shaking to the tread of Sherman's mighty columns. Another bridge two hundred feet long was flung across the Chickamauga Creek. The extreme north point of Missionary Ridge was not occupied by the enemy,—his right wing being further back, near the tunnel through which the railroad passed. This extremity, Sherman at once seized, thereby threatening Bragg's communications. In the meantime, a cavalry force was sent off eastward toward Cleveland.

Grant now had Sherman's army above, and Hooker's below him, and both on the same side of the river; while Thomas lay in front of Chattanooga. Missionary Ridge, extending southward from Sherman, passed in front of Chattanooga, where the centre lay.

General Bragg was amazed at the appearance of a powerful army on his extreme right, and immediately made arrangements to dislodge Sherman. In the mean time, Hooker, from below, moved against Lookout Mountain, and, by dark, carried the nose of it, thus opening up communications with Chattanooga. His advance up the steep sides of the mountain had been made with great celerity and skill. A thick fog for awhile concealed him, but, as it lifted before the sun, the cliffs above were seen crowded with the enemy, while their cannon sent a plunging fire from the heights. Grant, far down in the mist-shrouded valley below, could hear the thunder of guns, and crash of musketry high up in the clouds above, as though the gods were battling there. An eye-witness to the scene, friendly to the North, says of it:

"At this juncture, the scene became one of most exciting interest. The thick fog, which had heretofore rested in dense folds upon the sides of the mountain, concealing the combatants from view, suddenly lifted to the summit of the lofty ridge, revealing to the anxious gaze of thousands in the valleys and on the plains below, a scene such as is witnessed but once in a century. General Geary's columns, flushed with victory, grappled with the foe upon the rocky ledges, and drove them back with slaughter from their works. While the result was uncertain, the attention was breathless and painful; but when victory perched upon our standards, shout upon shout rent the air. The whole army with one accord, broke out into joyous acclamations. The enthusiasm of the scene beggars description. Men were frantic with joy, and even General Thomas himself, who seldom exhibits his emotions, involuntarily said, 'I did not think it possible for men to accomplish so much.'"

Before dawn, on the 25th, Sherman was in the saddle, and by the dim light which streaked the cloudy east, as if foretelling a stormy day, he rode along the entire line. A deep valley lay between him and the steep hill beyond, which was partly covered with trees to the narrow wooded top, across which was a breastwork of logs and earth, dark with men. Two guns enfiladed the narrow way that led to it. Further back arose a still higher hill, lined with guns that could pour a plunging fire on the first hill if it should be taken. The depth and character of the gorge between could not be ascertained. Just as the rising sun was tinging with red the murky rain-clouds, the bugles sounded the advance, and Corse taking the lead, briskly descended the hill, crossed the valley, and under a heavy fire began to ascend the opposite heights, and soon gained a foothold, though the spot where he stood was swept by the Confederate artillery.

It was in Sherman's advanced columns that Belcher's regiment fought that day. Mark Stevens, with his footsore and weary soldiers, fatigued with marches and midnight reconnoissances, were in the van. Mark was cool, and his soldiers were all veterans. Sis had recovered from his wound and was again in the ranks. Bill Simms was with him. Alec was near his captain loading and firing, as he advanced, at his former friends.

" We are going to have some hot work!" said Alec, during a brief lull in the attack, as they paused behind a large oak tree.

" Alec, do you believe in impressions?" asked Mark.

" What do you mean?" Alec asked fixing his eyes on the face of his cousin. " Now look here, Mark, for Heaven's sake don't go to making out that you are expecting something bad."

" Alec, I have passed through many conflicts without a scratch, but never have I before felt as I do now, and have felt, ever since we commenced the march on Missionary Ridge. If I should be slain, all my effects, my money and a letter which you will find addressed to my mother are in the pocket of my coat. You will also find a letter addressed to Elsie Cole, please send it to her."

" Do you know where she is ? "

" No."

Before more could be said, the order was given to advance and the great battle opened. For more than an hour it swayed back and forth in Sherman's front. Bringing up brigade after brigade, this gallant commander nobly strove to carry the lofty heights above him. By ten o'clock, it was one peal of thunder from top to base, while the smoke, in swift puffs and floating masses, draped it like a waving mantle. Corse, severely wounded, was borne to the rear, but the columns still stubbornly held their ground. At this point the battle raged furiously all forenoon. This most northern and vital position must be held by the Confederates at all hazards, for if once taken, their rear and all their stores at Chickamauga would be threatened. So here Bragg massed his forces, and at three o'clock P. M. was hurling column after column upon Sherman's advance, while gun after gun poured its concentrated fire on them from every hill and spur that gave a view of any part of the ground. Once the Union lines were partially forced back; but Sherman, by a skilful move, recovered his lost ground, and drove the Confederates to cover. His men were sternly held to their terrible work; but Sherman was growing impatient for Grant to move on the centre, as he had promised on the night before that he would. From his elevated position, he could see the flags of Thomas' corps waving in the murky atmosphere, but hour after hour passed away, and still they did not advance. The Confederates were still steadily massing their forces against Sherman, and his troops having fought from early dawn were almost exhausted.

For hours Grant sat on his horse, listening to the thunder of artillery on his right, as Hooker came down like an avalanche from the heights of Lookout Mountain, and the deafening uproar on his left, where Sherman, his favorite lieutenant, was hurling his brave columns on the batteries of the Confederates, and still they moved not. Thinking at one time that Sherman was too hard pressed, he sent a brigade to his relief; but Sherman, who had become thoroughly aroused at the resistance he was meeting, sent it back saying that he did not need it. And so, hour after hour, for six miles the battle flamed and thundered along the rocky crests, until, at last, the decisive moment looked for by Grant had arrived.

Thomas' corps was moving on the acclivity four hundred feet high in front. Upward, step by step, the irrepressible Thomas pressed his way. Bragg displayed wonderful generalship. He was confronted by Grant, Hooker, Sherman and Thomas, with forces vastly superior to his own, and yet held his post with great fortitude and bravery, until overpowered by odds and driven from the field.

It was in the last charge up the heights of Missionary Ridge, that Mark pressed forward in the extreme advance with Alec, Sis, and Bill Simms at his side. The enemy were but a few feet away. He saw Sis and a Confederate both fire at each other at the same moment not ten paces apart, and both missed. Sis began to reload as he advanced, and the Confederate did the same. As Sis had to climb up the steep and rocky acclivity, he discovered that the Confederate would get loaded first. The Confederate was already feeling for his cap, when Sis suddenly bounded forward, and with the butt of his gun knocked him down, fracturing his skull so that he died from the effects of the blow. They were soon so close that bayonets were used, then the sickening horrors of war were fully realized. One man went down with two bayonets through his body, the points crossing as they came out at his back.

Amid all the uproar and excitement, Mark felt a quick and sudden pain in his side, a mist came before his eyes and his head swam. Alec saw him, and leaping to his side cried:

" Mark, Mark ! "

He caught him in his arms and let him down

"MARK! — COUSIN! — OLD FRIEND, HAS IT COME TO THIS?"

easily. The captain closed his eyes, Alec glanced to the West. The sun was setting and the Confederates, broken and defeated, were flying from the victorious Union army. With tears in his eyes, the kind-hearted Alec turned his anxious gaze upon his captain lying on the ground as peaceful as if asleep, and said:

"Mark!—cousin!—old friend, has it come at last?"

28

CHAPTER XVII.

AN ETHER FANTASY.

WHEN Mark Stevens awoke, almost a week after the fight on Missionary Ridge, he was lying in a hospital with Alec at his side. He never forgot how that friend bent over him with tears of joy, and said:

"Thank God, you are better,—yes, thank God, you won't die."

"How long have I been here?" he feebly asked.

"A week."

"A whole week?"

"Yes, you are very weak. You almost bled to death."

"Were you wounded, Alec?"

"No. I took you in my arms and ran down that accursed hill, which I believe was bloody from top to bottom. I got detached to watch over you. Mark, Colonel Belcher is dead, and there is talk of——"

Mark shook his head. He felt that this was no time to talk of promotion. He was weak, very

354

weak; but the surgeon came along and, with an encouraging smile, said:

"You are better, my boy, but you must keep very quiet, for you have no strength to spare."

By a nod of his head, Mark intimated his willingness to submit to hospital regulations. Days wore on and Mark grew stronger, though the bullet was still in his side. At times it pained him, so that he wished that the surgeons had cut it out before he recovered consciousness. He soon became convinced that the operation would yet have to be performed, before he would fully recover. He talked with Alec about it one day, and he said he had heard the surgeon major say as much himself; so that Mark began to realize that some time in the future he would have to submit to the operation. Though he shuddered with dread at the thought, he was glad to know that he would be relieved of the burden, which was becoming oppressive to him.

It seemed like a dream, yet it was a reality,— that story he heard of a woman, young and fair, who had suddenly appeared like an angel of mercy on the field, and in the hospital, ministering to the wants of the wounded. Another Miss Dix had come, and all Chattanooga rang with her praise. She was kind and gentle alike to Confederate and Federal. Many a hero in blue or gray, blessed her name with his dying breath. The Women's Central Association for Relief, the United States Sanitary Commission, and Young Men's Christian Associations, were all doing good and noble work, but all these were not enough.

There were many evidences of individual heroism and exertion in relieving the sick and wounded. Scarce had the smoke of battle rolled away from about Missionary Ridge and Lookout Mountain, when there came from some place, no one knew where, one of the fairest of Columbia's daughters. Her sole mission was to do good, and her soft, tender hands soothed many a fevered brow, or bound up many a painful wound.

But she was searching for some one. General Sherman, who met her one day, ascertained that she was searching for a missing friend.

"Is he among the Federal troops or Confederates?" asked Sherman.

"He is a Federal," she answered. As she did not give his name, Sherman could not help her.

She found him at last. It came about through Alec. He had gone from the side of his wounded captain for a few moments to get a few whiffs of fresh air, with which, in spite of all the powerful disinfectants, modern science cannot fully supply a hospital. Alec was walking slowly down the street, reflecting on the past, the present, and trying to conjecture as to the future.

"How different—what changes!" he was thinking. "Who knows how it will end?" Then he almost ran against some one. He stopped and looked at the some one in astonishment, for he saw a pair of roguish blue eyes, saddened by care and grief, a wealth of golden hair, and a face which had never failed to wonderfully impress him. He bounded forward, and caught her hand, crying:

"What! Thunderation!—Old Nick and General Jackson! Can it be? By the Holy Jumping Moses, it is! Well, may I be teetotally smashed, girl, where did you come from?"

"Alec,—Alec Stevens, and in a Yankee uniform!"

"Yes, Elsie. I've turned over. I was a little in doubt about which side was right in this quarrel, and I've fought on both so as to be sure."

Elsie's face wore a look of anxiety. She had some curiosity to know Alec's history; but her desire to know the fate of Mark Stevens was far greater. She asked Alec about his cousin. Yes, he knew where he was, had, in fact, just come from his bedside. He was a captain now, and, if he survived the operation of cutting a ball of lead out of his side, he might be a colonel, as there was a vacancy. Alec would show her to the hospital where Captain Stevens was; but she must pass inspection by the surgeon major before she would be allowed to enter.

She had met the surgeon major, who knew something of the noble, self-sacrificing labors of this young woman; but the old major was a good judge of human nature, and readily saw that the young lady had something more than a general interest in the wounded captain. He held quite a lengthy interview with her before he decided to admit her to the ward where the wounded captain lay.

Even then, she was only admitted while he was under the influence of opiates, or sleeping, so that Mark was not sure, at first, that the sweet musical voice and soothing touch were not only the pleasant vagaries of a fevered vision.

Gradually he began to expect this sacred presence, and when he began to recover, felt fears that he might lose it. The presence grew more and more tangible, until he came to realize that she was something more than the baseless fabric of a dream. When he was able to be propped up in bed, she sat by his side and held his fevered hand. They did not talk of the past nor the future, for they were forbidden to talk at all. Sometimes he asked himself how she had come there, and wondered if she would remain until all was over one way or the other. She had relatives somewhere, why was she not with them? She did not speak of them to him, nor was he at liberty to ask her any questions. Since the appearance of Elsie Cole, Alec did not come near the hospital. He returned to his company, though he frequently inquired after the captain.

Though Mark grew stronger, he was assured that he must undergo the surgical operation. The bullet must be removed, and the sooner it was done, after he was strong enough to stand the operation, the better. He became able to sit up, and even walk about the room, and it seemed too bad to be cut and hacked to pieces by those scientific butchers.

Mark asked himself if he would have the nerve to face the ordeal coolly. Any man, who is not a poltroon, can find courage to fight when he is in danger, and excited, but a surgical operation, with all its calm, ghastly preparations, is another matter. To get on a table, lie down and take ether or chloroform, with the knowledge that one is to be carved, and aware that he has an even chance of never waking up again, calls for a pluck of a different order. At least, Mark thought so, and suffered from a secret fear that he might make a humiliating exhibition of himself.

Like one doomed to execution, the consciousness that it had to be endowed him with self-control. And like a man who is going to be hanged, he was anxious to have it over, and hastened things by helping the doctors to move and arrange the tables. He even rebuked one of the surgeons quite severely, who was rather late in coming.

"Thank God!" he mentally ejaculated between commands and queries as he lay stretched on his back with the ether funnel over his mouth and nostrils. At last the cursed thing that had made his life a load was to be put to the sword. The thing was personified to his mind, at that moment, as a personal enemy, and the thought that if he lived it must perish gave him a glow of revengeful satisfaction.

That first inhalation of ether went into his lungs like peppermint, and brought on a fit of coughing. After the third or fourth whiff, he squeezed the physician's hand, and experienced a desire to sit up and propose ether all round.

"Doctor," he said from under the paper cone, "this is delightful; it's as good as champagne."

"Whir, whir, whir-r."

"Heavens! doctor, this is most extraordinary. Here, here, here! This won't do at all!" "Tap-tap-tap-tap!" "Why, confound you, I'll knock your head off!" "B'rr b'rr b'rr! Whir, whir, whir-r-r-rip!" "Let go, you scoundrel! You

won't? Murder me, would you?" "B'rr, b'rr,
b'rr!" "Ha, ha, ha, ha!"

He came to consciousness in his coffin. The
darkness was black and so thick that to breathe it
stifled him. The weight of six feet of earth
pressed upon his breast. Although the coffin lid
was really between him and this mass, he panted
under its crushing pressure. The sweat burst
coldly through his skin, the blood rushed into his
brain, and it oozed from his eyes and ears. Each
hair tingled to its very end. He felt in an instant
that he should go mad and lay there in his rayless
prison shrieking, foaming and gnashing his teeth,
but was held from movement by the walls of wood
and earth. If he could turn and try to lift the lid
and the filled grave with his back, perhaps there
might be one chance in a million that the frenzied
strength of despair would prevail.

Turn! He might as well attempt to fly. The
lid was within an inch of his chest—his chin
touched it. His hands were by his sides and there
was not room to move them. His fingers and toes
answered to his will, and he could roll his head
from side to side. That was all.

To be a raving maniac in a bare, stone cell—
that would be freedom, happiness; but this!
Hissings and flashings of dazzling light within his
brain warned him. It was better to lie still and

die by suffocation, than to go mad and perish in a hurricane of impotent agony.

It would soon be over. The air in the coffin, already hot, humid and sickening with the odors of decay, could not last long. So he composed himself, closed his eyes, and all his consciousness was centred in the one purpose of keeping an iron clutch upon his will. Every other thought, whether of life or death, self, or those he loved, he held at bay.

There darted out of his memory a long, tunnel-like hall of stone, in which he had once sat grieving for a friend. It was very dark—dark as this grave in which he lay manacled, shackled and gnashing his teeth until they cracked. This tunnel-like hall was in the cemetery where he was buried. While he sat, his elbow on a little, wooden table and his head bowed upon his hand, far away at the end of the strange tunnel, a bright blue electric spark appeared, for an instant, like a minute star, and then came a faint ringing. Twice this flash and sound were repeated, and then all was as before, dark, damp, silent and sad.

In his coffin he understood, and a torrent of horror swept over him. His friend had been buried alive, and had sent this appeal from the tomb for succor. And he had sat there dumb and motionless, while the one whom he loved had lain and faced an awful death such as he was facing now; had gone through this ordeal, which no one can understand, until he has endured it! Oh, horrible! horrible!

He beat his temples on the coffin's sides in an ecstasy of remorse. Such dulness destined him thus to die. Some one should always be on the watch in that cavern ready to spring to the rescue of such poor buried wretches as touched the bell cord, with which, he now remembered, every coffin was provided.

There was hope then. They could dig him out before life was wholly gone.

He knew where the cord was,—just under the lid, above his left shoulder. He could not raise his hands to it, and his head was beyond it; but he thought he might raise his shoulder and press it against the knotted end of the cord, so as to pull it and ring the bell. Of course it would be easy enough. Those who arranged such matters knew what they were about.

He raised his shoulder.

The knotted cord, his only hope of life, was beyond his reach.

He must go mad. Life was within two inches of him, and he unable to reach it. If he could turn, his right shoulder in coming in contact with the knotted cord, would certainly pull it down-

ward and so ring the bell.   But turning was impossible.

No, it was not impossible.   He would turn if
it broke every bone in his·body to splinters.

The   lid—oh, curse that lid, with a world's

THEN A WARM, SOFT, LOVING HAND TOOK HIS.

weight upon it, it was as immovable as a mountain!   A living demon must be holding it against
his shoulder to keep him from rubbing the cord
which would ring away the darkness, the torture,
and the grave.   Forty men could not, all together,

possess the splendid, furious strength with which he steadily, surely turned. Crack, bones! Bleed, flesh! Roar, thunder! flash, lightning! Heavens! can it be——

"Well, sir, how are you feeling?"

"Hello, doctor! Haven't you begun the——"

"It's all over, my boy, and as pretty a job as I ever did in my life."

Then a warm, soft, loving hand took his. The mists gathered, but through them dimly he saw her face, and sank into a sweet, painless slumber.

CHAPTER XVIII.

"I HAVE A WIFE."

THE recovery of Mark Stevens was rapid. The bullet, which had been the thorn in his side, and the great hindrance to his recovery, being removed, his youth, strong constitution, and everything now was in his favor. During all that critical period in his illness, Elsie hovered over him, like an angel of mercy and love.

They spoke of neither the past nor the future. They talked of the present only, when they talked at all, which was seldom. Theirs was a silent devotion, and he was never happier than when she was at his side, holding his thin, wasted hand in hers; but he instinctively realized that this could not last always. She must go away. Elsie was like the angels. They approach nearer when comes the grim monster death, and recede with returning health. When he had recovered, she was gone; he knew not whither, nor could any one inform him. She had last been seen about the hospitals, flitting here and there, a ray of sunshine wherever she went. Then she disappeared as completely as if she had melted into air. On returning to his headquarters, he found Alec, and asked him whither she had gone.

" I don't know," the soldier answered, rubbing away on his gun barrel, which he was brightening.

" Did she tell you she was going, Alec?"

" No."

Alec seemed averse to talking on the subject, and Mark asked him no more questions about her.

" She is gone," thought Mark. " Perhaps it were better if we never saw each other again. In time I might forget her. No,—no, I could never do that,—though I will not allow myself to believe that Elsie Cole loves me. She feels grateful, because I saved her life; but she has surely repaid the debt with interest."

Mark was soon able to assume command of his company, and a part of the time commanded the regiment. After the severe struggle at Missionary Ridge and Lookout Mountain, a short season of rest was granted the regiment.

There was no slackening in the war, however. It raged in North Carolina, where General J. F. Foster, quartered at New Berne, was sending out raiding parties to scatter Confederate forces gathering here and there to recover the lost posts in that

State. Although Charleston had become a comparatively unimportant point in the grand theatre of war, its possession was coveted by the national government because of the salutary effect it would produce. General Quincy A. Gillmore, who succeeded General Hunter in the command of the Southern department, planned an expedition against Charleston by land and water. After a futile effort to capture Fort Wagner, he began a regular siege. With infinite labor, a battery was constructed in a morass, half-way between Morris and James Islands, upon a platform of heavy timbers standing in the deep black mud. When a lieutenant of engineers was ordered to construct it, he declared:

"It is impossible." His commanding officer replied:

"There is no such word as impossible; call for what you need."

Whereupon the lieutenant, who was a wag, made a requisition on the quartermaster for "one hundred men, eighteen feet high, to wade in mud sixteen feet deep;" and he gravely inquired of the engineer if these men might not be spliced if required. The lieutenant was arrested for contempt, but soon after released; when he built the redoubt with the services of men of ordinary height. Upon the redoubt was erected a Parrott gun, which they called "The Swamp Angel," that sent shells into Charleston, five miles away.

General Gillmore was ready for another attack on Forts Wagner and Sumter, on the 17th of August, and on that day the guns of twelve batteries and of the fleet opened upon them. Before night the walls of Sumter began to crumble, and its cannon, under the pressure of Dahlgren's guns, ceased to roar. The land troops pushed their parallels nearer and nearer to Fort Wagner; while the fleet continually pounded away, day after day, until the 6th of September, when General Terry was prepared to storm the latter work. Then it was ascertained that the Confederates had evacuated it, and fled from Morris Island. Gillmore took possession of Fort Wagner, and turned its guns on Fort Sumter, battering it terribly, and, it was thought, driving away the garrison; but when a force in boats attempted to seize the fort, they found a strong force there, which repulsed them with heavy loss. Late in October (1863), Gillmore brought his heaviest guns to bear on Sumter and reduced it to a heap of ruins. As a commercial mart, Charleston now had no existence. For months, not a blockade runner had entered its harbor. Wealth and trade had departed from the city where in 1861 the war between the States had begun.

24

In the West and Southwest, the war was on the decline. The Confederates reoccupied all Texas in 1863, and carried on a sort of intermittent warfare in Arkansas during most of that year. On the 20th of April, 1863, Marmaduke, the Confederate general, fought a strong Union force at Cape Girardeau, but was defeated and retreated to other territory.

General Banks, from his Red River expedition, marched to the siege of Port Hudson, and General Taylor, the Confederate, for awhile overran Louisiana and Texas; but the middle of July witnessed the fall of Port Hudson, and then Banks succeeded in forcing Taylor from the country eastward of the Atchafalaya. This was the last struggle of Taylor's forces to gain a foothold on the Mississippi.

At the opening of the third year of the civil war, 1864, there were many hopeful signs of success for the defenders of the cause of the North. Though the northern debt exceeded a billion dollars, the public credit was never better. Northern people stood for the government and trusted it with a faith that was unshaken. Those who trusted the government in its hour of adversity, made money. Many a man in but moderate circumstances in 1861, was a millionaire in 1871. The Confederate debt was almost as great as the

National debt, with a prospective increase during the year likely to double that amount. The Confederate government had contracted loans abroad, to almost $15,000,000, of which sum the *Southern Independence Association* in England (composed chiefly of British aristocracy) loaned a very considerable share; the security offered for the Confederate bonds being cotton to be forwarded, but which could not be delivered. Many producers in the Confederacy were unwilling to lend support to their own government in its distress, and withheld supplies; for they believed they foresaw the want of future value in the bonds and paper currency of the Confederates. The people in the South were no longer willing to volunteer for the military service; and President Davis and his associates at Richmond, in their great need, proceeded to the exercise of a drastic act which has no parallel in the history of any struggle. By the passage of a law they declared *every white man in the Confederacy, liable to bear arms, to be in the military service;* and that, upon his failure to report for duty at a military station within a certain time, he was liable to the penalty of death for a deserter.

While the authorities at Richmond were preparing to carry out these measures, they received a dispatch from Lord John Russell, the British Foreign Secretary, which deprived them of the last prop of hope for the recognition of the independence of the Confederate States from any foreign State, excepting that of the Roman Pontiff. That dispatch gave notice that no more vessels should be fitted out in Great Britain (nor allowed in British waters) for making war on the commerce of the United States by the " so called Confederate States." The last expression, ignoring the very existence of the Confederacy, was naturally very offensive to the heads of the government. President Davis made a sharp reply protesting against the " studied insult; " and from this time on to the end, the Southern Confederacy felt that England could no longer be looked upon as a trusted friend.

France, in the last year of the war, took advantage of the distracted condition of the country to violate the principles of the Monroe Doctrine sacred to every American; and, by the establishment of Maximilian as emperor of Mexico, overthrew a republic and set up an empire on the Western continent; but the ambitious Napoleon III. brought ruin upon Maximilian and himself.

Early in 1864, in order to more completely unify the army, Congress created the office of Lieutenant-General, and Ulysses S. Grant was nominated to fill the office. He became general-in-chief of the armies of the Republic, and fixed his headquarters with the Army of the Potomac.

In the Southwest, Sherman was making war terrible. The destruction of public and private property was enormous, and has only been excused on the ground that it was necessary to conquer so formidable an enemy as the South. Nevertheless the Christian must admit there was little of the humane or Christian about Sherman's war. But there is never anything Christ-like in war. No public property of the Confederates was spared, and in many instances private houses were burned. The station houses and rolling-stock of the railroads were reduced to ashes. The tracks were torn up, and the rails, heated by burning ties cast into heaps, were twisted and ruined, and by bending them, while red hot, around a sapling, converted into what the men satirically called "Jeff Davis neck-ties." General Sherman intended to push on to Montgomery, Alabama, and then, if circumstances appeared favorable, to go southward and attack Mobile.

In May, 1864, General John Morgan, a daring Confederate cavalryman, who had been a terror to Kentucky, Ohio, and Indiana, was forced out of Kentucky into East Tennessee, where he was surprised at Greeneville and killed, while trying to make his escape.

General Robert E. Lee was the master soldier of the war. Though an enemy to the North and its cause, though success for him would have overthrown what his noble ancestors helped build, and though his course has been condemned, we must regard him as the superior military genius of either army. The man, who came nearest being

his match, was General Meade, at Gettysburg. But for fighting and retreating, for holding together a poorly equipped and poorly fed army, for skilful flank movements, for fruitfulness in resources, and all that goes to make up a great military genius, Lee rises above any man in either the northern or southern armies.

GEN. ROBERT E. LEE.

When General Grant, flushed with the victories of the west, took up his head-quarters with the Army of the Potomac with the finest army ever on American soil, great things were expected, nor was the public disappointed; but had not Grant possessed inexhaustible resources, of men, money, arms, clothing and food, his bull-dog tenacity would have proved his ruin.

These two giants, with their splendid corps of officers, first met in the Wilderness, May 4 and 5, 1864, when the long stubborn conflict began. It was during this conflict that Grant sent his famous dispatch to the president: *"I propose to fight it out on this line if it takes all summer."*

General Grant had an army of one hundred and forty thousand men under such lieutenants as Sheridan and Custer, Sedgwick, Meade, and others. Lee had sixty thousand men, less than half of Grant's forces. In two days General Grant lost thirty thousand men, of which only five thousand were prisoners, while Lee's losses were but ten thousand. The battle of the Wilderness cannot be claimed as a victory for Grant, and the reckless loss of life can only be excused on the ground that the " hotter the war, the sooner would they have peace." May 7, 1864, Lee retreated toward Spottsylvania Court-House, the Union army following and still fighting. On the 8th the battle of Spottsylvania was fought with an indecisive result. On the 10th, the battle was continued with a loss of ten thousand on the Union side. The result was still doubtful. On the 12th, Lee and Grant again fought with an indecisive result. On the 13th, General Sheridan destroyed Lee's depot of supplies in his rear near Beaver Dam. By the 21st, Lee, being flanked by overwhelming masses brought against him, retired from Spottsylvania to the North Anna. On the 25th, General Stuart, the admired Confederate cavalry leader, was killed, and General Sheridan, who was fast rising in military fame, after performing a series of brilliant and daring deeds in Lee's rear, joined General Grant. Grant seldom lost a foot of ground that he had gained, and at any and all cost pushed on. While there may have been more brilliant officers in the field, he possessed the excellent faculty of " hanging on " to an extraordinary degree. His frightful losses of three to one of the enemy, would have disheartened any other general. Although he had lost an army of soldiers during the month of May, on the 27th of that month he crossed the Pamunky and flanked Lee at Hanovertown.

On June 1, 1864, the battle of Cold Harbor was fought, the result indecisive, but loss on both sides fearful. Though Confederate losses were much less than Grant's, they had no resources to draw from.

On the 15th, an unsuccessful assault of three days was made on Petersburg, with a loss on the Union side of ten thousand men. General Grant had been at the head of the Army of the Potomac less than three months, and had lost the enormous number of sixty-four thousand men, four thousand men more than comprised Lee's army in the beginning, and almost as many as were thought necessary, in 1861, to put down the rebellion. Lee's losses were a little over half as many. It was now quite evident that the war was to be a war of endurance. On the 20th of June, Petersburg was strongly reinforced by Lee, and Grant's advance checked.

In the west, General Sherman was following the plan of General Grant. In fact, there was a wonderful similarity between these officers. Neither seemed to know the word failure.

On the 15th of May, while Grant and Lee were fighting at Spottsylvania, Sherman, after a two days' fight, drove Johnston from Resaca, Georgia. Sherman pushed on after Johnston, and these giants again met at Kenesaw Mountains on June 27th. Johnston had been compelled to abandon his positions before the approach of Sherman's conquering columns. The Kenesaw Mountains overlook Marietta. Around these great hills and upon their slopes and summits, and also upon Lost and Pine Mountains, the Confederates had cast up intrenchments and planted signal stations; but, after a desperate struggle—fighting battle after battle for the space of about a month, while the rain was falling copiously, almost without intermission—the Confederates were forced to leave these strong positions. They fled toward the Chattahoochee River, in the direction of Atlanta, closely pursued by the Nationals. One of the corps commanders, Bishop Polk, was killed by a shell on the summit of Pine Mountain. So persistently did Johnston dispute the way from Dalton, in northern Georgia, to Atlanta, that when he reached the entrenchments at the latter place, he had lost nearly one-fourth of his army.

On the evening of July 2d, Sherman's cavalry threatened Johnston's flanks, also menacing the ferry at Chattahoochee, and the Confederates abandoned the Great Kenesaw, and fled. At dawn next morning, when the national skirmishers planted the stars and stripes over the Confederate battery on the summit of that eminence, they saw hosts of the enemy flying in hot haste toward Atlanta. At eight o'clock Sherman entered Marietta, close on the heels of Johnston's army. He hoped to strike the Confederates a fatal blow while they were crossing the Chattahoochee; but Johnston, by quick and skilful movements, passed the stream without molestation, and made a stand along the line of it. General Howard laid a pontoon bridge two miles above the ferry where Johnston had crossed, and at the same time there was a general movement of Sherman's forces all along the line. The imperilled Confederates were forced to abandon their works near the Chattahoochee, and retreat to a new line that covered Atlanta, their left resting on the Chattahoochee and their right on Peach Tree Creek. The two armies rested until the middle of July. The able and judicious leader, Johnston, was succeeded by Hood of Texas, a dashing but less cautious officer than his predecessor. Sixty-five days after Sherman had put his army in motion southward, he was master of the whole country north and west of the river on the banks of which he was resting (nearly one-half of Georgia) and had accomplished one of the chief objects of the campaign, namely, the advancement of the National lines from the Tennessee to the Chattahoochee.

The possession of Atlanta, the key-point of military advantage in that region, was the next prize to be contended for. About the 16th of July, the National army began its advance, destroying railways and skirmishing bravely; and on the 20th, the Confederates, led by Hood in person, fell upon the corps

GEN. W. T. SHERMAN.

of Howard, Hooker, and Palmer, with heavy force. The assailants were repulsed after a sharp battle in which both parties suffered severely.

There were indications that Hood intended to evacuate Atlanta; but when Sherman's troops moved rapidly toward the city, they encountered strong entrenchments. Before these, a part of Hood's army held their antagonists; while the main body, led by General Hardee, made a long, night march, gained the rear of Sherman's forces on the morning of July 22d, and fell on them with crushing weight and numbers. A terrific battle ensued, lasting many hours; and after a brief interval, one still more sanguinary was begun, which resulted in a victory for the northern troops, and the retreat of the Confederates to their works. General McPherson was that day killed by sharpshooters in the woods, and General John A. Logan took his place in command. On the 28th of July, another terrible battle was fought before Atlanta, and the Confederates were again driven to their lines; and from that time until the close of August, hostilities in that region were confined, chiefly, to raids upon railways and the interruption of each other's supplies. On the 31st of August, the forces of Howard and Hardee had a severe battle at Jonesboro, twenty miles below Atlanta, in which the Confederates were defeated. When Hood heard of this disaster, he perceived his peril, and blowing up his magazine at Atlanta, formed a junction with Hardee, and with his whole army soon recrossed the Chattahoochee. Hood had lost nearly half his infantry in the space of a few weeks. The Union army entered Atlanta September 2, 1864.

Mark Stevens, since his recovery and return to the command of his company, had seen active service. Though he had been promoted to major, he never lost interest in his company. For meritorious conduct, and through the influence of his cousin Mark, Alec, despite the fact that he had come, as he said, to serve the country as a private, and carry a musket, was made lieutenant. At Kenesaw Mountains, the mortality of the officers was very great and when the conflict was over Alec had a captain's commission.

While the army was operating about Atlanta just previous to the fall of that city, Major Stevens was sent with a force of one hundred and fifty men to a small village at the head of a creek to capture a Confederate colonel, who was reported to be lodging in a large stone house. He took with him Alec and his company, and a part of two other companies. The country was full of Confederate cavalry, and there was great danger of their detachment being cut off. The night was dark and, as the men began the march, a fine drizzle of rain commenced. Bill Simms said:

"This reminds me o' one night when I was with Gineral Percy."

Upon which a comrade put in:

"Oh, Bill Simms, for goodness sake give Gineral Percy an' all the rest o' us a rest."

"No talking in ranks! *Forward!*"

Away they marched in gloom, darkness and falling mist. Not one of the men knew the object of the expedition. That secret was known only to Mark and the two captains. For hours they marched in an unknown land. A forest loomed

up before them.   The major walked at the side of
his cousin Alec, leading the force, preceded by
the guide, a bright young mulatto, thoroughly
acquainted with the country.

About two o'clock in the morning, having
traversed a dark forest, they came in sight of the
village.   Mark and Alec held a short consultation,
after which they drew up their forces in a peach
orchard near the house.   Accompanied by Alec,
Bill Simms, Sis and Lieutenant Black, Mark went
to the big stone house, not over fifty paces away.

The night was dark and there was but one
light visible at a window.   This light was in the
gable.

The reconnoitring party went completely round
the house searching for some means of entering it
unperceived.   When they had reached the rear,
they were assailed by a ferocious dog, which Lieutenant Black ran through with his sword.

There was a broad piazza, or high porch in
front; and, finding no means of entering the building save the doors which were closed, Mark determined to demand admittance at the great front
entrance.   He left Lieutenant Black at the south
end of the house, Bill Simms was in the rear, Sis
at the north wing, while Alec was to remain on the
piazza, as it would be nearest to the major.   All
were to keep their positions unless summoned by

the major to come to his aid. Mark went to the door and rapped lightly. There being no response, he rapped again louder than before, and still receiving no answer, he struck the door with the butt end of his revolver, a blow which made it tremble.

Listening carefully, he was soon rewarded by a light footstep inside.

" That is surely a woman's footstep," he thought.

The door opened just a little, and he heard a whispered:

" Who are you?"

Quickly throwing all his force against the door, he pushed it open wide enough to enter, and sprang into a dark corridor. As he did so, he heard the voice of a negro woman exclaim,

" De good lawd a massy!" and the sound of retreating feet on the carpeted hall, fell on his ears; but some one remained, and he grappled with this person. The slender wrist he caught, he knew to be a woman's.

" Come, I won't harm you," he said in an undertone. " Get me a light. Lead me to a room where there is a light."

She made no answer, and he pushed her back toward the rear end of the hall, where there was a door opening into an apartment on the right. Into this he forced his prisoner. It was too dark to recognize her features. Pushing her into the apartment on the right, Mark took a match from his pocket and struck it, and lighted a candle that stood on the low mantel. Turning, he saw the face of his astonished prisoner, and, starting back with an exclamation of wonder, he gasped:

" Elsie!"

She stood giving him a look of cold, though tender reproach. For a full minute, neither spoke. Then recovering himself, he asked:

" Elsie, in Heaven's name, why are you here?"

" Do you come for any one in this house?"

" Is there a Confederate colonel here?"

" Yes." Her face was pale as death, and her voice faltered as she answered his question. " But he is wounded and would die if an attempt were made to remove him," she added in a broken voice.

Mark then asked:

" Has he any troops with him?"

" No, he is alone." He saw tears gathering in her eyes and asked:

" Elsie, is that colonel your father?"

" He is."

" God forgive me. I would die before I would harm him."

" Where are you going?"

" Back to camp to perjure myself," he answered. " I will swear there is no Confederate here."

"Mark, Mark!" She held her hand toward him, and he paused. "Will you do this for—for me?"

For a moment a flood of emotion swept over him, and he almost forgot himself. He had taken a step toward her, when he paused and said:

"Yes, and I would do a thousand times more."

Quickly wheeling about, he left the house and calling Alec, Black, and the others, returned to his troops in the peach orchard. In ten minutes they were on their way to their camp, which was reached at daylight. In a charge that day Lieutenant Black was killed. Mark never mentioned the affair to any one, until after the fall of Atlanta.

Three days after the capture of the city, he and Alec were together, when the latter said:

"ELSIE!"

"Mark, you remember the night we went to capture the colonel at the old stone house?"

"Yes."

"Well, I would like to know whom you saw there?"

25

" Elsie Cole. "

" I thought so. You need not have been afraid of telling me. I'd a been racked on the rack, burnt on the stake, drawn through a thorn thicket and squeezed to death in a cider-press, before I would have peached. "

" Alec, I never doubted you, but having been untrue to my trust, I did not want to make another an accessory to my crime. "

" He was there? "

" Yes. "

" Who was it? "

" Elsie's father. "

For a moment Alec was silent, then in his characteristic manner he seized his friend's hand and cried:

" Mark, I am proud of you, cussed if I ain't. You have showed yourself a man with a heart as big as an ox, and I know it. Talk about duty and sentiment and all that, but I would not give a tinker's cuss for a man who would sacrifice a friend, because he holds to a different notion of things. But, Mark, " and then his face grew more mysterious, and his voice dropped almost to a whisper, " tell me what all this mystery is? Why don't you propose to that girl, whom you love, and marry her? What is in the way? Is it me? If it is I'll swear I'll put myself out of the way very soon. "

" You are not in the way, Alec."

" Why don't you marry her, then?"

" *Because I already have a wife!*"

Alec uttered a yell and stared at his cousin as if he thought him suddenly gone mad.

CHAPTER XIX.

THE CLOUDS ROLL AWAY.

"Yes, Alec, I am a married man and have been all these years," continued Mark Stevens in a low, melancholy voice. "I don't blame you for starting and staring at me. There you have it all. Alec, —you know what a villain I am, and I would not blame you, if you cut my acquaintance entirely."

For several minutes Alec Stevens was silent. They had walked a long distance into the suburbs of the city, and reached a dismantled fort. Alec sat down on a gun-carriage and with his honest brow gathered into a knot, tried hard to solve the difficult and delicate problem.

Could it be possible that his dearest friend for whom he had so often risked his life, and for whom he would have staked his all, was a villain? Alec would not have listened to such an imputation from other lips, and even now it seemed impossible. Mark could not have been all these years living a double life. Alec's voice was somewhat husky, when he asked:

"Mark, when was it? Before the war began?"

"Yes, before I ever saw Elsie at your home in Florida," the major answered.

"Where is your wife?"

"I don't know. Heaven knows I would give all I possess to know."

"Did she desert you?"

"No."

"You left her?"

"No."

"Well, who?—how?—what in thunder happened to separate you anyway? Did the earth split in two and one slide off on each side?"

"We were torn asunder within two hours after we were married."

Alec sat on the cannon gazing in open-mouthed amazement at his cousin for several seconds, and, at last, finding voice, asked:

"Who did it?"

"I don't know."

"Well, but your wife's family name, you could surely find her by——"

"I never knew her name," Mark interrupted. "Nor do I know from whence she came."

"Oh, thunderation! Mark, are you mad—what kind of a cock-and-a-bull story are you telling me anyway?"

"Be patient and I will relate this melancholy

story, which may throw some light on the mystery that has enshrouded my life. When you left me in college, you know how ambitious I was to finish up my education, and get out into the great, busy world. After you left me at old Harvard, I studied so hard that my mind became confused. Horace, Plato and Integral Calculus became badly mixed in my brain, and I failed to sleep. I went to a physician, who instead of prescribing rest and fresh air for my insomnia, dosed me with bromide until my mind was full of wild fantasies, and then to cap the climax with his stupidity, hurried me off to an asylum for the insane.

"I have little knowledge of how I came there, and still less of what transpired while I was there. It seems my bromide delirium took a strange turn. My mind was full of horses and lovely maidens. Like Don Quixote, I imagined myself some knight of the past centuries, destined to rescue a fair lady from some enchanted castle, and one day while riding on horseback about the grounds with my attendant, we came upon a patient, fair and young, accompanied by her attendant, also riding on horseback. In my mad fancy, I supposed this the lady whom I was to rescue. I charged down upon the attendant, and with the affrighted girl fled through the open gate. She was a superb horse-woman, as I remember her now, and lovely as

Venus. In our mad ride, we outstripped our pursuers, went to a local preacher's house, about five miles from the institution, and were married. Within an hour after, we were both arrested, and taken back to the institution, from which my friends immediately removed me, and in a few weeks I recovered. My recollection of the whole affair is vague and dream-like, yet it has left a lasting impression on my life."

At the conclusion of Mark's story, Alec gave vent to a prolonged whistle and exclaimed:

"Shades of the Arabian Nights, Don Quixote outdone! I'll be hanged if I know whether to laugh or cry. Mark, have you made any great effort to learn who your insane bride was?"

"Yes, I have searched everywhere, and done everything possible to find her. All that I could learn is that her parents, who were wealthy, became indignant at the carelessness of the officials and removed her. I did hear an unreliable story about her recovering almost immediately on her removal. She had been entered under an assumed name. Her friends hoped that she might recover, and the world never know that she had been in such an institution. She was from some distant state, and every clew to her identity is lost."

"What are your recollections of the affair?"

"Very meagre. I seemed actuated by some

inward impulse wholly uncontrollable. Horace, Ovid and bromide badly befuddle the brain, and bring up strange fancies."

"I suppose you remember how she looked?"

"Yes," he answered slowly and sadly. "To me she was the perfection of beauty and grace. She was young, childlike and innocent; but whether dark or fair, I have no recollection. She was no type. In beauty she stood alone, no antecedents, no followers and no successors. To me she is an ideal, a dream, bright as the morning, fair as the day, when there is not a cloud in the sky. Did I love her then? Yes. Do I love her yet? I certainly do, but as the recollection of a bright dream which it is a pleasure to recall. You may call me still mad, but through all these years, I have felt a moral obligation to this wedded unknown. I never loved any one more than I love her. I never loved any one so ardently as I love Elsie Cole; yet with all my love for Elsie, there constantly rings in my ears, the word 'duty, duty and honor to the one whom you wedded in the darkest hour of your existence!'"

A serio-comic expression took possession of Alec's features as he responded:

"Mark, I'll be hanged if I believe you have recovered your good sense yet."

"Why?"

"That marriage is no marriage at all. That wife was a dream, and I think you got too much of Ovid's Metamorphoses in your noggin. You were drunk on lore and bromide, and you have not got sober yet. After all that has passed between you and Elsie, you love each other. That other marriage was a dream,—forget it and have a real wedding."

"I can't."

"Why?"

"My honor."

"Tell Elsie all about it. She is a sensible girl and will laugh at such a notion. A contract made when neither party is *compos mentis* is wholly invalid. Elsie will look over all that, unless she is not the girl I take her to be."

"But the other?"

"Oh, the dream-wife. Why she is nothing to you. Forget her."

Mark slowly shook his head as he answered:

"Alec, I don't blame you for thinking me still mad. You do not know, and the world can never know, how strangely I am impressed by the dream-wife as you call her. It was not all a dream. To me she is more reality than dream. I have seen her a thousand times since, and if I should dwell long on her I would go mad in earnest. I can't explain to you how her vision rises before me every time I have thought of matrimony, and madly as I love Elsie, this figure comes between us when I think of her and says, 'I am your wife, will you desert me?' What can I do under such circumstances?"

"I swear, I don't know," Alec answered. Soon after, they rose from the gun and went back to their camp. Mark watched his cousin, as he went to his quarters and murmured:

"He is the most remarkable man I ever knew. He loves Elsie as devotedly as I; yet, knowing me to have been a villain all these years, he still insists on our marriage. Alas, poor Alec, there never lived another such as you."

The above occurred on November 13th, and on the morning of November 14, 1864, Sherman marched from Atlanta with sixty-five thousand men, in two columns, commanded respectively by Generals Howard and Slocum, and preceded by General Kilpatrick with five thousand cavalry, on his famous march to the sea. The army subsisted by ravaging the country, wherein they found ample supplies, leaving a desolate waste of smoking and blackened ruins behind. They also met very little opposition on their march of thirty-six days through the heart of Georgia. It was a military promenade, requiring very little skill in the performance, and as little personal prowess.

On that march, Mark often wondered what had become of Elsie and her father. Were they sharing the hard fate of these poor people, who were rendered homeless and deprived of the means of sustaining life? Sometimes his heart almost rebelled against Sherman's cruel orders. When he saw women and children, some of the latter of tender age weeping at sight of blazing homes, he thought, " What a monster is war!" Why is it that the weak and innocent are the greatest sufferers?

Finally, as the Federal army approached the Atlantic seaboard, they attacked and captured Fort McAllister, on the Ogeechee River. That was on the 13th of December, and four days later, Sherman appeared before Savannah and demanded the surrender of that city. Hardee was there with fifteen thousand men, and on the 20th abandoned the city and fled to Charleston. On the 21st, Sherman entered the city in triumph. By his march through Georgia, he discovered that the Confederacy in that region had lost its strength. To every observer it was quite apparent that its days were numbered.

November 8, 1864, Abraham Lincoln had been re-elected to the presidency of the United States by an overwhelming majority over General McClellan, the Democratic nominee. His re-election was conclusive evidence to the world and to himself that his course in putting down the Confederacy was approved by the North, and on the 19th of December, he issued a call for three hundred thousand men to finish the war. On the 25th of November, an attempt was made to burn New York, but it failed. On the 30th, Hood with forty thousand men attacked General Schofield eight miles from Nashville, where, with only seventeen thousand troops, he successfully resisted four desperate assaults of the enemy, and then fell back to Nashville and joined Thomas. Hood's loss was reported at six thousand. On the 15th and 16th of December, Hood was defeated by General Thomas, and fled, pursued by the victorious Federal troops.

On December 6th, Mr. Chase, ex-secretary of the treasury, was appointed chief justice of the United States supreme court. On December 20th, General Stoneman captured some Confederate forts, salt works, lead mines and railroad bridges at Saltville, in East Tennessee.

The year 1864 closed in general disaster to the Confederacy, Sherman had broken the Confederate power in Georgia, destroying its communications with the States on the Mississippi, and taken Savannah. General Thomas had broken up Hood's army in Tennessee, and Grant had closely beleaguered the southern army in Virginia, within Richmond and its defences; while Sheridan had quite ruined the army of Early in the Shenandoah valley.

As the year 1865 dawned, the end was drawing near. On January 15th, Fort Fisher on the coast of North Carolina was captured by General Terry. On the 16th, a magazine exploded, killing and wounding three hundred Union men. On the 17th, a Federal monitor was blown up by torpedoes in Charleston Harbor. On the 20th, the southern troops evacuated Corinth, Mississippi. On the 3d, General Hood surrendered his command in the southern army to General Taylor. On the 21st, General Breckenridge became the Confederate secretary of war, and southern commissioners sought a peace interview with the president, hoping yet to save something; but the opportunity had long since passed. Two days later, congress, by joint resolutions, voted to submit an amendment called the 14th Amendment, abolishing slavery, and nine States ratified the amendment within the next month.

On the 5th of February, General Grant was defeated at Hatcher's Run, where he had met a similar defeat on 27th of October. On the 17th, Columbia, South Carolina, was burned. On the 18th, Sherman took possession of Charleston, and

Major, now General, Anderson raised the flag over Fort Sumter, which he had been compelled to lower, after a most gallant resistance, four years before.

Strange emotions swayed the breast of Mark Stevens as he entered the city of Charleston after the flames had been extinguished. What a sad change in the once proud, gay southern city. Many elegant mansions which had stood in the town when he left were in ashes or ruins. And the once happy families—where were they? He wandered to the beautiful suburban home of Colonel Cole. It was deserted now. No glad, laughing eyes met him at the gate. No gay, happy voice was there to welcome him. He walked through the silent halls, heavily oppressed with woe. All were gone. Not even the echo of an old familiar song remained.

The house had been used alternately as hospital, a barracks and a stable. It was sadly defaced, and the carpets and most of the furniture had almost entirely disappeared. He found one parlor chair, minus the upholstering, in the hall. An old, decayed sofa, faded and worn and only the shadow of its former self, was in one of the upper chambers.

He wandered to her favorite room, and almost shed tears. Oh, what a change! In one corner was the skeleton of her piano, at which she used to sit and sing such songs as seemed to charm the seraphims; but it was husky now and gave forth only discordant sounds. It was all that was left to remind any one of the fair being, who, in the years gone by, had been the joy and sunlight of a happy home. There is little consolation in wandering about the tombs of buried happiness, and Mark returned to his regiment.

He met Alec, who had been wandering about the ruined city. For once, the light of mischief had gone out of his eyes, and in a voice of sadness, he said:

"It don't look like Charleston. It's not the Charleston we used to know. I've been all over it and don't see much that's familiar. I was up at the church and saw where a shell had torn away all but two of the ten commandments: 'Thou shalt not kill,' and 'Thou shalt not commit adultery;' but this will soon be over. The rebels are everywhere following my example, deserting and coming back to the old flag."

On the 4th of March, Lincoln was inaugurated for his second term. On the 10th, General Bragg was defeated at Kingston, North Carolina. On the 8th of February, the Confederate congress adjourned and never met again.

When Sherman left Charleston in pursuit of the rebels, Mark and Alec were both glad to leave the dismal place. Charleston seemed only to mock them as the grinning skeleton of a once-beloved friend. After a three days' rest at Fayettesville, Sherman moved his army forward in another distracting march, puzzling his antagonists. On March 16th, while moving toward Goldsboro, his troops fought twenty thousand Confederates under General Hardee at Averysboro and defeated them.

Mark's regiment was with Slocum's division of Sherman's army, and the day after the fight at Averysboro, they wheeled to their right, crossed South River, swollen by rains, and took the road to Goldsboro, whither Howard, farther east, was marching, "wallowing along the miry roads."

On the 18th, both wings were within a few miles of the place, and Sherman, thinking there would be no more opposition to his advance, left Slocum and started across the country to see Howard. He had gone scarce six miles, when he was startled by the sudden, angry roar of cannon behind him, evidently coming from the spot where Slocum's army lay. While listening to the heavy explosions, wondering what they could mean, a staff officer galloped up and quieted his anxiety by saying it was merely an affair between Carlin's division and the Confederate cavalry, and that the latter were in full retreat. In a few moments, other officers arrived with the alarming intelligence that Johnston's whole army near Bentonville had assailed Slocum. Comprehending at once the new, dangerous position of affairs, he sent word back to Slocum to stand solely on the defensive, until he could forward troops to his relief. Officers immediately dashed off over the country, bearing dispatches—one to Blair, to make a night march with his corps, to Falling Creek church, and with three divisions of the Fifteenth Corps, to come up in Johnston's rear, from the direction of Cox's bridge,—another to Howard to move at daylight on Bentonville, leaving his wagons behind.

While thus engaged, couriers arrived from Schofield and Terry. Ordering the former to march on Goldsboro, and the latter to move to Cox's bridge, ten miles above, and establish a crossing there, he once more gave his individual attention to Slocum, and the unexpected battle thus suddenly thrown upon him.

He found the latter not the least alarmed. He had chosen an admirable position and placed his artillery so as to sweep the front. He then sent Morgan's division to establish another line about half a mile in advance. Against this Johnston advanced in overwhelming numbers and hurled it back in confusion, capturing three guns and caissons. Slocum, seeing the heavy force opposed to him, at once deployed the two divisions of the

26

Fourteenth Corps, under General Davis, and hurried forward at their utmost speed the two divisions of the Twentieth Corps. A line of barricades was hastily prepared, and the whole force put strictly on the defensive. In the mean time, Kilpatrick, aroused by the roar of artillery, came thundering down the roads and massed his squadrons on the left. It was now four o'clock in the afternoon, and Slocum had hardly got ready to meet the enemy, when they came pouring in upon him like an avalanche. In three massive columns they swept up to his frail barricades and threatened by mere weight of numbers to carry everything before them. Mowed down by Federal batteries and the deliberate volleys of infantry, the first column recoiled, when the second, undaunted by the repulse of the first, charged with a cheer; but right in its path stood Davis' Corps—which had won such signal honors on the bloody field of Chickamauga—and stopped it with one terrible blow. The whole fury of the attack spent itself in less than an hour, and yet in that time the enemy had made six successive assaults, and in the last charge had broken Slocum's line; but it rallied and, charging in turn, drove Johnston back. So close and desperate was the combat, that many of the Confederate dead lay within the lines of the government troops and around the headquarters of the generals.

It was in that last mad charge, that Mark happened to be near Sis, when the brave boy dropped his gun. Leaping from his saddle, he ran to him and caught him in his arms as he was sinking to the earth. His face bore a peaceful look, almost to be envied in all that turmoil and uproar. Mark spoke to him, shook him, then gently laid him on the ground soaked with his own blood, and folded the arms of the youth across his breast. They found him thus when they came next day to bury the dead.

Mark had the third horse shot under him that day. He sat on the fourth, under a tree, when he heard a wild, whirring noise, then came a blinding flash as if a bolt of lightning had struck his head. There was a deafening explosion, and it seemed as if the tree had been torn up by the roots. He felt himself sinking. Horse and rider went down, and he was conscious of his steed making some spasmodic plunges, while it uttered one or two almost human cries of agony.

Mark was carried to the rear. Though his horse had been killed by the explosion of the shell, he had not been touched. A branch torn from the tree had struck his shoulder and he was badly shocked, bruised and insensible when taken to the rear. When he recovered, the fighting was over for the present.

As has been stated on another page, many of the Confederates, in their wild, impetuous charge, rushed into the Union lines. Alec saw a fine opportunity to cut off a small detachment of these, and, by a skilful flank movement, dashed into their rear and swooped up the entire party, whom he quickly marched to the rear. The party was led by two brave young officers, whose uniforms were faded and mud-stained, and whose hard-pinched features told of privation and suffering for a cause which they now knew to be hopelessly lost. Alec led the two young Confederates aside and said:

"You fellows are brave as hedgehogs, and I am going to parole you, and give you the liberty of the camp. I know that men so brave as you must be honorable——"

"Alec Stevens, a Yankee! Heavens! is it possible?" interrupted one.

"Dick——Dick! what, great guns! tar and pitch! is it really you? Why, I thought you were off on a ship somewhere."

Dick hastily explained that he had been aboard the *Alabama* when she sank, and that he came to America with his cousin Charley Cole to try battling for the Confederacy on land; but both Dick and Charley, for the other was Charley, wanted to know how Alec had "flopped." Alec made an explanation, declaring that he had felt just like a fool all the time he was fighting the old flag. It is doubtful if his explanation was satisfactory to the prisoners; but Charley Cole said:

" I think that you did a wise thing, Alec, whether you acted from principle or not, for the bottom is knocked out of the Southern Confederacy, and the old tub is sinking. "

" You are right there, boys; but now that this present little squall is over, make yourselves at home. Here is a cracker apiece to amuse your stomachs, until supper is ready. I must go and look after our major. The last I saw of him he was batting off a shell with his elbow, and I want to see if there's enough left of him to hold a funeral over. I will be back soon, and we will talk over old times and enjoy ourselves. "

Alec expected to find Mark dead, and was rejoiced to learn that he was alive and not seriously injured. The major had been badly shaken up, and the surgeon declared that he must be kept quiet for a few hours.

That night Mark lay in a hospital tent on the field listening to the far-off thunder of cannon and the rattle of musketry, which seemed to proclaim to everybody that the four years' storm was subsiding. It was midnight, and he was in a semi-conscious state produced by the narcotics of the surgeon, when he heard the nurse ask some one:

"When did you come?"

"I reached the camp but two hours ago, heard of his injuries and, after a long search, found him."

How like the tender notes of a fairy's shell, as she winds them mellow and clear on the glistening beach, enchanting the sailor, sounded those silver tones. He half opened his eyes, and, weak as he was from the shock, he could have sworn he saw Elsie at his side, arrayed in riding habit, her face very white, but beautiful as ever. He tried to speak, but could not. The power of the drug held his tongue. He heard her ask:

"Is he dangerously hurt?"

"Oh, no," the nurse answered. "It is only a shock to his nervous system, and with proper care he will be over it in a day or two. He is very still now; but it is the effect of an opiate the doctor gave him. There is a widow lady living just across the street. You had better go there and stay until morning."

"I will. At eight I will call, for perhaps by that time I can see him?"

"Perhaps."

Mark again sank into a state of unconsciousness. He awoke next morning and was trying to settle in his own mind the incidents of the preceding night, when Alec came bounding into the tent crying:

" By George, Mark!—thunder and lightning!—
it's all right——" He was almost out of breath
with running and excitement. " I've been all night
working on it, and have just got it fixed. The
problem of five years is solved."

" What do you mean, Alec? What problem
have you solved?"

" Your problem. You,—Great Jehosaphat!
don't you understand me? It's you. You married the right girl after all."

" Alec, are you crazy?"

" No; but you have been all along, or you
might have saved yourself lots of trouble and me
too. I tell you, you married the right girl. Look
here," and he held up a clipping from an old
newspaper. Mark glanced at it, and saw that it
was one of the many accounts of his mad flight and
marriage from the insane asylum.

" Where did you get that?" he asked.

" Charley Cole and Dick Stevens were captured
yesterday, after that shell kissed your face. We
talked nearly all night, and after I had told them
everything else, I told them about you and Elsie
and your runaway from the madhouse with a girl
whom you never knew, never expect to know, and
never will know. Then Charley, he up and says
that girl you eloped with and married, while your
head was full of Horace, Ovid and bromide, was

his sister, Elsie. They had been on a visit in the North, and Elsie, for a temporary nervous trouble, was treated by a quack on bromide, until she had a bromide delirium and was taken there under an assumed name———"

"Elsie! Elsie!" cried Mark at this moment, leaping to his feet and clasping in his arms the beautiful woman who had just entered the tent. "It was you, after all. Oh, Elsie, our love in madness has been perpetuated through all these years. Tell me, darling, you who accepted me for better or for worse, when our minds were clouded, will you still do so, now that the clouds have rolled away?"

Her head rested on his shoulder, and she faintly sobbed:

"Yes!"

Alec, who had retreated to the door at the startling and romantic dénouement, paused for a moment to gaze on the scene, and muttered:

"To think, I have been five years courting another man's wife! It makes me feel like a fool."

"TO THINK, I HAVE BEEN FIVE YEARS COURTING ANOTHER MAN'S WIFE!"

CHAPTER XX.

CONCLUSION.

THE great struggle was almost over. General Grant captured Richmond April 3d. President Davis had fled to Danville. On the 9th, terms were agreed upon between Grant and Lee for the surrender of the latter's army at Appomattox, and next day Lee delivered his farewell address to the army. On the 12th of April, Lee's army, numbering 27,805, was surrendered at Appomattox Court House. The same day, Stoneman defeated the Confederates at Salisbury, North Carolina, and General Conly occupied Mobile, Alabama.

The valiant little South was at last overwhelmed with defeat; but it took four years to do it. Four years, with more than two millions of men and billions of money. Of the two millions of soldiers, two hundred and seventy-five thousand had died on the field of battle and in the hospitals. It has been stated by the adjutant-general of the Confederate army, since the close of the war, that the available Confederate force during the entire war was six hundred thousand men, and that they never had more than two hundred thousand in the field at any one time. This is the only official data we have, and it must be taken as correct. He states that the Confederate force opposing Grant, Sherman and Thomas at the close of the contest was only one hundred thousand. According to the best authority, the Union forces were a million, if they did not exceed that number. According to the best statistics obtainable, the Federal army lost more from deaths on the battle-field, in the hospitals and wounded, than the entire southern army ever enrolled. Victory was won, but we can see at what a terrible price. The contest was fearful, and the cost great. The lost in killed and wounded is not the only loss, and in fact not the greatest. There are hundreds of thousands, disabled by diseases contracted in the army, many thousands of whom are unable to earn a livelihood, and are pensioners on the bounty of a grateful country, that never forgets its brave defenders.

A few weeks before the surrender of Lee's army, yet when all seemed to read the inevitable, there was a handsome, talented young actor, playing an engagement at De Bar's Opera House in St. Louis. The name of this actor, a promising young tragedian, was John Wilkes Booth, the son of the elder Booth. Critics had said that John Wilkes Booth would never equal his father, as an exponent of Shakespearian tragedy, and some think that his sensitive nature was soured and he was jealous of the reputation of his sire. He was a handsome man with a magnificent forehead and fine face. He wore a mustache, as many actors did in those days. One night, Booth played " Richard III." with James Carden, an English actor, in the role, as Richmond. Those who saw Booth that night never forgot him. The soul of the murderous Richard seemed to have found its way back to earth, and taken lodgment in Booth's body. So intense was the interest, that several ladies, unable to endure the strain, were taken away by their escorts. It was a relief when the play was over, and they could breathe freely. Shortly after the performance, Booth was seen to enter a restaurant in company with a lady, who proved to be Maggie Mitchell, the sparkling soubrette, then attracting the attention of the world. The appearance of Booth and Miss Mitchell attracted no special attention. A boy showed them to a private dining room, and waited on them himself. Being a youngster, he heard more of their conversation than he should, and soon discovered that Booth was making violent love to Miss Mitchell, who had evidently rejected him. Booth was very much in earnest, and, finally working himself into a passion, he straightened himself up and, with a dramatic gesture, said:

"Maggie Mitchell, I love you! You know I speak the truth. Should you reject me now, you shall never, so help me God, hear another word of love from me; and I swear to you that when next you hear from me, it shall be in connection with some terrible and desperate deed." *

Miss Mitchell, who, up to this time, had been tolerably composed, began to cry bitterly. This aroused in Booth's breast the sense of the gentleman, inherent in him, and he attempted to soothe her. He had entirely forgotten the boy, who stood at the other end of the room a spellbound spectator. At sight of the lad, the actor's eyes suddenly flashed with anger, causing the youngster to tremble in his shoes; but Booth said nothing beyond asking for some water. The boy brought it, and in a few moments Maggie Mitchell became somewhat composed, and they left the restaurant.

John Wilkes Booth was a moody man, who seemed brooding over real or imaginary wrongs. Sunday, April 9, 1865, he passed almost entirely

---

* The above is from the personal statement of a waiter in Merkle's restaurant, in 1865, on the corner of Sixth and Chestnut Streets, who was the boy in question, and saw and heard the above. This statement was first published in the Cincinnati *Tribune* a year or two ago.

alone with an actor named Charles Chrone, who for a long time played " leads and heavies" in Ben De Bar's St. Louis stock company. Mr. Chrone

" WHEN NEXT YOU HEAR FROM ME, IT SHALL BE IN CONNECTION WITH SOME TERRIBLE DEED."

says that he discovered that there was something on Booth's mind that day, and he tried to get at the trouble, but was unable to do so. His nature was peculiar. He was sometimes enthusiastic and jolly; but usually he was taciturn, and seemed to be meditating on something. Chrone supposed his present melancholy was the result of some adverse criticism on his ability as an actor, in which he had been unfavorably contrasted with his father.

On the fatal April 14, 1865, Booth was seen in Washington City. About midday, he went to Ford's theatre on Tenth Street. Harry Ford saw him sitting on the steps, and, knowing his strong southern sentiments, said:

"Well, Booth, President Lincoln and General Grant are going to witness Laura Keene in the 'American Cousin' to-night!" Booth raised his fierce eyes to the manager and gave him a silent stare. With a laugh, Harry Ford added: "Yes, Lincoln and Grant will occupy one box, and Lee and Davis another."

At this, Booth broke forth with:

"Lee!—Lee is a coward and a traitor to his country, or he would never have surrendered. He should have died at his post, and could have whipped Grant yet."

He went away and was seen no more about the theatre, until after the curtain had rung up and the performance begun. Then he came to the theatre, and as he passed the box-office, he looked into the window, and, putting his arm through, placed a cigar, which he had partly smoked, on a shelf inside, and said, in mock heroic style:

> "Whoe'er this cigar does displace
> Must meet Wilkes Booth face to face."

Then he passed into the theatre, and later in the evening, while Mr. Ford and his assistant Joe Sessford were in the treasurer's office, they heard a pistol shot. They thought at first that it was the pistol fired by Mr. Harry Hawk, as Asa Trenchard in "Our American Cousin;" but Sessford said it was too early in the evening, and suggested that it must be an accident. They opened a little window and, looking into the theatre, saw Booth crouching on the stage, with a knife in his hand. Even then, they could not tell what had happened, and no one seemed to know. They at first thought that some one had insulted Booth, and he had pursued the man across the stage, and several minutes elapsed before they learned the terrible truth.

While the interest of everybody was attracted to the stage, Booth had entered the theatre unperceived, made his way to the president's box and, with a Derringer pistol, shot him in the back of the head. The sharp report startled, stunned and petrified everybody. The president sat bolt upright for a moment, then swayed and sank forward, while the assassin, leaping on the stage, holding a gleaming dagger in his hand, shouted:

" *Sic semper tyrannis !* " He was booted and spurred for the night ride, and shouting to the audience: " The South is avenged !" escaped by a back stage door, mounted a horse that was in readiness for him, dashed across the Anacostia, and found temporary shelter in Maryland. In the excitement and confusion, it was noticed by some that he was quite lame, and limped as he ran from the stage.

Laura Keene the actress was one of the first to realize the awful truth. She saw the president swaying in his chair and ran to him as he fell. She clasped his dying head in her arms, and his life-blood stained her beautiful robes, while her tears mingled with those of the grief-stricken and horrified friends and relatives. The president never spoke after he was shot. He was carried to a house near, and expired next morning at twenty-two minutes past seven o'clock. There was a conspiracy to kill Lincoln, Johnson, the vice-president, and Seward, secretary of state. An assault was made on Seward, and both he and his son were dangerously stabbed; but they recovered. For awhile, there was the wildest excitement in Washington. People believed that there was a general and wide-spread conspiracy to overthrow the country by assassination; but the conspiracy evidently never extended beyond a few deluded fanatics, who should have been kept in madhouses to prevent their doing injury.

Near Front Royal, in Virginia, there still stands the old Garrett Homestead. About the 18th day of April, Captain Jett and a handsome young man, who was quite lame, came to the house. Jett told Mr. Garrett that the stranger was a wounded Confederate soldier; that he had surrendered with Lee's army and gone home to Maryland, where they demanded that he take the oath of allegiance, which he would not do, and that he was now on his way to join Johnston's army in North Carolina.

"Of course, in that case, I will do what I can for him," said the farmer, who had entertained some suspicions that they were not what they pretended to be.

This handsome stranger had very little to say. He spent most of his time alone, or with Mr. Garrett's son William, who had been a Confederate soldier. He talked most with the children, and especially a little three-year-old girl, of whom he became very fond, and called his little blue-eyed pet. For hours he would lie on the grass in the yard alone and speak with no one. While playing with some of the younger children on the grass, a little girl saw on his arm the tattooed initials "J. W. B."

27

"What are those letters for?" she asked.

"Why, child, those are the initials of my name, —James W. Boyd."

This was the name by which Captain Jett had introduced him. Mr. Boyd claimed to be from Baltimore, and stated that he was there when the Massachusetts troops were attacked. When he came to the Garrett house, he had a very rude pair of crutches; but William Garrett, who had been wounded in the Confederate army, and still had a fine pair of crutches, gave them to him. William Garrett also had a Confederate uniform, which the pretended Mr. Boyd wanted, and agreed to exchange with him.

"I am going back into the army and need your uniform; and you are going to be a citizen and need my citizen's clothes," he argued.

It was well for Mr. Garrett that the exchange was not made.

There was nothing whatever in the man's manner that would lead one to suspect that he was the terrible criminal he afterward proved to be. The first night he was at the Garrett house, he slept in the same room with Jack and William Garrett. The next day, he was with William Garrett most of the day, without arousing his suspicions. William had a pistol, and they went to shoot at a mark. The stranger claimed to be an excellent marksman, and said that he could fire five balls in succession through a knot-hole in the gate some two inches in diameter. Taking a position about two rods off, he fired all five shots and, leaning on his crutches, sent William to ascertain the result. As he could find no mark of the bullets on the gate, Boyd insisted that they had all gone through the knot-hole in the gate. When they came to reload the pistol, however, they found all the five bullets still in it, and he laughed as heartily as any at the mishap.

One day, while the family were at dinner, Jack Garrett, who had been to town, brought a paper in, saying:

"President Lincoln has been shot, and they have offered one hundred thousand dollars for the man who did it."

"Gracious! don't I wish he would come this way, and I could capture him!" said William.

The lame stranger turned his melancholy eyes upon him, and asked:

"Would you betray him for one hundred thousand dollars if you could?"

"I would, indeed. One hundred thousand dollars is a great lot of money."

The stranger turned away and became thoughtful, and had very little to say after that. Some time after that, the man called Harold came from

Bowling Green, and he and Boyd were seen talking together for a long time. This was the first time that Mr. Garrett had his suspicions fully aroused. On the way back from the woods, they paused near the fence and held a long conversation. Then Boyd came to the house and was standing on the porch in his shirt-sleeves, when some soldiers passed down the road toward Bowling Green. He seemed very uneasy, and Mr. Garrett said to him:

" You seem very much excited. Have you been doing anything that makes you afraid of soldiers? If you have, you will have to find some other place to stay than here. "

" Oh, no, " he quickly replied. " I did get into a little difficulty over in Maryland, and one man I believe was killed ; but it was nothing with which the soldiers could possibly have anything to do. " Shortly after this, he and Harold again went off into the wood and did not come back until nearly night.

Meanwhile, Mr. Garrett and his two sons had discussed the matter well, and finally decided that the two men must be members of Mosby's band, and that their object perhaps was to steal horses. On their return, Mr. Garrett informed them that they could not sleep in the house.

" Why can't we sleep in the house?" the lame man asked. This man, as the reader supposes, was none other than John Wilkes Booth. " If you will not let us sleep in the house, let us sleep under the house."

"That would not do, for the dogs would get after you."

"Let us go into one of the outbuildings, then," plead the lame man. To this Mr. Garrett finally consented, and they went into the barn, which was filled on one side with corn-blade fodder, the other side containing a lot of farming utensils and furniture belonging to refugees from Front Royal. After they went to the barn, William Garrett, still fearing they might be horse thieves, went out and locked the door with a padlock on the outside, so they could not get out without making a noise; but on returning to the house he was still not satisfied, and told his brother Jack they would take their pistols and go and sleep in the corn crib near the barn, that they might be ready to prevent any attempt to steal their horses.

About two o'clock in the morning, they were awakened by a terrible commotion at the house, and both Jack and William ran to see what was the trouble. They found their father in his night clothes in the custody of the soldiers, who threatened to kill him if he did not reveal the whereabouts of the two men. Jack Garrett, coming up, said:

"I will show you where the two men are," and

the officers released Mr. Garrett and took his two sons into custody. " The men are in the barn," Jack added.

" Show us the way," commanded the officer, and a moment later the soldiers had surrounded the barn, while Jack and William were kept under arrest. One of the detectives called the name of Booth and demanded his surrender, and, unlocking the door, pushed Jack Garrett in, with orders for him to go and tell the others to come out. Jack Garrett, trembling with dread, approached the point where Booth was lying on the corn blades and said:

" The soldiers are here after you, and they want you to surrender. If you don't come out, they threaten to burn the barn and destroy our property."

" Get out of here, young man, or I will take your life," Booth whispered, desperately. " You have betrayed me."

Jack Garrett tried to convince him of the folly of resistance and appealed to Booth to prevent the destruction of property. Booth grew violent, threatened to kill him, and Jack came out and told the officer that he would not surrender. The officer then placed the Garrett brothers a short distance from the barn and set a light directly in front of them. Two men were placed to guard them with instructions to kill them at the first shot Booth or his companion fired at any of the soldiers.

Booth, who had been watching the proceeding through a crack in the barn, on hearing the order of the officer, shouted at the top of his voice:

" That is unfair; those men are innocent. These people do not know who I am."

The officer revoked the order he had given, and Colonel Conger, one of the detectives, ordered William to pile dry brush against the corner of the barn, so that it could be fired. He had commenced doing this, when Booth called to him:

" Young man, you had better stop that. If you put any more against that place, I will shoot you."

Colonel Conger then ordered William to stop, and Lieutenant Baker began a parley for the surrender of the fugitives. Booth was determined from the first that he would not be taken alive, and he so informed Lieutenant Baker. Harold, however, wanted to give himself up, and Booth, after calling him an arrant coward, virtually drove him out of the barn into the hands of the officers. Another long parley between Baker and Booth ensued, during which Booth begged the officer to draw his men off fifty yards, then twenty-five yards, and at last came down to ten yards, and give him a chance for his life.

" Be fair, captain," said Booth, coolly—" be fair and give me a show for my life. I could have killed you a dozen times to-night; but I took you to be a brave man. Now give me a chance for my life."

"You must surrender," replied Baker. "We came to take you prisoner, not to kill you."

"I will never be taken alive," retorted Booth. "You may make up your mind I will fight to the death."

Hardly had the last words died upon his lips, before a blaze shot up among the dry fodder. Colonel Conger had, during the talk, slipped around to the back of the barn and, lighting a handful of dry straw, had passed it through a crack in the boards and fired the building. The combustible material inside the barn burned like tinder, and in a moment the whole inside of the building was a blaze of light, and in the middle Booth was seen leaning on his crutches, with his carbine in his hands, trying to get a shot at his enemies. He could not see beyond the light which surrounded him, while those outside could see plainly. At last when the fire was fast approaching him, he started for the door as if about to take his last desperate chance for life. He had only advanced a step or two, when Boston Corbett, a sergeant, got an aim at him through a crack. There was a sharp report, and Booth dropped his crutches and fell, shot through the neck.

Lieutenant Baker and William Garrett ran into

"BOOTH WAS SEEN LEANING ON HIS CRUTCHES, TRYING TO GET
A SHOT AT HIS ENEMIES."
(See page 434)
After an original drawing by Freeland A. Carter.

. . . give . . . a chance for

. . . . . . and Baker. **We**
. . . . . not to . . . you . .
. . . . retorted Booth.
. . . . . I . . . .

. . . . his lips.
. . . . the dry . . .
. . . . around
. . . . . . a handful of
. . . . . .
. . . .
. . . . and a
. . . . with a
. . . .
. . . .
. . . . **He**
. . . .
. . . .

the burning building and carried him to the house and laid him on the porch with his head toward the door. He made several efforts to speak; but only inarticulate gurgling sounds issued from his wounded throat. They tried to place him on a mattress; but he would not let them; nor would he allow them to put a pillow under his head. He was suffering such intolerable agony, that to move him was torture. He could utter but few words for the wound was in his throat.

. " Tell mother," he began, and then the detective who bent his ear close to his lips heard him add, " that I died for my country."

The detectives would allow no one to come near him, for they wanted all the secrets he had to reveal. They were constantly bending over him, to catch any word he might utter. When they wanted anything they ordered the Garrett girls, who pale and horrified stood on the porch gazing on the scene, to bring it to them. Pieces of cloth saturated with brandy were frequently held to Booth's lips, and he sucked it eagerly. This seemed to revive him for the time being; but he was of course growing weaker all the while. An eye-witness to the scene said:

" I can never forget the sad scenes of that night. They fixed themselves indelibly upon my mind. I remained around during all the bustle that attended the affair and looked on, little realizing the meaning of what was passing. Booth died just as the sun came up."

This is the history of America's greatest assassination. What inspired John Wilkes Booth to kill the great and good man, just as he was bringing the nation from turmoil, war and bloodshed to peace, is a mystery to this day. Booth had never been active in politics and certainly was deranged. His was not a family of warriors or desperadoes, but scholars. No one had ever before deemed him capable of a desperate or cruel act. His brother Edwin Booth lived to be one of the world's greatest Shakespearian exponents. Undoubtedly the shadow of the great historic crime that inseparably connected the name of Booth with that of Lincoln lay, throughout all his subsequent life, upon the melancholy spirit of Edwin Booth, who died this year (1893), and in the same year, almost at the same time, Ford's Theatre, in which the tragedy occurred, and which had since been used by the government as a national museum, fell and buried a number of employees in its ruins.

There has never been known such a funeral on this continent as that of the martyr president. His body was taken in solemn procession to his home in Springfield, Illinois, by way of Baltimore, Philadelphia, New York, Albany and western cities, everywhere receiving tokens of respect and grief. Funeral honors were displayed in many cities of the land.

On the 18th of April, General Sherman arranged the preliminaries for the surrender of all the remaining Confederate forces under General Johnston, commanding the southern army in North Carolina, with the consent of the Confederate secretary of war and President Davis. This included the basis of a general peace, and a policy of reconstruction; but the Federal government rejected the proposition and ordered hostilities to be resumed. On the 26th of April, Johnston finally surrendered.

Nearly all the armed Confederates had now surrendered. General Kirby Smith and a few men leading the lives of guerillas rather than soldiers were still at large. President Davis at last lost hope and began his flight across Georgia, doubtless intending to make his way to Mexico. On the 10th of May, he was captured in Georgia. On the 26th of the same month, General Kirby Smith, the last leader of a military organization, surrendered his command, and the last shadow of war passed away, leaving the glorious Union stronger and more firmly cemented than ever before, and so, let us hope, it will remain until time shall be no more.

We must not end this volume without personal mention of some of the characters in the story, in which the reader may have some interest. Notwithstanding Dick Stevens failed to build up a great southern empire, Miss Lorena Lancaster, the English beauty, kept her promise, and a year after the war closed she became his wife, and they to-day form one of the happiest families in Charleston. Nearly all our southern friends came out of the war financial wrecks; but they went to work with a hearty good will, building up the devastated country, and it is hoped that the South will soon reach its former power and glory, and even surpass it. They have learned a sad lesson;—let us forgive them, take them by the hand, call them brothers, and remember their wrongs no more.

Alec Stevens fared better than most of his southern relatives. His father's plantation suffered little, save, as Alec puts it, " in the loss of a hundred worthless niggers." Alec got over his love affair with Elsie Cole, when he learned that all the time she had been the wife of another. He soon made another discovery which was very important to his future happiness. It was that his cousin Clara was a very sweet, amiable girl, and that she was very kind to him, even though he had turned Yankee. He found that he could talk to her without " feeling just like a fool," and the upshot of the whole thing was, he and Clara were married shortly after her brother Dick brought home his wife from

England. Colonel Cole survived the war but a few months, and his son Charles, after vainly trying to resurrect the lost fortune of his parents, went to California, where he has been extensively and profitably engaged in fruit growing.

Bill Simms lives at Rising Sun, Indiana, and is regarded as the champion liar of the town. He draws a pension of twenty-two dollars per month, quite sufficient for his modest wants. He is a member of the " G. A. R." and spends most of his time around Grand Army headquarters, or the offices of examining boards, telling stories of the war and "trying for an increase." One, to hear Bill and put any confidence in one-half he says, need not be surprised that victory should perch on the banners of Grant and Sherman, so long as they had Bill Simms with them. And they would be at a loss to tell what those generals would have done, if Bill Simms had not been along.

In Boone County, Kentucky, near the old original Stevens homestead, lives Major Mark Stevens, now past the meridian of life. He is happy with his children and grandchildren about him, while his wife, once known as the " Peerless Elsie of Charleston," seems to still possess a matured beauty, to him more lovely than when she outshone the splendor of the southern sun. The major is not rich, but "well-to-do in the world." He often looks back over the past twelve generations of the Stevens family, to the time when his first ancestor, Hernando Estevan, touched the western continent with Columbus.   By stories of their forefathers for the last four hundred years, in establishing this great republic, he tries to inspire his children and grandchildren with a love for this land of the free and home of the brave, which should be dear to every American, whether native or adopted, and which we trust may forever remain one, complete and indissoluble UNION.

APPENDIX.

CHAPTER I.

ANDREW JOHNSON AND THE RECONSTRUCTION.

At no time during the great struggle of our country was Abraham Lincoln more needed than at his death. After the conflict of arms came the conflict of reorganization, and the same hand that had steered the ship of state safely through the dangerous reefs was now needed to land her in port. Six hours after the death of President Lincoln, Andrew Johnson, his constitutional successor, took the oath of office as president of the United States, which was administered by Chief Justice Chase.

It was believed by many, that the assassination of President Lincoln, was only part of a plan, in which the murder of the cabinet ministers and prominent Republicans was contemplated. Jefferson Davis and many prominent southern people were thought to be in the plot, and large rewards were offered for them; but there was never any evidence implicating the chief or any of his officials. It seems to have been only a plot concocted by a few fanatical, maddened and disappointed southerners about Washington.

After the terrible convulsions produced by the civil war, by which a deep-rooted social system had been overthrown, by the enactment, early in 1865, of the XIII Amendment to the national constitution, the country was far from gliding at once into that peace

28   488

and tranquillity, which was so much desired. The XIII Amendment was as follows:

"SECTION I. Neither slavery nor involuntary servitude, except as punishment for crimes, whereof the party shall have been duly convicted, shall exist within the United States, or any place subject to their jurisdiction.

"SECTION II. Congress shall have power to enforce this article by appropriate legislation."

The slave was free; now what was going to be done with him? That was a serious question in that day. It is a serious question at this day. The leaders of the Republican party were eager to have the black become a citizen of the United States with all the rights and privileges of any white man. The Democrats claimed that their pretended sympathy for the negro was only to get his vote, to perpetuate that party in power. Thus the unfortunate black man has been a bone of contention, much to his detriment, between the two great political parties ever since he became a political factor.

President Johnson took a preliminary step toward reorganization, on April 29, 1865, when he proclaimed the removal of restrictions on commercial intercourse between all the States. A month later he issued a proclamation stating the terms by which the people of the late seceded States, with specified exceptions, might receive full amnesty and pardon, and be reinvested with the right to exercise the functions of citizenship, supposed to have been destroyed by participation in the insurrection. This was followed by the appointment of provisional governors for seven of those States which had formed the original fabric known as the "Confederate States of America," clothed with authority to assemble citizens in convention, who had taken the amnesty oath with power to reorganize State governments, and secure the election of representatives in the national congress.

When Andrew Johnson was inaugurated president, there were painful apprehensions among men who knew him intimately, that he would not act with the party in power. He was from Tennessee and was strongly suspected of Democratic proclivities, which at this time were repugnant to the Republicans. His nomination and election on the ticket with President Lincoln, has proved the folly of political compromises. The Republicans claimed that they had put down the rebellion, and that they should have the reorganization. A pilot was needed at the helm, possessed of a combination of moral and intellectual forces of a rare order, strong and unswerving convictions, sobriety of conduct, firmness of will, a thorough knowledge

ANDREW JOHNSON.

of men, an accurate and impartial judgment, a willingness to take counsel, a clear perception of righteousness, and all the acuteness of a true statesman.

Much as historians and politicians have attempted to mask the cause of the quarrel between Johnson and his Republican cabinet and congress, it arose on the very subject it might have been expected to rise, " the enfranchisement of the negro." Johnson was a southern man with all the prejudices and instincts of a southerner. Although of humble parentage, by his own indomitable will and energy, he had worked his way up, until he now occupied the chief place in the

nation. He was loyal to his government in its hour
of peril; but he could not bring himself to believe in
the doctrine of enfranchisement of the negro. Not
only did it smack of the "doctrine of equality," offensive to every southern man, but he seriously doubted
the propriety of placing the ballot in the hands of a
horde of ignorant blacks who must become the tools
of scheming politicians. The Republican party,
partly from a sense of right to men made citizens of
the United States, and partly from hope of perpetuat-
ing their party in power, held that now that the slave
was free, he should be made a citizen. Johnson,
driven to extremes, proposed to make intelligence the
test, to grant every negro capable of reading the
Amendment that made him free, or who owned a certain amount of property, the right to vote. This did
not answer the purpose of the opposition, who knew
that there were perhaps not a dozen negroes in Mississippi who could read or write. The negro problem
was far from being solved, and wise and patriotic men
began to seriously consider the matter. Of course
the colored vote of the South far exceeded the white
vote, and many thinking men, regardless of party, to-
day doubt the propriety of turning the government
of those southern States over to that mass of unintel-
ligent beings.

The quarrel between Johnson and the Republican
party grew more and more acrimonious. The president was charged with being more friendly to the late
enemies of his country than its defenders. As in all
quarrels, both parties were to blame. Johnson was
stubborn and unwilling to take advice from any one.
The Republicans believed that the enfranchisement
of the negroes would give them the "Solid South."
They did not understand the negro, or they would
have seen that, as a political factor, he would be more

likely to turn against them, than act with them. The negro does not live for the past, nor the future, but for the present. The result is that the Republicans were surprised and disappointed in him, though hardly willing even to this day to admit it.

The quarrel between the Republicans and Johnson became more and more earnest. People looked with great anxiety to the assembling of congress, hoping for some relief from the impending danger.

The 39th Congress assembled December 4, 1865, and took up, among the first orders of business, the subject of reorganization. On the first day of the session, congress agreed by a joint resolution to appoint a joint committee to be composed of nine members of the house and six of the senate, to "inquire into the condition of the States which formed the so-called Confederate States of America, and report those entitled to be represented in either house of congress, with leave to report at any time by bill or otherwise; and until such report shall have been made and finally acted upon by congress, no member shall be received in either house from the so-called Confederate States, and all papers relating to the representatives of the States shall be referred to said committee." This body was known as the "Reconstruction Committee."

This act of congress was a virtual condemnation of the action of the president. It was an interference of the representatives of the people with his policy of reorganization, and he was highly offended. His opposition to the legislative branch soon became open and active. In his public addresses, he displayed, in a most unguarded way, his antipathy to the legislative branch of the government. He exercised the veto power as no other man save Grover Cleveland has done. In February, 1866, he vetoed an act for enlarging the operations of the Freedmen's Bureau, which had been established for the relief of freed refugees, and for the cultivation of abandoned lands. In March, he vetoed an act known as the Civil Rights Law, which was intended to secure to all citizens, without regard to color or previous condition of servitude, equal rights in the republic. These acts became law by the constitutional two-thirds vote of both houses. The president was soon involved in a bitter quarrel with his cabinet, and all resigned save Edward Stanton, secretary of war. He was urged to remain, and, by doing so, became an object of the president's bitter hatred.

Notwithstanding the quarrel between congress and the president, the work of reorganization went on; and on the 29th of July, after a long and laborious session, congress adjourned. The president had by proclamation on April 2d, formally declared the civil war at an end. The first fruits of the congressional plan of reorganization were seen in the restoration of the State of Tennessee to the Union, six days before the adjournment of congress.

Meanwhile, notable events in the foreign relations of the government had occurred. The emperor of France had been informed by Secretary Seward that the continuation of French troops in Mexico was not agreeable to the United States; and on April 5, 1866, Napoleon's minister for foreign affairs gave assurance to our government that those troops should be withdrawn within a specified time. This was done; and the Grand Duke Maximilian of Austria, whom Louis Napoleon had, by military power, placed on the throne in the neighboring republic, with the title of emperor of Mexico, was deserted by the perfidious ruler of France. The deceived and betrayed Maximilian, after a struggle against the native republican government for awhile, was captured at Queretero and shot, and his loving wife, Carlotta, overwhelmed by her misfortune and grief, became hopelessly insane. Such was the sorrowful ending of one of the schemes of the emperor of France for the gratification of his ambition. He had longed to aid the Confederates, with a hope that the severance of our Union would give him an opportunity to successfully defy the " Monroe Doctrine," and extend the dominion of the Latin race on the American continent, as well as monarchical institutions. It is thought by well-informed historians, that Louis Napoleon picked a quarrel with Mexico, solely to seize that weak country, and have the soldiers on the frontier ready to aid the southern Confederacy; but the quarrel and seizure of Mexico came too late. Already the war of the rebellion was waning, and it was ended before he could render any effective aid.

There is no doubt that the English ministry was anxious to render service to the cause of the Confederacy. In fact, our country has never had a foreign or domestic quarrel, in which Great Britain did not openly or secretly espouse the other cause. The British government not only desired to aid the Confederacy, but did so, until the enormous reserve power of the United States alarmed them, when they abandoned the insurgents, whom they had deceived with false promises, and sneeringly called their political organization the " so-called Confederate States of America." Notwithstanding this faithlessness to their traditions and fairly implied, if not absolutely stated, treaty stipulations on the part of the rulers of Great Britain, our government was faithful to them all. When, in 1866, a military organization of Irish residents in our country, known as the Fenian Brotherhood, associated for the avowed purpose of freeing Ireland from British domination, in May and June, for a formidable invasion of the neighboring British province of Canada, the United States Government, instead of investing them with "belligerent rights," was true to its pledges to Great Britain concerning neutrality laws, interfered and suppressed the warlike movement. Though these are events of the past and should not be cherished in hatred, we would be foolish to forget what may be to our interest to remember, in order to guide our footsteps aright in the future. There is no reason why Great Britain and the United States, both people of the same language and nationality, should not be friendly. They are of one common ancestry, and save the political difference in their governments, there is little difference in their tastes and desires. It is gratifying to note that, in 1866, a peaceful bond of union was formed between the two countries, by the successful establishment of permanent telegraphic communication between the two countries.

On May 15, 1866, the president vetoed a bill admitting Colorado. On the 29th of this month, General Winfield Scott, the hero of two wars, died at West Point, New York.

Trouble between the white and colored races in the South began soon after the war, and continues yet. It was no more than might have been expected when the negro was made a political factor. On July 30th, there was a great riot in New Orleans, in which many colored people were killed.

On December 14, 1866, congress passed a bill granting the elective franchise in the District of Columbia to persons "without any distinction on account of color or race." The president vetoed the bill, on the 7th of January, 1867, when it was immediately passed by the constitutional majority of both houses in its favor.

On the same day, Mr. Ashley of Ohio, arose in his place, and charged " Andrew Johnson, Vice-president and acting-president of the United States, with the commission of acts, which, in the estimation of the constitution, are high crimes and misdemeanors, for which he ought to be impeached." He arraigned the president on the following charges: (1) In that he has corruptly used the appointing power; (2) in that he has corruptly used the pardoning power; (3) in that he has corruptly used the veto power; (4) in that he has corruptly disposed of public property of the United States; and (5) in that he has corruptly interfered in elections, and committed acts which, in the contemplation of the constitution, are high crimes and misdemeanors. Mr. Ashley also offered a resolution, instructing the committee on the judiciary to make inquiries on the subject. This resolution was adopted, and was the first move in the impeachment of Andrew Johnson, president of the United States, which terminated in his trial in 1868. On March 1, 1867, Nebraska was admitted as a State.

An act was passed for limiting the authority of the president in making official appointments and in removal from office. Among other provisions, was one to deprive him of the power to remove a member of the cabinet without permission of the senate, declaring they should hold office for and during the term of the president by whom they had been appointed, and for one month thereafter, subject to removal by and with the consent of the senate. This law, known as the "Tenure of Office Act," was vetoed by the president, when it was passed over his veto by a large majority. The fight between the legislative and the executive powers of the government from this on became doubly acrimonious. Congress passed laws depriving him of the power to grant amnesty and pardon to those who had been engaged in the great rebellion, for a military government in the disorganized States, which were divided into five districts: 1st, Virginia, 2d, North and South Carolina, 3d, Georgia and Alabama, 4th, Mississippi and Arkansas, and 5th, Louisiana and Texas.

The thirty-ninth congress closed its session at midday, March 4, 1867, and twelve hours after, the first session of the fortieth congress was begun. The fight between the president and the new congress was not one whit less bitter. Both were petulant, aggressive and foolish. A hundred side issues became involved, so that the main subject of dispute was almost hidden. Johnson was charged with seeking to destroy the government. This charge was as foolish as it was false. He had been loyal to the Union during the war of secession, and no sane man, looking at the matter with unprejudiced eyes, can for a moment believe that he ever harbored such an idea. He wished to forgive the southern people at once and take them back as "erring brothers." Perhaps he had his own political schemes as well as his Republican opponents. They wished to enfranchise the negro to perpetuate their party in power. He wished to issue a general amnesty to the late Confederates, in order that they might have an opportunity to aid the Democratic party.

The "Tenure of Office Act" was a slur on Johnson, and congress seemed determined to strip him of official power. In violation of the act, he removed the secretary of war, Mr. Stanton, and put General Grant in his place. Johnson's personal friends were amazed at this and declared that he had gone too far. At the second session of the fortieth congress, the strife showed no signs of abating. The president's annual message was so offensive in tone and temper, that, when the usual resolution was offered in the senate to print it, Mr. Sumner took fire and vehemently denounced it as a "libel and insult to congress." Wiser and less impulsive counsel prevailed, and, while "the tone and temper and doctrines of the message" were decidedly condemned, it was thought best to print it.

On December 5, 1867, the judiciary committee offered the following resolution:

"*Resolved*, That Andrew Johnson, president of the United States, be impeached of high crimes and misdemeanors." After a long debate, the resolution was rejected by a decided majority.

A week later, the president sent to congress a message, in which he gave his reasons for removing the secretary of war, which not being satisfactory, the senate reinstated Stanton, January 13, 1868, and General Grant retired from the office. The strife was far from being over, for, on February 21st, Mr. Johnson issued an order directing Mr. Stanton to vacate the office of secretary of war, also another order to Adjutant-General Lorenzo B. Thomas to enter and take the place of the deposed secretary. Mr. Stanton refused to be deposed in this manner, and congress was driven to a frenzy. On the following day, February 22, 1868, the house of representatives, by an almost strictly party vote of 126 to 47, "*Resolved*, That Andrew Johnson, president of the United States, be impeached of high crimes and misdemeanors."

The charges against him were, (1) unlawfully ordering the removal of Mr. Stanton as secretary of war, in violation of the provisions of the "Tenure of Office Act;" (2) unlawfully appointing General Lorenzo B. Thomas as secretary of war *ad interim;* (3) substantially the same as the second charge, with the additional declaration that there was, at the time of the appointment of General Thomas, no vacancy in the office of secretary of war; (4) conspiring with Lorenzo B. Thomas and other persons to the House unknown, to prevent, by intimidation and threats, Mr. Stanton, the legally appointed secretary of war, from holding his office; (5) conspiring with General Thomas and others to hinder the execution of the Tenure of Office Act, and, in pursuance of this conspiracy, attempting to prevent Mr. Stanton from acting as secretary of war; (6) conspiring with General Thomas and others to take forcible possession of the war department; (7) and (8) substantially charged conspiring to prevent the execution of the Tenure of Office Act, and for taking possession of the war department; (9) charged that the president called before him the commander of the forces of Washington and declared to him that a law, passed the 30th of June, 1867, directing that "all orders and instructions relating to the military operations, issued by the president or secretary of war, shall be issued by the general of the army, and, in case of his inability, through the next in rank," was unconstitutional and not binding on the commander of the department at Washington, the intent being to induce the commander to violate the law and to obey the orders issued by the president directly.

For the impeachment and prosecution of the president of the United States, the house of representatives appointed the following managers: Thaddeus Stevens of Pennsylvania, Benjamin F. Butler of Massachusetts, John A. Bingham of Ohio, George S. Boutwell of Massachusetts, James F. Wilson of Iowa, Thomas Williams of Pennsylvania, and John A. Logan of Illinois.

Two additional charges were adopted against the president, on March 3, 1868. The first charged him with making inflammatory speeches, during a journey he made through the country. The second that the president had in August, 1866, in a public speech in Washington, declared that congress was not a body authorized by the constitution to exercise legislative powers. The Democratic members of the house, forty-five in number, entered a formal protest to the whole proceeding. This makes the impeachment of Andrew Johnson purely a partisan measure, and it was wholly unworthy patriotic Americans, acting in their cool, sober senses. Johnson had not the power to check the fiery, impetuous course of the politicians, flushed with victory over the South, as Lincoln could have done, had he lived, and as he did do during his administration.

The United States senate was organized into a high court of impeachment, with Chief Justice Salmon P. Chase as president, and on March 30th, the trial began. The details of that trial are too long for this volume. It continued until May 25th, when the president was acquitted. Secretary Stanton left the cabinet, and General John M. Schofield was appointed secretary of war in his place.

North Carolina, South Carolina, Georgia, Alabama, Mississippi, Louisiana and Texas, having ratified the amendments, and having, by the adoption of a State constitution, approved by congress and by the election of national senators and representatives, complied with prescriptions of congress, took their places as revived States of the Union. The perfect reorganization was not effected until the spring of 1872, when, on the 23d of May, the remaining States having taken their places with their sisters, every seat in congress was filled, for the first time since the winter of 1861.

In the Summer of 1868, General U. S. Grant and Schuyler Colfax were nominated for president and vice-president of the United States on the Republican ticket, and Horatio Seymour of New York and General Frank P. Blair of Missouri, for president and vice-president on the Democratic ticket. The election resulted favorably to Grant and Colfax.

During the year 1868, there was considerable trouble with Indians on the frontier. It was at this time that General Sherman is accused of saying, "There is no good Indian, but the dead Indian." The expression is consistent with a soldier whose trade is blood; but to a humane man and a Christian, it is wholly repugnant. Besides, the statement was in contradiction of facts. Missionaries and educators among the Indians have proved that there are many good Indians. In his report in 1875, Commissioner E. P. Smith says:

"The civilization of the Indian is not only entirely possible, but is fairly under way." He reported that out of the entire Indian population within the domain of the United States (278,963 souls), 40,638 men and boys supported themselves by the labor of their own hands. About one-sixth of the barbarian population in our republic had become producers. "Five years ago," said the Commissioner, "10,329 Indian families were living in houses. This year shows 19,902; a gain of 92 per cent." He also reported that the number of children attending school was 10,600. The increase has been very satisfactory since, and the red man, under honest treatment, and in the light of Christian development, will soon become a respected and valuable citizen.

February 26, 1869, the following resolution, as the fifteenth amendment, passed both houses:

"SECTION I.—The right of citizens of the United States to vote shall not be denied or abridged by the United States, or by any other State, on account of race, color, or previous condition of servitude.

" Section II.—The congress, by appropriate legislation, may enforce the provisions of this article."

The turbulent administration of Andrew Johnson came to an end March 4, 1869. On the day he retired, he issued a long address to the people of the United States in vindication of his conduct. It is too soon yet to say just how much Johnson and the Republicans were to blame, or to fasten the blame on either. The whole contest was a political battle over partisan issues, and though it did not appear in the impeachment at all, the great question between Johnson and Congress was extending the elective franchise to the negroes. The Republicans won, and it is doubtful if the whites or the blacks are any better off for it, and certain it is, the Republicans were losers in the game.

CHAPTER II.

GRANT'S TWO ADMINISTRATIONS—"ALABAMA" CLAIM
—TROUBLE WITH SPAIN—CORRUPTION OF OFFI-
CIALS—THE "WHISKEY RING."

ULYSSES SIMPSON GRANT was inaugurated president
of the United States March 4, 1869. His cabinet
was as follows: Hamilton Fish, secretary of state;
George S. Boutwell, secretary of treasury; John A.
Rawlins, secretary of war; Adolph E. Borie, secretary
of the navy; Jacob D. Coxe, secretary of the interior;
A. J. Creswell, postmaster-general, and E. Rockwood
Hoar, attorney-general.

The beginning of President Grant's administration
was bright with hope and promise. The only cloud
that darkened the firmament was the unsettled account for the depredations committed by the *Alabama*,
fitted out in England by tacit sanction of the British
government. To effect a peaceful solution of the
problem, Reverdy Johnson of Maryland was sent to
England, in 1868, to negotiate a treaty for that purpose. The treaty was rejected by the American senate. Johnson was recalled, and J. Lothrop Motley
was appointed minister to the British court, charged
with the negotiation of another treaty for the same
purpose; but Mr. Motley met with no greater success than his predecessor.

The reduction of the national debt over $600,000,-
000 in the space of three years and eight months, at
the accession of President Grant, made the outlook

encouraging. The country was prosperous. Returning soldiers, with back pay and bounties, were purchasing farms, horses and cattle, and spreading money all over the country. In 1864, a law was passed providing for a separate bureau in the treasury department, the chief officer of which was called the comptroller of the currency, whose office is under the general direction of the secretary of the treasury. It also provided for the formation of private banking associations, within defined limits, to have existence for twenty years, the stockholders to be equally liable to the extent of the stock for the debts and contracts of the bank. Every such association was required, preliminary to the commencement of banking, to transfer bonds of the United States to an amount not less than $30,000, and not less than the capital stock paid in. Then the asso ciation was entitled to receive from the comptroller of the currency, circulating notes equal in amount to twenty per cent of the current market value of the bonds transferred, but not exceeding ninety per cent of the par value of such bonds. The government of the United States was thus made the basis of security for the redemption of paper currency, and that circu-

ULYSSES S. GRANT.

lating medium was of equal value in all parts of the United States. This was the formation of national banks, which system, in 1875, was made free, without any restrictions as to the amount of circulating notes that might be issued by the comptroller of the treasury. The system is condemned by certain classes and upheld by others.

At an early period of Grant's administration, an important amendment to the national constitution was proposed by Mr. Julian of Indiana, for securing the ballot to women, in the following terms:

"The right of suffrage in the United States:—citizens, whether native or naturalized, shall enjoy the right equally, without any distinction or discrimination whatever, founded on sex."

This never became a law. It was thought that the fourteenth amendment, declaring "that all persons, born or naturalized in the United States and subject to the jurisdiction thereof (without any allusion to sex) are citizens of the United States and the State wherein they reside," clearly gave women the rights and privileges of citizens.

An important event of 1869 was the completion of the Pacific Railroad, thus uniting the Atlantic and the Pacific coasts by a band of steel. The impressive ceremony of laying the last "tie" and driving the last "spikes" took place on May 10, 1869, in a grassy valley, near the head of the great Salt Lake, in Utah. It was performed in the presence of many hundred people of various nationalities, including Indians of the plains. That "tie" was made of laurel wood, brightly polished, its ends bound with silver bands. The "spikes" were three in number. One of solid gold came from California; another of solid silver from Nebraska; and a third, composed of gold, silver and iron, was furnished by the citizens of Arizona. That great railway crosses nine mountain ranges in its passage of about three thousand four hundred miles, between New York and San Francisco by way of Chicago.

Early at the close of the war, the subject of a ship

canal across the Isthmus of Darien, to connect the waters of the two oceans, was brought before the American people, and has occupied much public attention ever since, though it has not become a reality. In 1871, the United States and Great Britain, having agreed to arbitrate the *Alabama* claim, the tribunal for that purpose assembled at Geneva, in Switzerland, where Count Sclopis was chosen to preside. After several meetings, in September, 1872, the tribunal decided that the government of Great Britain should pay to the government of the United States, the sum of $15,500,000 in gold, to be given to citizens of the latter country, for losses by depredations of the *Alabama* and other Anglo-Confederate cruisers.

On October 10th and 12th, 1871, there occurred at Chicago the great fire, in which over $300,000,000 was lost. Many insurance companies were forced to make assignments. It is said that the fire originated from a cow kicking down a lamp. It was during this year that the Grand Duke Alexis of Russia paid the United States a visit and made a tour through several States and Territories. On January 2, 1872, Brigham Young, the great Mormon chief, was arrested for murder, being charged with complicity in the Mountain Meadow massacre. He was not convicted; but a jury found a Mormon official named Lee guilty, and he was afterward executed. On March 7th, three members of the Kuklux Klan were convicted and sentenced to twenty years in the penitentiary. The Kuklux Klan was a southern organization to prevent negroes from enjoying the elective franchise.

May 3, 1872, the Liberal Republicans, in convention at Cincinnati, nominated Horace Greeley for president, with B. Gratz Brown of Missouri for Vice-President. Mr. Greeley, the eminent editor of the New York *Tribune*, and one of the greatest men of his age, had been an earnest advocate of abolition, and was thought to be one of the stanchest Republicans in the nation. He was loyal and true; but

HORACE GREELEY.

when the Confederates surrendered, he believed the war over and was willing to take them by the hand and forgive them. He became one of the bondsmen for Jefferson Davis, which made him repugnant with the mass of Republicans, who seemed to still sniff the smoke of battle. Horace Greeley was not the political mountebank that he has been accused of being. He was a humane man. His love of humanity made slavery of the blacks hateful, and his love of humanity revolted at the oppressive means suggested to humiliate the conquered people of the South. His views on the tariff were thoroughly Republican and not far from the ideas held by the party to-day.

The Republican party had determined to renominate General Grant. Though Grant had not evinced any brilliant statesmanship, yet he had made no serious mistakes, and his brilliant military record made him popular. On June 6, 1872, he was renominated. William H. Seward, Lincoln's secretary of state, stabbed on the night of the president's assassination, died October 14, 1872. The presidential election resulted in the election of Grant and Wilson. On the 25th of November, after the election on the 5th, Horace Greeley died, at the age of 62.

On the 9th of this month a destructive fire broke

out in Boston, resulting in a loss of about $75,-000,000.

President Grant's second term of office began March 4, 1873. It was an intensely cold day at the national capital; but the inaugural ceremonies were performed as usual, in open air, at the east front of the capitol. Chief Justice Chase administered the oath of office. It was one of the last public acts of that distinguished jurist. His health had been failing for some time, in consequence of a paralytic stroke in 1872, and he died two months after the imposing ceremonies. President Grant's second cabinet was as follows: Hamilton Fish, secretary of state; William A. Richardson, secretary of the treasury; William W. Belknap, secretary of war; George A. Robeson, secretary of the navy; Columbus Delano, secretary of the interior; John A. J. Creswell, postmaster-general. Changes in the personnel of the cabinet afterward took place, and only Mr. Fish remained in General Grant's cabinet during the eight years of his administration.

At the close of the third session of the forty-second congress, which closed March 4, 1873, at noon, there was rushed through the infamous salary-grab bill. Had this law been enacted prior to the presidential election, it would have materially aided Horace Greeley. By this law, the president's salary was raised from $25,000 a year to $50,000 a year, payable in monthly instalments. The salary of the vice-president was fixed at $10,000; chief justice of the supreme court, $10,500, and the associate justices at $10,000 each; the heads of the several departments, attorney-general and speaker of the house of representatives at $10,000 each, and senators and representatives at $7,500 each. President Grant signed this bill, and it became a law, just before he began his second term of office.

The South was in a miserable condition. Intelligence under the ban of rebellion was disfranchised, and ignorance and imported politicians called "carpet baggers" controlled the country. It was still under military rule. Ignorance, to a certain extent, ruled intelligence in local affairs. The enfranchised negro was about the only citizen in the South entitled to vote or hold office. Local offices were in many cases held by negroes incapable of reading or writing. There was a gradual lightening of the burdens of taxation which the war had imposed, and this made the masses of the people hopeful for the future. The protective tariff, proposed as a war measure, was proving beneficial in peace. Manufacturing industries sprang up all over the land; labor was in demand, and wages were good. This soon began to attract the attention of the laboring people of the old world. The wage earner in the United States was receiving double the wages the laborer received in the old world, and emigration from Europe poured into America in one continuous stream. In the year 1873, the emigration reached the unprecedented figures of 473,000. The great panic of 1873 prostrated thousands of commercial and manufacturing institutions, cutting off, or reducing the wages of thousands of people, which put a check to emigration, though it has never ceased. The vast unoccupied lands in the western States and Territories have been rapidly filling up with foreign emigrants and people from the overcrowded eastern States.

November 6, 1873, an American vessel named the *Virginius* was captured by Spanish authorities near Cuba. Her crew and persons aboard of the vessel were accused of aiding the insurgents in Cuba. They were taken to Santiago, Cuba, where several were shot. This brought about some diplomatic correspondence with Spain. It was supposed that General

Grant would stubbornly insist on satisfaction, which Spain seemed not in the least inclined to give. One of the men killed by the Spanish authorities was a citizen of Iowa, and it was declared that he was in no way connected with "filibusters," if any of them were. To the surprise of all, the matter passed away and was hushed up. Some of the newspapers at the time intimated that Secretary Fish had a son or a son-in-law at this time interested in some financial matters in Spain, and that this probably accounted for the unsatisfactory way in which the matter ended.

Through the unwise "peace policy" of President Grant, by continuing the vicious system of treating the Indians as foreigners and at the same time wards guarded by rapacious and unscrupulous agents, who swindled and continually excited their righteous anger, the Modocs became incensed and took up the hatchet. In their mountain fastnesses and lava beds, they made a desperate resistance. General Canby and Reverend Dr. Thomas were commissioned to treat with them, and were treacherously murdered by the infuriated Modocs.

The government became roused, and the Modocs were driven to their lava beds and forced to surrender. Captain Jack and three of his companions were tried by a court-martial and hanged at Fort Klamath, in Oregon, October 3, 1873.

The trouble originating in the South from giving the negro the elective franchise was renewed in 1874, and in fact in every biennial, or quadrennial election, there are reports of outrages in the South, until people have come to expect trouble at the polls when an election is held.

A report of the discovery of gold in the Black Hills caused the government to send Mr. Jenny, government geologist, to make a survey of that region. He was escorted into the reservation by six companies of cavalry and two of infantry. The Sioux, at once suspecting that they were to be deprived of their lands, began their dances and prepared for war. In 1876, a campaign against them was organized. The general plan was for the military force to make a simultaneous movement under experienced leaders, in three columns,—one from the department of the Platte, led by General Crook; one from the department of Dakota, commanded by General Terry; and a third from the Territory of Montana, led by General Gibbon. The latter was to move with his columns down the valley of the Yellowstone, to prevent the Sioux from escaping northward. General Custer, at the same time, pushing across the country from the Missouri to the Yellowstone, was to drive the Indians toward General Gibbon, while General Crook was to scout the Black Hills and drive out any of the hostile Sioux that might be found there. The expedition was under the chief command of General Alfred H. Terry, a brave, judicious and experienced officer. He and his staff accompanied Custer from Fort Abraham Lincoln to the Yellowstone River. On their arrival in the vicinity, about June 1, 1876, by communicating with General Gibbon, they learned that the Indians were in that neighborhood, in large numbers, and well supplied with munitions of war.

The reports of scouts caused a belief that the Indians, with their great movable village, were in the meshes of the net prepared for them near the waters of the Big Horn and Little Horn, Powder and Tongue rivers (tributaries of the Yellowstone), and Rosebud Creek. The concentrated troops began to feel for themselves. On the 17th of June, Crook had a sharp fight with a superior force of Sioux, who were thoroughly armed and equipped, and he was obliged to retreat. Terry and Gibbon met at the mouth of the Rosebud. Custer was there, at the head of the stronger column, consisting of the whole of the 7th regiment of cavalry, composed of twelve companies, and was ordered to make the attack. He and Gibbon marched to the vicinity of the Big Horn River. Custer arrived first and discovered an immense Indian camp on a plain. He had been directed to await the arrival of Gibbon, to co-operate with him, before making the attack; but, inferring that the Indians were moving off, he directed Colonel Reno to attack them at one point with seven companies of the cavalry, while he dashed off with five companies (about three hundred men) to attack at another point. A terrible struggle ensued on the 25th of June, 1876, with a body of Indians, five to one of the white men. The savages were led by a chieftain named "Sitting Bull," a man with more than ordinary ability, and who, had he been Christianized and civilized, might have been a power in the land. Custer and almost his entire command were slain. Two hundred and sixty-one were killed and fifty wounded. With General Custer, perished two of his brothers, a brother-in-law, and other gallant officers; but the Indians were finally driven from their lands to a reservation set apart for them, and a peace established.

The Territory of Colorado was admitted as the thirty-eighth State in the year 1876.

General Grant's second administration was saddened by some of the most gigantic frauds and swindles ever brought to light against government officials and prominent men in political circles. During the latter part of the year 1875, disclosures were made of a wide-spread conspiracy among the United States revenue officers, distillers and others to defraud the government of its revenue on whiskey. This was known as the "whiskey ring." O. E. Babcock, President Grant's private secretary, was one of the accused, but on trial was acquitted.

The "whiskey ring" seemed to have its headquarters in St. Louis, though there were branches extending to Kansas City and St. Joseph. It was wholly within the ranks of Republican officials and Republican leaders, whose object was to increase their own wealth by violating the law and defrauding the government. Respectable Republicans kept aloof from the gigantic fraud, and saved their good names from reproach. Those familiar with the ring and its schemes understand its strenuous and persistent efforts to dominate and control city, State and national politics.

For six years, all else had to yield to or feel its influence. The chief Republican paper of St. Louis and Missouri was the *St. Louis Democrat*, owned by Fishback, Houser and William McKee, all three having an interest in it. This paper, from its skill and enterprise, had gained a wide influence during the war. March 23, 1872, William McKee and D. M. Houser sold their shares in the *Democrat* to Fishback & Co. for $456,000. On July 18, 1872, McKee and Houser established a new Republican paper, called the *Globe*, which it is supposed derived its first vigor from the proceeds of the whiskey ring frauds, though there is no evidence that Mr. D. M. Houser, or any one else, connected with the paper, save McKee, had anything whatever to do with the whiskey ring frauds. The emoluments of the whiskey frauds, according to the statement of General McDonald, reached the enormous amount of $2,786,000. Of this, it is said that McKee of the *Globe* received $300,000. On March 19, 1875, McKee and Houser purchased the *Democrat* from Fishback & Co., and, consolidating it with the

Globe, it became the *St. Louis Globe-Democrat*, which name it bears to-day.

The power of the whiskey ring was almost unlimited. Scarce any dared oppose it, and he who did was crushed by the weight of its influence. Republican State conventions were manipulated in its interest, and Chauncey I. Filley, the Republican leader then and now in the State, because he would not accede to the wishes of the ring, was retired from the State committee. He was, at the time of its exposure, by Geo. W. Fishback to Secretary Bristow, postmaster of St. Louis. These gigantic frauds on such a wholesale plan could not go entirely unnoticed. On May 10, 1875, seizures were made by two revenue officers going to St. Louis for that purpose after Fishback had given into the hands of Bristow the sworn proof. The parties in St. Louis who aided in furnishing the information were Jesse B. Woodward, an attorney, and Myron Coloney, a special agent.

On May 15, 1875, the commissioner of revenue was superseded by Commissioner Pratt of Indiana, and in June, McDonald, Joyce and Fitzroy were indicted. In July, General John B. Henderson was appointed special attorney to assist Colonel Pat Dyer, the district attorney, in the prosecution of the frauds. Henderson, being a politician, hesitated to incur the displeasure of the great opposing newspaper, and a ring that had gained such a wonderful power. He consulted with Mr. Filley, the postmaster, also a prominent Republican, who wielded wide influence in the State and nation. Mr. Filley said that the way to favor was to "stand up for the country and the right," and Henderson, having his spiritual strength renewed, decided to take hold and prosecute with a vengeance.

Henderson had been an applicant for a foreign mission in 1872, and President Grant, having been informed of a personal attack made by Henderson on him, refused to appoint the general. It is said by one who knew Grant well, that he never overlooked a personal attack. On being appointed to prosecute the whiskey ring, Henderson could not resist the temtation to vent his spleen on the president, and he declared that the whiskey frauds were a ring that extended to the White House. Henderson was at once removed, and Hon. James O. Broadhead, an eminent lawyer and Democratic statesman, was appointed in his place. General Grant, in making this appointment, gave utterance to the famous order:

" Let no guilty man escape !"

November 4, 1875, McKee and Maguire were indicted for " conspiracy to defraud the government." In September, John A. Joyce was indicted in the western district court at Jefferson City for failure to report official investigation. On November 13, Joyce was sentenced to three years in the penitentiary and $2,000 fine. McDonald was convicted in the same month. W. O. Avery, a clerk in the commissioner's office, was tried at St. Louis and convicted December 3d. In February, 1876, Babcock was acquitted by a jury. On February 1st, William McKee was convicted. The same day collector of internal revenue Con. Maguire plead guilty. McKee was fined ten thousand dollars and sentenced to two years in the county jail. Maguire was sentenced to six months in the county jail. In St. Joseph, John L. Bittinger was, on April 15, 1876, sentenced to two years in the State penitentiary, and to pay a fine of one thousand dollars. Other members of the ring were more or less punished ; but there is no doubt that many of the guilty escaped. So many prominent politicians, newspaper men and men wealthy and occupying high places in society, were perhaps never before convicted by their own political friends.

The Republican party in Missouri has never yet gotten over the blighting effects of the whiskey ring. Ever since, the State has been Democratic. Chauncey I. Filley, the great Republican organizer and leader, refused to sign a petition or write a letter for the pardon of William McKee of the *St. Louis Globe-Democrat*, and has ever since been the object of that paper's hate. Mr. Filley gives the following reason for declining to sign a petition, or write a letter to President Grant for the pardon of William McKee:

" I declined to sign a letter or petition for the pardon of McKee, not upon any personal grounds, but because he, as an intelligent man and publisher of a great newspaper, whose duty it was to be faithful to the public as a public educator, had been false to his public and individual duty, and the means of suborning and contaminating so many young men, and so many public officers, federal, State and city, that he had no claims for consideration, and should be made to suffer for his own acts, and to atone for the homes he had destroyed, as well as the lives of so many who fell under his blight."

Filley has never ceased to feel the effects of his refusal. William McKee died in 1879, and a statement published in many of the leading papers and never to our knowledge denied, is to the effect that he called his wife, Joseph McCullagh, editor of the *St. Louis Globe-Democrat*, and D. M. Houser, its manager, to his death-bed, and made them promise never to cease to fight Chauncey I. Filley so long as he lived and the *Globe-Democrat* existed. Whether such an obligation was imposed on the survivors of William McKee or not, it has been acted upon. When Filley organized the shattered ranks of the Republican party in his part of the nation, after the defeats of 1870 and 1874, and led them to victory in 1876, 1880 and 1888, the *Globe-Democrat* assailed him, and soon had the ear of the administration turned against him in each case. Filley went down in 1892, and so did the Republican party. The *Globe-Democrat* and its followers are denominated the "silk-stocking" faction of the Republican party, while Filley and his followers are called "hoodlums." Both pseudonyms are misnomers, as one can see by the history of the origin of the factions.

SAMUEL J. TILDEN.

1876 was not only a presidential year, but also the year of the great centennial exposition, celebrating the one hundredth anniversary of American Independence. The centennial exposition was held in Philadelphia. Rutherford B. Hayes of Ohio and William A. Wheeler of New York were nominated for president and vice-president of the United States on the Republican ticket at Cincinnati, June 16, 1876. Belknap, secretary of war, left the cabinet, and on June 17th, B. H. Bristow, secretary of the treasury, resigned.

On the 28th and 29th of June, Samuel J. Tilden and Thomas A. Hendricks were nominated for president and vice-president of the United States on the Democratic ticket. The election was so close that for months it was in doubt. At last an electoral commission was agreed upon, and the result was that Hayes and Wheeler were declared elected. The commission was very unsatisfactory, and we hope will never be resorted to again.

CHAPTER III. ·

MANY evil things were said of the manner in which President Hayes was elected. He was called the "Fraudulent President;" but whatever may be said of the fraud, if there were a fraud, which placed him in the presidential chair, P r e s i d e n t Hayes was no party to it himself. He found himself chief magistrate of a mighty nation, and perhaps in as trying a position as ever a man was placed in time of peace. He proved himself conscientious and worthy of the high trust reposed in him. His cabinet was, William M. Evarts of New York, secretary of state; John Sherman of Ohio, secretary of the treasury; George W. McCrary of Iowa, secretary of war; Richard W. Thompson of Indiana, secretary of the navy; Carl Schurz of Missouri, secretary of the interior; David

RUTHERFORD B. HAYES.

M. Key of Tennessee, postmaster-general, and Charles Devens of Massachusetts, attorney-general.

Mr. Hayes at once set about a much needed reform in the South. He realized that the war had ended twelve years before, and that a standing army was no

463

longer necessary in the South. He believed the people of the South capable of controlling their own affairs without the intervention of federal or military authority, and South Carolina and Louisiana, being left to themselves, declared the Democratic nominees for governor of those two States elected. The Southern States have been solidly Democratic ever since and are rapidly recovering from the devastation of war.

Mr. Hayes, on June 22, 1877, issued the following circular letter to all government office holders:

"SIR :—I desire to call your attention to the following paragraph in a letter addressed by me to the secretary of the treasury on the conduct to be observed by officers of the government in relation to elections:

"'No officer shall be required or permitted to take any part in the management of political organizations, caucuses, conventions, or election campaigns. Their right to vote and express their views on public questions, either orally or through the press, is not denied, provided it does not interfere with the discharge of their official duties. No assessments for political purposes on officers or subordinates should be allowed. This rule is applicable to every department of the civil service. It should be understood by every officer of the general government that he is expected to conform his conduct to its requirements.'"

The summer of 1877 was memorable for the Nez Percé (Pierced-Nose) Indian war in Idaho. The history of this war is only another record of a series of aggressions and impositions of the white men upon the red. The Nez Percés were first discovered in 1803, by a party of explorers. They were quite friendly and continued so until about twenty years ago. They were organized, like most of the tribes west of the Rocky Mountains, with no general chief. An Indian agent was sent among them, who forced upon them a principal chief, whose only recommendations were that he could speak English, and could be controlled in the interest of the agent. They waited patiently for the appointed chief to die, that they might again enjoy their old political system; but when this event did transpire, another chief was chosen in opposition to "Joseph," a member of one of the most illustrious families of the tribe. He was the father of Joseph, the leader of the band in war. Old Joseph withdrew in disgust from the councils of the Nez Percés.

The Nez Percés had lived from time immemorial in the Wallowa valley, distinguished for its wealth of roots and fishing. The white men envied them their lands, and by various treaties, which they in their ignorance could not understand, provided them with reservations and annuities. Old Joseph and his band refused to go upon the reservation, and remained in their ancestral home in the Wallowa valley. So did many others who refused to become parties to the treaty.

In 1871, old Joseph died and left his son Joseph at the head of his band. Like his father, he denied the right of a portion of the tribe to give up their lands. Not having signed the treaty, they determined to remain in the Wallowa. White people came into the valley for the purpose of crowding them out. The oppression of the Indians became terrible and, as might be supposed, resulted in war. Joseph, at the head of a few followers, made a gallant fight. A distressing war continued from June until the second month in Autumn of 1877, when, on the 5th of October, Joseph and his band surrendered to General Nelson A. Miles at Eagles' Creek, Montana Territory. Joseph in his speech said to General Miles:

"Tell General Howard I know his heart. What he told me before I have in my heart. I am tired of fighting. Our chiefs are all killed. Looking-glass

30

is dead. The old men are all dead. It is the young men who must say yes or no. He who led the young men is dead. It is cold, and we have no blankets. The little children are freezing to death. I want time to look for my children and see how many of them I can find. May be I shall find them among the dead. Hear me, my chiefs! I am tired. My heart is sick and sad. From where the sun now stands, I shall fight no more forever."

A more pathetic speech has not been heard since the time of Logan the famous Mingo chief.

Since the death of Custer, Sitting Bull, the terrible Sioux, and his followers had been at large. General Terry, commander of the military department of the Northwest, was placed at the head of the commission, and on hearing of the surrender of the Nez Percés, and considering it a favorable time to negotiate, started for the rendezvous of Sitting Bull, near Fort Walsh, where they met the chief, who rejected the proposals of peace made by the commissioners, and the commission returned. The British authorities gave Sitting Bull notice that if he should attempt to cross the border with hostile intentions, he would have the English as well as the Americans for his enemies. In 1881, about one thousand of Sitting Bull's followers surrendered; but it was several years before the chief would consent to be placed on a reservation.

January 1, 1879, was the time set for the resumption of specie payment, and as the time drew near, timid persons began to fear a panic; but resumption, like many anticipated evils, proved a blessing. In 1878, the "Bland Silver Bill," of which Mr. Richard Bland of Missouri was author, became a law. It provided for the coinage of silver dollars of the weight of $412\frac{1}{2}$ grains and that the rate of coinage should be at least $2,000,000 a month, and not more than $4,000,000. In the fall of 1878, the yellow fever prevailed as a fearful epidemic in the region of the Lower Mississippi, from Memphis to New Orleans. In his annual message, the president called the attention of congress to the necessity for investigating the causes of the epidemic. The senate appointed a committee to act in the matter in conjunction with one from the house, and $50,000 was appropriated.

On January 1, 1879, the much-dreaded specie resumption came. In fact, under the wise management of Secretary Sherman, it had been reached weeks before. As the time approached, all dread of the monster passed away, and, instead of producing the financial panic predicted by so many, 1879 was the most prosperous year the nation had seen since the war.

On the Pacific coast there has long existed a strong prejudice to the Chinese, and in 1879 the matter was brought to the attention of congress in an effort to restrict Chinese emigration. A bill was passed to that effect; but the president vetoed it.

Early in the Autumn of 1879, there was an uprising of the Ute tribe of Indians. They murdered N. C. Meeker, the Indian agent at White River, and for several weeks held his wife and daughter in captivity. Major Thornbreak of the United States Army was sent with a force to suppress the hostiles, and in a battle with them on Milk River, he and ten of his men were killed. The Indians were finally subdued, and the captives released.

1880 was another presidential year. General Grant's friends set on foot a movement to break the precedent set by George Washington, which until this year had been respected by the most ambitious politician America had ever produced. Early in the year, in fact, the year before General Grant was announced as a candidate for the "third term," he had taken a tour around the world, and an admiring press had given him a liberal amount of laudation. His chief opponent was that brilliant statesman, James G. Blaine. Roscoe Conkling and General John A. Logan were the special champions of General Grant.

This mistake, to a considerable extent, dimmed the lustre which General Grant's name had already acquired. The campaign was very bitter, and some hard things were said of the general who had received the sword of Lee. The convention was held in Chicago, and the ex-president was accused of imperialism and Cæsarism. Washington was held up in contrast with the third-term candidate. The salary grab, the whiskey frauds, and many other things for which the general was not responsible were charged against him. The Young Men's Republican Club from New York had their headquarters at the Palmer House, and with them was a chorus of excellent singers and a number of orators, the lay of whose songs and the burden of whose speeches were against the "third term."

It soon became evident that safety to the party lay in a compromise candidate. The galleries rang with applause whenever James A. Garfield, who was a delegate, appeared in the convention hall, and the delegates wisely decided that he was the coming man. General Grant received 306 votes; but the Blaine and Sherman men went to Garfield, and he was nominated for president, with Chester A. Arthur for vice-president.

The Democrats nominated General Winfield Scott Hancock, a brave soldier in the late war, with William H. English for vice-president. The National (Greenback) party nominated General John B. Weaver of

Iowa and Benjamin J. Chambers of Texas. The Prohibition candidates were Neal Dow of Maine and
A. H. Thompson of Ohio. Gar-
field and Arthur were elected.

President Hayes' adminis-
tration was prosperous and,
save the Indian troubles, peaceful from beginning to end.
Honor was never done him during his life, and the world cannot honor him now. Mrs.
Hayes was more nearly a Mar-
tha Washington, in her sweet
Christian-like spirit and simplicity, than any woman who
has ever graced the White
House. Her character was a
power for good. Unlike the
weak ladies who preceded her,
she refused to allow liquors to

WINFIELD SCOTT HANCOCK.

ever appear on her table. No foreign diplomat was
ever known to taste wine in the White House while
she presided over it. It is to be regretted that her
successors have not all followed her example.

GARFIELD.

President Garfield's constitutional advisers were:
secretary of state, James G. Blaine of Maine; secretary of the treasury, William Windom of Minnesota;
secretary of war, Robert Todd Lincoln of Illinois,
son of President Lincoln; secretary of the navy,
William H. Hunt of Louisiana; secretary of the interior, Samuel J. Kirkwood of Iowa; postmaster-general, Thomas L. James of New York; attorney-general, Wayne McVeagh of Pennsylvania.

Soon after the inauguration of President Garfield and the selection of his cabinet, there sprang up a bitter fight between Senator Roscoe Conkling and the administration. Conkling, still smarting under his defeat in his efforts to nominate General Grant for the "third term," and the elevation of his personal enemy Mr. Blaine to the highest place in his cabinet, became doubly bitter against President Garfield.

Conkling, Logan and all the supporters of Grant were styled "Stalwarts," while the Republicans that had opposed him for the "third term," were called "Half-Breeds." Judge Robertson had been a New York delegate to the Chicago convention, and refusing to be bound by the unit rule which they sought to impose on the delegates to insure the State for Grant, and being friendly to Blaine, he incurred the displeasure of Senator Conkling and all his followers. A foolish custom has prevailed for many years in public affairs at Washington. Not only is it foolish but dangerous. That custom is to allow the congressmen and senators from each State to select such persons as they choose, and nominate them for the various federal offices within their State or district. Congressmen and senators are elected to make laws for the people, and not as patronage brokers. Besides, the system is dangerous in this, that it enables a wily and corrupt politician to perpetuate himself in office, by having that powerful weapon, patronage, by which he can sway his constituents as a master does his slaves with the lash. Garfield and some of the best of our presidents, have paid little attention to this rule.

When President Garfield appointed Robertson collector of New York, Conkling became enraged and resigned his seat in the senate, and Senator Thomas C. Platt followed his example. They went home relying on being returned by the New York legislature then in session in Albany. The legislature failed to return them, and Conkling became soured and retired from politics, though Thomas C. Platt has ever remained loyal to the party of his choice.

President Garfield's administration was full of bright promise. The country was at peace with all the world and was never more prosperous, and everybody felt that a long era of good times was at hand. Among the army of office seekers who had been prowling about Washington, was one, Charles J. Guiteau, who wanted a foreign mission. But little attention was paid him, until, mad with a desire for notoriety, on July 2, 1881, he shot President Garfield, in the depot at Washington City, as he and Mr. Blaine were about to take the train. From the very first, it was feared the wound was mortal. For long weeks, the president lingered be-

JAMES A. GARFIELD.

tween life and death, and the people waited with deepest anxiety. As a last resort, he was taken to the seacoast at Elberon, where he died, September 19, 1881.

Charles J. Guiteau was arrested and put in prison. While incarcerated, Sergeant Mason of the United States Army fired at him, but missed. Mason was promptly arrested on a charge of assault with intent to kill, was tried and convicted.

Guiteau's trial was a farce. He was defended by his brother-in-law Mr. Scoville. The prisoner was more like a low comedian in a farce comedy than a man on trial for his life, and he continually interrupted the proceedings with the most ridiculously foolish remarks. There can be little doubt of Guiteau's insanity, and it is even questionable if he was accountable for the act. Nevertheless, public opinion was greatly against him, and he was convicted on January 25, 1882, and hanged on the 30th of the following June.

ARTHUR.

The constitutional successor of James A. Garfield was Mr. Chester A. Arthur. The first change Mr. Arthur made in the cabinet was in November, 1881, when Secretary Windom was succeeded by Judge Folger of New York. On January 1, 1882, Mr. James resigned as postmaster-general and was succeeded by Mr. Howe.

Slight trouble between Chili, Peru and the United States gave rise to some diplomatic correspondence. Mr. William H. Trescott was sent as a special envoy to Chili and Peru. These countries were at war with each other at the time; but after some delay and trouble, matters, so far as the United States of America were concerned, were adjusted.

CHESTER A. ARTHUR.

The famous " star route" trials were during the administration of Arthur. Senator Dorsey, and second assistant postmaster-general Thomas J. Brady were indicted for defrauding the government in postal contracts, were tried and acquitted.

During this year, the United States contested the right of any European power to guarantee the neutrality of the Panama canal, maintaining that the United States had the sole right so to do. It intimated an intention of withdrawing from the Clayton-Bulwer treaty, wherein a joint guaranty of those powers was established. This position was taken by the United States because of the changed condition of affairs since that treaty was made. Then the United States made concessions to England, because possessed of resources and wealth too limited for so arduous an undertaking. Now the country was larger, twice as populous and richer by far. Above all, its possessions on the Pacific coast would be exposed to attacks from the enemy in case the neutrality of the canal were guaranteed by European powers alone.

The Mormon question, which has for years been troubling Americans, was the occasion of some restrictive legislation during President Arthur's administration.

With Germany, an extensive correspondence took place, not on such lofty subjects as the rights of American citizens, or treaty obligations, but on that harmless, necessary animal, the American hog. In consequence of alleged discoveries of trichinæ in pork imported from the United States, the question was, in 1878, raised in Germany as to the advisability of allowing its consumption. After much correspondence, the "American hog" was, for a time, prohibited from taking European tours.

A panic, started early in 1884, almost prostrated business. General Grant and his son had gone into business in New York City with a man named Ward. General Grant seems to have given little attention to the business in which he had staked his all, but entrusted it to Ward and his son. Ward evidently proved too much for his son. The concern went down in ruins. Ward was arrested for swindling and sent to the penitentiary. Other banks tumbled in ruins, and the panic became general. It was over a year before the country fully recovered, and confidence was restored.

There were two notable deaths during Arthur's administration. One was the poet Henry W. Longfellow, who died March 24, 1883, and the other the great philanthropist, Peter Cooper.

It was Arthur's desire to be his own successor; but the Republican convention, which met in Chicago, nominated James G. Blaine of Maine and John A. Logan of Illinois for president and vice-president of the United States. The Democratic party nominated Grover Cleveland, of New York, and Thomas A. Hendricks of Indiana. General Butler was nominated for president on the Greenback ticket, and John P. St. John of Kansas on the Prohibition ticket. The

BENJAMIN F. BUTLER.

campaign was the most exciting and enthusiastic since the hard-cider campaign of 1840. Conkling sulked in his tent. George William Curtis, who had been in the convention that nominated Mr. Blaine, went over to the Democracy. Henry Ward Beecher declared for Cleveland, yet Mr. Blaine went to work with an energy such as no candidate has ever displayed. He still had a few faithful leaders, and with these he entered into the conflict. He made a grand, noble fight; but he lost New York by a few hundred, which gave the election to Grover Cleveland.

CHAPTER IV.

CLEVELAND'S ADMINISTRATION AND THE CAMPAIGN OF 1888.

JAMES G. BLAINE was for years known as the Gladstone of America. His defeat was a surprise to his friends, but Mr. Blaine himself had predicted it, before he was nominated. The week before the meeting of the Republican national convention in 1884, on Thursday, Mr. Blaine telegraphed Murat Halstead at Cincinnati, saying he would be glad to see him at his residence in Washington, before the convention assembled. Late next day, Mr. Halstead rang the door bell of Blaine's house, which was on the opposite side of Lafayette Square from the place where Blaine died. He took Mr. Halstead into his back parlor and said he had sent for him on an impulse, and did not know but that he had caused him a journey without sufficient errand to warrant it, and it might seem very peculiar and unreasonable. He added:

JAMES G. BLAINE.

"I am alarmed about this convention." Mr. Halstead assured him there was no reason for alarm so far as he was concerned, for things were going his way as well as his friends could desire.

"Ah, that is what I am afraid of," answered Mr. Blaine. "As the case stands I shall be nominated, and I do not desire to be, and it ought not to be. It would be a mistake. I ought not to be nominated, for I could not carry New York. The Arthur administration would be inefficient, at least, and faction would do its work. I could not carry New York, and defeat is certain without that State. We might work ourselves up, during the campaign, to the belief that we could carry the essential State; but at last we should miss it, may be just a little, but enough. I feel that there is no doubt about it. Why should we be defeated, when we can name the candidate, a ticket certain to be elected? Put up William Tecumseh Sherman and Robert T. Lincoln, and we shall go right through to certain victory. The names of Sherman and Lincoln would be irresistible. I have written fully to General Sherman and he understands my views. He says 'No' of course; but he has a sense of duty through which he may be controlled. I want you to assist at Chicago to carry out the Lincoln and Sherman programme. I wanted to see you to tell you so myself, that there might be no mistake about it, that you could act with the knowledge that I do not want to be a candidate, and should not be, and the reasons why. I have said so many times to William Walter Phelps among others, and to friends now in town from Virginia."

Mr. Halstead listened with profound surprise and concern. Through State and personal associations he was for the nomination of John Sherman, and asked:

"You could not make the ticket John Sherman and Robert Lincoln?"

Mr. Blaine doubted the ability of John Sherman to get the nomination, or carry New York even if he did get it, whereas General Sherman was a certainty.

Mr. Blaine's excuse for not having spoken sooner, was because there was one thing needful, the prevention of the nomination of Arthur, whose candidacy would be a fatality. Arthur was skilfully managing the whole power of the administration to secure the nomination; but he would be slaughtered in New York and Ohio. Mr. Blaine added that he had not seen the time when he could safely withdraw in the positive terms that would carry conviction, that he was really out of the field, without preparing the way for Arthur's success in the convention, and defeat of the party at the polls. Mr. Halstead assured Mr. Blaine it was now too late to recede. That he could not convince Mr. Blaine's friends in the convention that he was in earnest or not a traitor. Mr. Blaine was nominated, was deserted by Carl Schurz, George William Curtis, Henry Ward Beecher, and many others, who had heretofore claimed to be Republicans, while Roscoe Conkling sulked, if he did not give his secret influence to the Democracy, and Mr. Blaine, as he predicted, was "beaten at least just a little."

GROVER CLEVELAND.

On March 4, 1885, Grover Cleveland was inaugurated president of the United States with the usual ceremonies. His cabinet advisers were as follows: Thomas F. Bayard, secretary of state; Daniel Manning, secretary of the treasury; William C. Whitney, secretary of the navy; William C. Endicott, secretary of war; L. Q. C. Lamar, secretary of the interior; Augustus H. Garland, attorney-general, and William F. Vilas, postmaster-general. During the latter part of Mr. Cleveland's administration, another cabinet position was created, called the department of agriculture, and Norman J. Colman, of Colman's *Rural World*, St. Louis, Mo., was appointed secretary of agriculture, which position he held but a short time, retiring with the administration.

After twenty-four years, the Democratic party again held the reins of government. An attempt was made to change the tariff, by the introduction of the " Mills bill," of which Mr. Mills of Texas was the author; but it was checked in the Senate, which had a Republican majority, and failed to become a law. The Mills bill, however, formed the issue for the next campaign. The first business that attracted the attention of the new administration was the civil war raging in the Central American States, to the detriment of American interests there. A naval force was dispatched to the scene of disturbance, and a force of marines landed to protect life and property at Aspinwall, which had been occupied and burned by one of the belligerent forces.

About the time of the election of Mr. Cleveland, the public was shocked and grieved by the report that General Grant, the distinguished soldier, was afflicted by an incurable disease, a cancer of the tongue. The last act of President Arthur was signing a bill restoring him to his rank in the army; but the old hero was not destined to hold the honor long. Bowed down with financial trouble and affliction, his last days were full of pain and sorrow. He died, July 23d, at Mount MacGregor, and on August 8th his remains were taken to New York. The body lay in state two days in the city hall, and was then transported to a spot on the banks of the Hudson in Riverside Park, which the city had assigned for that purpose. The procession which accompanied the funeral car was immense. The president, vice-president and cabinet, as well as ex-Presidents Hayes and Arthur, Generals Sherman and Sheridan, and hosts of his old comrades, who came from far and near to pay the last honors to their chief, were present.

On the 28th of November, Vice-President Hendricks died suddenly. By his decease before the meeting of congress, the succession to the presidency, in case of the death or disability of the president, was left undetermined. By the constitution, congress has the power to provide for filling the vacancy in case of the president's and vice-president's death or removal; but congress had not yet been organized. When it did meet, on the 7th of December, the senate elected Senator John Sherman its president *pro tempore*, the acting vice-president thus being the leader of the opposition to the president's policy. So great was the anxiety felt at this unexpected state of affairs that, by the advice of his cabinet, the president declined to attend the funeral of his colleague. Various proposals have been made with a view to settling beyond peril the question of succession. In the early part of 1883, a bill for this purpose was brought in, and the death of Mr. Hendricks again called the attention of congress to this important matter. A bill prepared by Senator Hoar was finally passed. By its provisions in case of the death of both president and vice-president, the functions of the office are to be discharged, until an election can be held under the articles of the constitution, by the cabinet officers, in the order of the authority of their offices.

Among the chief events of Grover Cleveland's administration, not already mentioned, were the dedication of the Washington Monument, February 21, 1885; the publication of the revised Old Testament, May 15th; the arrival of Bartholdi's statue of Liberty in New York, July 15th; the blowing up of Flood Rock, in East River, New York, October 10th. On October 29th, General George B. McClellan died. On December 8th, William H. Vanderbilt, the great New York millionaire, died suddenly of heart disease, with which he had long been afflicted, and which had for years been a cloud upon his life.

The year 1886 was also notable for the death of many prominent men. General Winfield S. Hancock died February 18th; Horatio Seymour, Democratic statesman, died February 12th; John B. Gough, the noted temperance lecturer, died February 13th; Judge David Davis died at Bloomington, Illinois, June 26th; Samuel J. Tilden died August 4th; Ex-President Chester A. Arthur died November 18th, and General John A. Logan died December 18th. Scarcely any of these men were far enough advanced in life to have died of old age.

During the month of May, there were great labor agitations throughout the United States, and on the fourth of that month occurred the Haymarket riots in Chicago, during which, one of the rioters called anarchists threw a dynamite bomb, which exploded and killed and wounded a number of police. Seven of the accused were sentenced to be hanged, and one to serve fifteen years in the penitentiary. On November 10th, 1887, Governor Oglesby commuted the sentence of Samuel Fielden and Michael Schwab, two of the anarchists, to imprisonment for life. The same day, Louis Ling, one of the anarchists, committed suicide, and on August 11th, August Spies, A. R. Parsons, Adolph Fisher and George Engel were hung. In 1893, Governor Altgeld of Illinois pardoned the remaining anarchists in prison, who are now at large.

On June 2, 1886, Mr. Grover Cleveland, president

of the United States, was married to Miss Frances Folsom.

Early in 1887, an interstate commerce law was enacted. On March 8th, the Rev. Henry Ward Beecher died. On August 10th, there was a terrible railroad accident near Chatsworth, Illinois, in which nearly one hundred persons were killed.

There arose in congress some bitter discussion on the question of American fisheries. It was reported that Canadian authorities had been imposing on American fishermen. That able American, Senator Fry of Maine, declared that "England had played the bully with the United States," and the silver-tongued orator from the Sunflower State, Senator John J. Ingalls of Kansas, raised his powerful voice in the interest of American liberties. Efforts were made to adjust the matter of American right and more clearly define the three-mile limit as contemplated in the treaty with Great Britain, also to include the scal-fishery question in Alaskan waters; but these are still disputed points that may at some time in the future cause trouble.

From March 12th to 14th, 1888, occurred a terrible blizzard in New York city, such as was never known before. Ex-Senator Roscoe Conkling, being caught in that blizzard, contracted a severe cold in his head, from the effects of which he died August 5th. On October 1st, President Cleveland signed the Chinese Exclusion Bill.

The year 1888 was a presidential year. The Republican convention at Chicago in 1888 had many candidates, all prominent and able men. New York asked for Chauncey M. Depew. Ohio was divided between John Sherman and the brilliant statesman William McKinley. Kansas put forth her talented John J. Ingalls. Iowa had Senator Allison, and

31

Michigan had General Russell A. Alger, the great statesman, soldier, financier and philanthropist. Illinios was divided between Walter Q. Gresham and Robert T. Lincoln, while Indiana advanced the claims of Benjamin Harrison.

The Democrats met in national convention at St. Louis, June 6th, and nominated Grover Cleveland and Allan G. Thurman. During the same month, the Republicans met at Chicago and nominated Benjamin Harrison of Indiana for president and Hon. Levi P. Morton for vice-president. Streeter was the labor candidate, and the prohibition candidate, Gen. Clinton B. Fisk. Harrison was a grandson of William H. Harrison, and his managers raised the old Tippecanoe enthusiasm of 1840. Old campaign songs, badges and medals, that had slumbered for almost half a century, were resurrected and brought to swell the campaign. The ball-rolling, and everything that would rouse the early patriotism and enthusiasm of the nation was brought to bear, and Harrison and Morton were elected November 6, 1888.

The latter part of Cleveland's administration witnessed a slight cloud in the firmament with Germany over that country's aggression in the Samoan Islands. It was claimed that Germany was trying to secure a ruler in Samoa whom they could control in the interests of that nation. This matter was not adjusted during Cleveland's administration.

Almost the last official act of President Cleveland was to sign a bill admitting as States, North and South Dakota, Montana and Washington. He retired on the 4th of March and went to New York, where he engaged in the practice of law.

CHAPTER V.

BENJAMIN HARRISON was inaugurated president of the United States March 4, 1889. His cabinet advisers were: secretary of state, James G. Blaine; secretary of the treasury, William Windom; secretary of the navy, Benjamin F. Tracy; secretary of war, Redfield Proctor; secretary of the interior, John W. Noble; attorney-general, Wm. H. H. Miller; postmaster-general, John W. Wanamaker; secretary of agriculture, Jeremiah M. Rusk.

The first thing requiring the attention of the new administration was the settlement of the Samoan difficulty. A peaceful and satisfactory adjustment was quickly made.

Oklahoma, a portion of the Indian Territory, was opened up for settlement April 22, 1889, and in a month the wilderness became a well-populated country.

On the 30th of April of this year was the centennial celebration of the inauguration of George Washington, as first president of the United States. The celebration was observed with appropriate ceremonies all over the land.

On May 31st and June 1st of this year, there occurred the greatest disaster ever known in the history of America, the Johnstown flood. A dam on the Conemaugh lake gave way, and the whole valley was flooded. Thousands of lives were lost, and property amounting to millions of dollars was destroyed.

From August to December, the Clan-na-Gael, or Cronin murder trials attracted the general interest of the public. The Clan-na-Gael was an Irish political society on the Fenian order, having for its object the liberation of Ireland, and Cronin, who was a member of the society, it was claimed, had revealed some of its secrets, for which, it was claimed, he was murdered. At least, he mysteriously disappeared. Three men accused of his murder got life sentences, and another, John Kunze, was sentenced to three years in the penitentiary.

BENJAMIN HARRISON.

The year 1890 was eventful. Samuel J. Randall, Democratic statesman, died April 13th. As the fourth century had almost elapsed since the discovery of the New World by Columbus, it was decided to hold a quadro-centennial celebration in the form of a Columbian exposition and world's fair. A world's fair bill passed the senate April 21st, and on the 25th, President Harrison signed it, making it a law. Idaho became a State, July 3d, 1890. Gen. Clinton B. Fisk, the great temperance advocate, died July 9th; Gen. John C. Fremont, the explorer, July 13th.

The new Republican congress had formulated a new tariff bill, arranged by Hon. William McKinley, known as the "McKinley Bill." This bill passed both houses, was signed by the president, October 1st, and went into effect October 6th. Early in December of this year, there was an outbreak of the Sioux Indians, who, it is reported, were driven to desperation on account of the scarcity of food. They began their ghost dances, and soldiers were hurried to their reservation. There were some skirmishes with them, in which several Indians were killed. It was reported by the newspapers that even the women were fired upon. On the 15th, Sitting Bull, the great chief, was killed.

Chicago having won the World's Fair in the contest between many of the prominent cities of the United States, the president issued a proclamation on the 24th of October, announcing the fact that the World's Fair would be held in that city in 1893.

On December 31st, Gen. F. E. Spinner, ex-treasurer of the United States, died. January 29, 1891, William Windom, secretary of the treasury, died. February 13th, Admiral David D. Porter died. On the next day, February 14th, Gen. William T. Sherman died.

On March 14th, a mob of American citizens broke open the jail in New Orleans, in which there were eleven Italians, who had been accused of murdering David Hennessey, a police officer, and hung them all. Some of the Italians had been tried for the murder and acquitted by a jury. As some of the lynched men had never been naturalized, the Italian government demanded satisfaction and temporarily withdrew their minister.

April 7th, 1891, P. T. Barnum, the great American showman, died.

On the 9th of July, this year, ground was broken for the exhibition at the fair grounds in Chicago, and after that time the work of erecting enormous buildings went steadily forward until they reached completion, making the grandest exposition buildings the world has ever known.

During the winter of 1891 and 1892, the United States of America became embroiled in a quarrel with our sister republic Chile. The unfortunate affair which was the immediate cause of the trouble occurred in the streets of Valparaiso on October 16, 1891. A party of sailors from the United States cruiser *Baltimore*, then lying in the harbor at Valparaiso, went on shore and were attacked by a mob of Chileans. The Chileans were armed with pistols and knives, while the American sailors were unarmed. In the fight, a boatswain's mate was dragged from a street car by a mob and shot to death. Five other men, William Turnbull, a coal heaver; John Hamilton, a carpenter; David N. Andrew, a painter; George Panter, a coal heaver, and John W. Talbot, an apprentice, were dangerously wounded with bayonets. Turnbull died from the effects of his wounds. Thirty-five other sailors were arrested by main force and dragged through the streets of the city and locked up in prison.

Captain Schley of the *Baltimore* made a careful investigation and reported it to the government at Washington. President Harrison made a demand for full satisfaction for the insult. Many of the opposition papers thought Harrison a little severe, especially as it had only been a few common sailors who had been killed and maltreated; but Harrison believed the life of a common sailor as dear to him as that of an admiral, and was determined in his demand for reparation. Chile was a little slow, and he was on the eve of asking congress to declare war, and had already ordered many war ships to the Chilean coast, when that government hastened to make such reparation as they could. The attack on the American sailors is said to have resulted from hatred of the United States, from some supposed meddling on the part of that government in the war with Balmaceda.

July 6th, 1892, witnessed one of the most terrible conflicts since the war, at Homestead, Pennsylvania. At this place, is located the Carnegie iron and steel works. Owing to the lowering of wages, the hands to the number of several hundred struck, and the Carnegie iron works officials at once brought a body of Pinkerton's detectives from Chicago, Philadelphia and New York, armed with Winchesters. They came in a boat partially bullet-proof. The workmen assailed the boat, and for ten hours a conflict raged in which a number were killed and wounded, when the Pinkerton detectives surrendered and were led through the town by the victors to a hall where they were imprisoned, until they could escape the fury of the mob.

During the latter part of President Harrison's administration, the annexation of the Hawaiian Islands to the United States became an absorbing topic in diplomatic circles, and was freely discussed in the newspapers. Some of the natives and American citizens had overthrown the government, dethroned the queen, and set up a provisional government, in the form of a republic with Mr. Dole at the head, and sent commissioners to the United States to ask to be annexed to this nation. The party in power seemed friendly to annexation, and President Harrison submitted a treaty to the United States senate, but a change of administration interrupted the proceedings.

The year 1892 being a presidential year, the Republicans renominated Benjamin Harrison for president with Mr. Whitelaw Reid of New York for vice-president. The Democratic Party nominated Grover Cleveland of New York for president and Mr. Stevenson of Illinois for vice-president. The Populists, or People's Party, which had gained considerable strength, nominated General Weaver of Iowa at the head of its ticket. General Bidwell of California was the standard-bearer of the Prohibition party.

Cleveland and Stevenson were elected president and vice-president of the United States.

The mortality during Harrison's administration was great.   His own family and his political associates were very unfortunate. The daughter and wife of Secretary Tracy perished in a conflagration which consumed the house. President Harrison's wife, an estimable Christian lady, died during the campaign which witnessed her husband's defeat.   On January 16, 1893, Rutherford B. Hayes, ex-president of the United States, died.   On January 11th, Gen. Benjamin F. Butler died, and on January 27th, at 11 A.M., Hon. James G. Blaine died.   Phillips Brooks and Union General Doubleday died the same month.   During the month of February, Confederate General Beauregard died. During this month, Hon. William McKinley suffered great financial losses from having indorsed notes for friends.   He was heavily embarrassed, but refused aid, saying that he would redeem all the obligations he had assumed for others.   McKinley was, in 1892, elected governor of Ohio, the greatest honor the State could confer upon him.

WILLIAM McKINLEY.

During the campaign of 1892, Judge Walter Q. Gresham announced his intention to vote for Grover Cleveland.   That announcement alone no doubt carried thousands of votes to the Democratic candidate. He was rewarded by Mr. Cleveland with the first place in his cabinet, that of secretary of state, an appointment astonishing to both Republicans and Democrats. The remainder of the cabinet is as follows: secretary of the treasury, John G. Carlisle of Kentucky; secretary of war, Daniel S. Lamont of New York; attorney-general, Richard Olney of Massachusetts; postmaster-general, Wilson S. Bissell of New York; secretary of the navy, Hilary A. Herbert of Alabama; secretary of the interior, Hoke Smith of Georgia; secretary of agriculture, J. Sterling Morton of Nebraska.

On March 4, 1893, Grover Cleveland took the oath of office for a second time as president of the United States.

Reference has been made to the dethronement of the queen of the Hawaiian Islands, during President Harrison's term. There was a division of opinion in regard to the subject of annexation, and unfortunately this division seemed to assume the form of a political question. Mr. Cleveland withdrew from the senate the treaty which Mr. Harrison had submitted and dispatched Hon. James H. Blount of Georgia as special commissioner, or minister plenipotentiary and envoy extraordinary to the Hawaiian islands to make full inquiry as to what part the minister of the United States and the officers and sailors of the United States man-of-war had taken in dethroning the queen. The theory of the president, based on the report of Commissioner Blount, was that the queen of the Hawaiian islands had been overawed by United States officers, including the minister and the captain of the man-of-war, and that her abdication was only temporary, with the understanding that her cause might be submitted to the government of the United States, and she be restored if found to be in the right.

This representation induced ex-Minister John L.

Stevens to publish a letter giving his version of what
had happened at Hawaii. Mr. Stevens stated that
on the death of King Kalakaua, his sister Liliuokalani
succeeded him to the throne, and surrounded herself
with libertines and gamblers, taking her paramour
to live with her in her palace. The biennial legislature of 1893 voted out the queen's immoral ministry. She seemed for a while to acquiesce, but, aided
by her friends, she carried by bribery the opium and
lottery bills, which were odious to the more intelligent
and honorable people of her country, and then forced
out the Wilcox-Jones ministry, and appointed in their
places four of her palace retainers, two of whom the
legislature and a responsible public had recently and
repeatedly rejected. Minister Stevens was absent
from Honolulu at the time on board the *Boston*. As
he was coming into the harbor at noon on January
14, 1892, the legislature was prorogued. The revolutionary edict of Hawaii's misguided queen, was about
to be proclaimed; rumors of it had already reached
the public ear. A few minutes before the appointed
hour for the *coup d'état*, immediately upon Minister
Stevens reaching the legation from the *Boston*, he
was urged to go at once to the British minister, and
ask him to accompany him to the queen, and try to
dissuade her from her revolutionary design; but it
was too late. The maddened and misguided woman
had already launched the revolution. Saturday night
told every intelligent man in Honolulu that the Hawaiian monarchy was at an end forever. There was a
great mass meeting on January 16th, representing the
wealth, influence and patriotism of the islands. They
resolved to be no longer ruled by an immoral queen,
but to overthrow her, set up a provisional government,
and then ask to be annexed to the United States, so
they might be protected by that great power. They

appointed a "committee of public safety," which appealed to Minister Stevens to land a force of men from the *Boston*, lest a riot and incendiarism should burst forth in the night, for no reliable police force longer existed, and whatever there was of force was then in the control of the usurpers, and lottery gamblers, who had inaugurated the revolution by forcibly ejecting the Wilcox-Jones ministry. Minister Stevens concluded his statement as follows:

"Under the diplomatic and naval rules which were and are imperative, the United States minister and naval commander would have shamefully ignored their duty, had they not landed the men of the *Boston* for the security of American life and property, and the maintenance of public order, even had the committee of public safety not requested us to do so. As American representatives, five thousand miles away from our government, we could not have escaped the responsibility, even had we desired to do so. Fortunately, the commander of the *Boston*, and those under his command had no desire to shirk their duty. On shore and in perfect order, they stepped not an inch from their line of duty. They never lifted a finger to aid the fallen monarchy nor the rising provisional government. The former sought their aid, but neither party had the least assistance of force by Captain Wiltse and those under his command. *All assertions to the contrary, by whomsoever uttered, are audacious falsehoods without a semblance of truth.*"

On November 10, 1893, the secretary of state issued a letter in which it was intimated that it was the intention of the president to restore the queen to her throne in accordance with the knowledge gained by the report of Commissioner Blount. This announcement caused excitement all over the United States, and for weeks the papers were full of rumors. The

Hawaiian question unfortunately became more a party issue, which always hinders a fair and impartial investigation. One of the conditions upon which President Cleveland proposed restoring the queen was that she should grant general amnesty to all those who had been concerned in the revolution that dethroned her. This she at first refused to do, but after it was too late she assented to the condition.

In accordance with Mr. Cleveland's instructions, Minister Willis, who succeeded Mr. Stevens, on December 22, 1893, went to Mr. Dole, the president of the Hawaiian government, and in the name of the United States demanded that the provisional government should abdicate in favor of the deposed queen. This President Dole took under advisement, and finally refused to do, and for many days, even up to this writing, great excitement has prevailed in the Hawaiian Islands and in the United States. On January 10, 1894, Mr. Gresham announced that the policy of the administration of "restoring the queen had been dropped."

The summer of 1893 was noted for the great World's Fair held in Chicago. It was officially opened May 1st, and closed October 30th of that year. It was the most successful exhibition ever known, and exceeded in attendance even the Paris exposition. As an educational feature, the World's Fair has perhaps done more for the American people, than any exhibition since the formation of the government. Among the many distinguished visitors at the Columbian exposition was the Duke of Veragua, who is said to be a lineal descendant of Christopher Columbus.

As early as April, 1893, evidences of a business depression were discernible, which in May culminated in a financial panic. From that time to the end of the year and into the first month of 1894, the present writing, the depression increased. Some financiers thought the cause of the sudden and unexpected "hard times" was the "Sherman Law," which provided that the secretary of the treasury should purchase 4,500,000 ounces of silver bullion every month to be hoarded away in the treasury, on which treasury notes were issued payable in coin, which were invariably paid in gold. Though this law was known as the "Sherman Law," and was enacted as a compromise to prevent "free silver," Senator John Sherman denied any responsibility for it.

President Cleveland called an extra session of congress to meet August 7th, and take action on the silver question, and after a long session and many debates, the Sherman Law was repealed on November 1, 1893. It was predicted that "good times" would be restored as soon as the iniquitous silver law was "wiped off the statute books," but the prediction failed. Financial matters grew worse. Railroads were seriously affected, and at this writing, more than one-fifth of the railroads of the United States are in the hands of receivers. Corporations and individuals failed for millions, and factories closed their doors, throwing many thousands of people, dependent on their daily labor for support, out of employment. Millionaires, common people, and paupers suffered.

Disasters went on multiplying until it is estimated that more than fifty-five millions of dollars were lost in failures in 1893.

There were State elections in many of the States on November 7th. Greatest interest centred in Hon. William McKinley, who was a candidate for reelection for governor of Ohio. The election was on purely party lines, for both Governor McKinley and his opponent were men of unimpeachable characters. The tariff became the issue, and McKinley won by a majority of nearly ninety thousand. New York also went Republican, and other States showed Republican gains.

On January 1, 1894, New York City had half a million unemployed people, many of whom were destitute and suffering, while the proportion in Chicago and other cities was equally great.

The principal events of the year 1893, not already mentioned, were the opening of the Cherokee Strip, September 16th; the assassination of Carter Harrison, mayor of Chicago, by an ex-policeman, October 28th; the strike on the Lehigh Valley Railroad, which for a while tied up the business of that great thoroughfare, but which, thanks to prudence, reason and justice, was amicably settled; the steps taken for the erection of a monument at Wakefield, Virginia, to mark the birthplace of George Washington, and the unveiling in New York City, on November 25th, of the statue of Captain Nathan Hale, the young patriot who was hanged by the British for a spy.

The year 1894 dawned gloomy and depressing on our glorious republic, yet the American people are ever hopeful, and through the darkest clouds the sun may sometimes break forth in radiance and glory. We are at peace with all the world, while the crowned heads of Europe constantly watch each other with suspicion. Though financial panics have wrought disaster to countless thousands, the American people are not a nation to despair, and already the people are grasping all the vital questions of the day with a boldness and patriotism that will soon set matters right, and this model republic which we have traced from its formation will then enter upon a new era of prosperity and will grow in strength and glory with each additional age of wisdom.

THE END.

HISTORICAL INDEX.

32

CHRONOLOGY.

PERIOD XII.—AGE OF UNION.

FROM A.D. 1854 TO A.D. 1894.

1854. KANSAS-NEBRASKA BILL, repealing Compromise of 1850, passed,—March 8.

KANSAS TERRITORY formed,—May 30.

NEBRASKA TERRITORY formed,—May 30.

OSTEND MANIFESTO issued by American ministers, Oct. 21.

1855. KANSAS TROUBLES; emigration from slave and free States.

NIAGARA SUSPENSION BRIDGE completed.

1857. JAMES BUCHANAN inaugurated president,—March 4.

DRED SCOTT DECISION; opinion delivered by Chief Justice Taney,—March 6.

TROUBLE with Mormons in Utah; military sent by the United States.

1858. MINNESOTA admitted into the Union,—May 11.

FIRST MESSAGE by the Atlantic cable,—Aug. 16.

1859. OREGON admitted into the Union,—Feb. 14.

JOHN BROWN seized United States arsenal at Harper's Ferry,—Oct. 16.

VICTORIA BRIDGE, Montreal, opened.

1860. SOUTH CAROLINA seceded,—Dec. 20.

1861. *Star of the West* fired upon off Charleston Harbor,—Jan. 9.

KANSAS admitted into the Union,—Jan. 9.

CONFEDERATE GOVERNMENT organized at Montgomery, Ala.,—Feb. 8.

JEFFERSON DAVIS. president; Alexander H. Stephens, vice-president,—Feb. 9.

COLORADO TERRITORY formed,—Feb. 28.

DAKOTA TERRITORY formed,—March 2.

NEVADA TERRITORY formed,—March 2.

ABRAHAM LINCOLN inaugurated president,—March 4.

FORT SUMTER, S. C., bombarded by Beauregard,—April 12.

UNITED STATES ARSENAL at Harper's Ferry destroyed by Federals,—April 18.

GOSPORT NAVY-YARD destroyed by Federals (Norfolk, Va.),—April 20.

BATTLE OF PHILIPPI, W.VA. ; Confederate defeat, June 8.

BATTLE OF BIG BETHEL, VA. ; Pierce defeated,—June 10.

BATTLE OF ROMNEY, VA. ; Federal victory,—June 11.

BATTLE OF BOONVILLE, MO.; Lyon victorious,—June 17.

BATTLE OF CARTHAGE, MO. ; Gov. Jackson and Sigel ; indecisive,—July 5.

BATTLE OF RICH MOUNTAIN, W. VA. ; Rosecrans victorious,—July 11.

BATTLE NEAR CENTREVILLE, VA.,—July 18.

CONFEDERATE CAPITAL changed to Richmond, Va., —July 20.

BATTLE OF BULL RUN, VA. ; McDowell defeated, —July 21.

BATTLE OF DUG SPRING, MO. ; Lyon victorious,—Aug. 2.

BATTLE OF WILSON'S CREEK, MO. ; Lyon killed,—Aug. 10.

BATTLE OF HATTERAS INLET, N. C. : Federal victory,—Aug. 28, 29.

COLUMBUS, Ky., seized and fortified by Confederates,—Sept. 4.

GRANT occupied Paducah, Ky.,—Sept. 6.

BATTLE OF LEXINGTON, Mo. ; Price defeated Mulligan,—Sept. 17–20.

BATTLE OF BALL'S BLUFF, or Edwards' Ferry; Baker killed,—Oct. 21.

SCOTT retired and McClellan appointed general-in-chief,—Nov. 1.

BATTLE OF PORT ROYAL ENTRANCE, S. C. ; Federals victorious,—Nov. 7.

BATTLE OF BELMONT, Mo. ; Grant and Polk, indecisive,—Nov. 7.

MASON AND SLIDELL taken from the *Trent*,—Nov. 8.

1862. BATTLE OF MILL SPRINGS, KY. ; Thomas victorious,—Jan. 19, 20.

FORT HENRY, Tenn., captured by Foote,—Feb. 6.

BATTLE OF ROANOKE ISLAND, N. C. ; Burnside victorious,—Feb. 8.

FORT DONELSON, Tenn., surrendered to Grant,—Feb. 16.

BATTLE OF PEA RIDGE, ARK. : Curtis victorious,—March 6–8.

THE *Virginia* (*Merrimac*) destroyed the *Cumberland* and *Congress*, at Hampton Roads, Va.,—March 8.

BATTLE between the *Virginia* (*Merrimac*) and *Monitor*, at Hampton Roads, Va.,—March 9.

BATTLE OF NEW MADRID, Mo. ; Pope victorious,—March 14.

BATTLE OF NEW BERN, N. C. ; Burnside victorious,—March 14.

BATTLE NEAR WINCHESTER, Va. ; Shields victorious,—March 23.

BATTLE OF PITTSBURG LANDING, OR SHILOH, Tenn. ; Grant defeated Beauregard ; A. S. Johnson killed ; 20,000 men lost ; April 6–7.

ISLAND No. 10, with 6,000 men, captured by Foote and Pope,—April 7.

BATTLE OF FORT PULASKI, Ga. : Gillmore victorious,—April 10–12.

FARRAGUT'S FLEET passed Forts Jackson and St. Philip, La.,—April 24.

NEW ORLEANS, La., captured by Farragut's fleet, —April 25.

NEW ORLEANS, La., occupied by Federals under Butler,—May 1.

BATTLE OF WILLIAMSBURG, Va. ; McClellan victorious,—May 5.

NORFOLK, Va., captured by Wool,—May 10.

HANOVER COURTHOUSE, Va., captured by Fitz John Porter,—May 27.

BEAUREGARD evacuated Corinth, Miss.,—May 27.

BATTLES of Seven Pines and Fair Oaks, Va. ; McClellan victorious,—May 31 and June 1.

LEE appointed to chief command of the Confederate army,—June 3.

GUNBOAT FIGHT near Fort Pillow, Tenn.,—June 6.

DAVIS, successor of Foote, captured Memphis, Tenn.,—June 6.

SEVEN DAYS' BATTLES in Virginia ; McClellan and Lee,—June 26 to July 1. (Mechanicsville, June 26 ; Gaines' Mill, 27 ; Chickahominy, 28 ; Savage's Station, 29 ; White Oak Swamp, 29–30 ; Glendale, 30 ; Malvern Hill, July 1.)

BATTLE OF CEDAR MOUNTAIN, Va. ; Jackson victorious ; Winder killed,—Aug. 9.

SIOUX WAR in Minnesota began,—August.

POPE'S BATTLES, between Manassas and Washington, D. C.,—Aug. 26 to Sept. 1. (The more important were Groveston, Aug. 29; second Bull Run, 80; Chantilly, Sept. 1; victorious campaign for Lee; Kearney and Stevens killed.)

BATTLE OF RICHMOND, Ky.; Kirby Smith victorious,—Aug. 80.

INVASION OF MARYLAND by Lee; crossed the Potomac near Point of Rocks,—Sept. 4–7.

BATTLE OF SOUTH MOUNTAIN, Md.; McClellan victorious,—Sept. 14.

HARPER'S FERRY, with 12,000 men, surrendered to Jackson by Miles,—Sept. 15.

BATTLE OF ANTIETAM, Md.; McClellan and Lee,—Sept. 17.

MUNFORDSVILLE, Ky., captured by Confederates,—Sept. 17.

BATTLE OF IUKA, Miss.; Rosecrans victorious,—Sept. 19–20.

BATTLE OF CORINTH, Miss.; Rosecrans victorious,—Oct. 8–4.

BATTLE OF PERRYVILLE, Ky.; unsuccessful attack by Bragg.—Oct. 8.

BATTLE OF PRAIRIE GROVE, Ark.; Blunt victorious,—Dec. 7.

BATTLE OF FREDERICKSBURG, Va.; Lee victorious, Federals lost 12,000 men,—Dec. 18.

BATTLE OF KINGSTON, N. C.; Foster victorious.—Dec. 14.

BATTLE OF STONE RIVER, or Murfreesboro, Tenn.,—Dec. 81 to Jan. 8. (One of the fiercest of the war,—Rosecrans victorious.)

1863. EMANCIPATION PROCLAMATION, issued by Lincoln,—Jan. 1.

BATTLE OF FORT HINDMAN, or Arkansas Post; McClernand victorious,—Jan. 11.

SECOND EXPEDITION to the Yazoo; Grant arrived at Young's Point, La.,—Feb. 2.

ARIZONA TERRITORY formed,—Feb. 24.

NATIONAL BANK ACT approved,—Feb. 25.

IDAHO TERRITORY formed,—March 3.

THIRD EXPEDITION to the Yazoo, under Porter,—March 15.

FORT SUMTER, S. C., bombarded by the Federals; Du Pont unsuccessful,—April 7.

GRIERSON'S CAVALRY raid through Mississippi; left La Grange, Tenn.,—April 17.

BATTLE OF PORT GIBSON, Miss.; McClellan victorious,—May 1.

BATTLE OF CHANCELLORVILLE, Va.; Lee victorious; Federals lost 18,000 men,—May 2, 8.

BATTLE OF FREDRICKSBURG, Va.; Early victorious,—May 8, 4.

BATTLE OF RAYMOND, Miss.; McPherson victorious,—May 12.

BATTLE OF BIG BLACK RIVER, Miss.; McClernand victorious,—May 17.

BATTLE OF VICKSBURG, Miss.; Federals repulsed,—May 22.

BATTLE OF PORT HUDSON, La.; Federals repulsed,—May 27.

BATTLE OF BRANDY STATION, Va., by cavalry; Gregg victorious,—June 9.

MARYLAND AND PENNSYLVANIA invaded by Lee,—June.

WEST VIRGINIA admitted into the Union,—June 19.

MORGAN'S RAID crossed the Cumberland River, near Bucksville, Ky.,—June 27.

BATTLE OF GETTYSBURG, Pa.; Meade and Lee; 50,000 men lost,—July 1–3.

BATTLE OF HELENA, ARK.; attack by Holmes repulsed; Prentiss victorious,—July 4.

SURRENDER OF VICKSBURG to Grant by Pemberton,—July 4.

PORT HUDSON, La., surrendered to Banks,—July 8.

RIOTS in New York City; opposition to the draft, —July 13–16.

JACKSON, Miss., destroyed by Sherman,—July 16.

FORT WAGNER, S. C., captured by Federals,— Sept. 6.

CHATTANOOGA, Tenn., occupied by Crittenden,— Sept. 8.

LITTLE ROCK, Ark., occupied by Steele,—Sept. 10.

BATTLE OF CHICKAMAUGA, Ga.; Bragg victorious; Rosecrans lost 16,000 men,—Sept. 19, 20.

BATTLES of Chattanooga and Lookout Mountain; Federals defeated Bragg,—Nov. 23–25.

BATTLE OF KNOXVILLE, Tenn.; Longstreet raised the siege,—Dec. 4.

1864. SHERMAN'S RAID, from Vicksburg; reached Meridian, Miss.,—Feb. 14.

BATTLE OF OLUSTEE, or Océan Pond; Finnegan defeated Seymour,—Feb. 20.

BANKS' Red River Expedition moved up the river, March 12.

BATTLE OF MANSFIELD, or Sabine Crossroads; Banks defeated,—April 18.

BATTLE OF PLEASANT HILL, La.; Banks victorious,—April 9.

BATTLE OF FORT PILLOW, Tenn.; captured by Forrest,—April 18.

PLYMOUTH, N. C., surrendered to Confederates under Hoke,—April 20.

BERMUDA HUNDRED seized and intrenched by Butler,—May 5.

BATTLES OF THE WILDERNESS between Grant and Lee; 30,000 men lost,—May 5–7.

33

SHERMAN'S GEORGIA CAMPAIGN, with 110,000 men, began at Chattanooga, Tenn.,—May 7.

BATTLE OF SPOTTSYLVANIA COURTHOUSE, Va.; 20,000 men lost,—May 10.

BATTLE OF RESACA, Ga.; Sherman defeated Johnston,—May 13–15.

BATTLE OF NEWMARKET, Va.; Sigel defeated,—May 15.

BATTLES OF NORTH ANNA, Va.; Federals victorious,—May 23–27.

MONTANA TERRITORY formed,—May 26.

BATTLES OF DALLAS, Ga.; Sherman victorious,—May 25–28.

BATTLE OF TOTOPOTOMOY CREEK, Va.,—May 30.

BATTLE OF COLD HARBOR, Va.; Grant repulsed by Lee,—June 1–3.

BATTLE OF PETERSBURG, Va.; Grant repulsed; 10,000 men lost,—June 16–18.

SIEGE OF PETERSBURG, Va., by Grant, begun,—June 18.

THE *Alabama* sunk by the *Kearsarge*, off Cherbourg, France,—June 19.

BATTLE OF KENESAW MOUNTAIN, Ga.; Sherman repulsed,—June 27.

INVASION OF MARYLAND by Early; Washington, D. C., threatened,—July 9–14.

BATTLE OF MONOCACY, Md.; Early defeated by Wallace,—July 9.

BATTLES at Atlanta, Ga.; Sherman victorious: McPherson and Walker killed,—July 22–28.

CHAMBERSBURG, Pa., attacked and burned by McCausland,—July 30.

BATTLE OF PETERSBURG; explosion; Federals repulsed,—July 30.

BATTLE OF MOBILE BAY, Ala.; Farragut victorious,—Aug. 5.

WELDON RAILROAD, running south from Richmond, seized by Federals,—Aug. 18.

BATTLE OF BEAM'S STATION, Va.; Weldon Railroad; Hancock repulsed,—Aug. 25.

BATTLE OF JONESBORO, Ga.; Sherman victorious, —Aug. 31 and Sept. 1.

ATLANTA, Ga., occupied by Sherman,—Sept. 2.

BATTLE OF WINCHESTER, Va.; Sheridan victorious,—Sept. 19.

BATTLE OF FISHER'S HILL, Va.; Sheridan victorious,—Sept. 22.

NEVADA admitted into the Union,—Oct. 31.

BATTLE OF FRANKLIN, Tenn.; Schofield victorious,—Nov. 30.

FORT McALLISTER, Ga., captured by Hazen,— Dec. 13.

BATTLE OF NASHVILLE, Tenn.; Thomas victorious,—Dec. 15–16.

SAVANNAH, Ga., occupied by Sherman's army,— Dec. 22.

1865 FORT FISHER, N. C., captured by Porter and Terry, —Jan. 15.

SHERMAN's march northward from Savannah, Ga., —Feb. 1.

COLUMBIA, S. C., surrendered to Federals; Sherman's march,—Feb. 17.

CHARLESTON, S. C., occupied by Federals; Sherman's march,—Feb. 18.

WILMINGTON, N. C., captured by Schofield,— Feb. 22.

LINCOLN began second presidential term,—March 4.

BATTLE OF AVERYSBORO, N. C.; Slocum victorious,—March 16.

BATTLE OF BENTONSVILLE, N. C.; Slocum victorious,—March 19.

ARMIES of Sherman, Terry, and Schofield united at Goldsboro, N. C.,—March 23.

BATTLE OF FORT STEDMAN, at Petersburg, Va.; indecisive,—March 25.

BATTLE OF DINWIDDIE COURTHOUSE, Va.; Sheridan victorious,—March 31.

BATTLE OF FIVE FORKS, Va.; Sheridan victorious,—April 1.

BATTLE OF PETERSBURG, Va.; Grant carried outer lines,—April 1, 2.

BATTLE OF SELMA, Ala.; Wilson captured the city,—April 2.

PETERSBURG AND RICHMOND occupied by Grant,—April 3.

LEE surrendered to Grant at Appomattox Courthouse, Va.,—April 9.

MOBILE, Ala., occupied by Canby,—April 12.

PRESIDENT LINCOLN assassinated at Washington, D. C.,—April 14.

ANDREW JOHNSON inaugurated president,—April 15.

THIRTEENTH AMENDMENT to the Constitution declared in force,—Dec. 18.

1866. FENIAN RAIDS into Canada.

TENNESSEE reconstructed by Act of July 24.

CIVIL WAR proclaimed to be at an end,—Aug. 20.

1867. NEBRASKA admitted into the Union,—March 1.

RECONSTRUCTION ACT passed over president's veto, March 2.

TENURE OF OFFICE ACT passed over president's veto,—March 2.

DOWNFALL OF MAXIMILIAN in Mexico (shot at Queretaro),—June 19.

ALASKA purchased of Russia,—June 20.

DOMINION OF CANADA established,—July 1.

1868. SECRETARY STANTON declared removed from office by President Johnson,—Feb. 21.

JOHNSON'S IMPEACHMENT trial begun,—March 80.

JOHNSON acquitted by a vote of 85 to 19, not two-thirds,—May 26.

ARKANSAS reconstructed,—June 22.

ALABAMA, Florida, Georgia, Louisiana, and North Carolina reconstructed,—June 25.

WYOMING TERRITORY formed,—July 25.

FOURTEENTH AMENDMENT to the Constitution declared in force,—July 28.

GENERAL AMNESTY proclaimed by President Johnson,—Dec. 25.

1869. ULYSSES S. GRANT inaugurated president, —March 4.

PACIFIC RAILROAD (Union and Central) completed, —May 10. (Length, 1,910 miles; cost, $252,-000,000.)

WOMAN SUFFRAGE in Wyoming,—Dec. 6.

1870. VIRGINIA reconstructed,—Jan. 27.

MISSISSIPPI reconstructed,—Feb. 8.

FENIAN RAIDS in Canada resumed.

TEXAS reconstructed,—March 80.

FIFTEENTH AMENDMENT to the Constitution declared in force,—March 80.

WAR between France and Germany began, July 19, ended May 10, 1871. (Sales of arms difficulties in the United States resulted from this war.)

1871. NATIONAL PARK established in Yellowstone Valley, —Feb. 28.

LEGAL-TENDER LAWS declared constitutional by Supreme Court,—May 1.

FIRE AT CHICAGO, Ill.; estimated loss, $300,000,-000,—Oct. 10-12.

TREATY OF WASHINGTON, providing for arbitration on the *Alabama* claims, etc., agreed upon by Joint High Commission,—Dec. 15.

CIVIL SERVICE REFORM COMMISSION, established by the act of March 8, promulgated report Dec. 19.

1872. NATIONAL BUREAU OF EDUCATION established,—Feb. 8.

GENEVA AWARD ; $15,500,000 awarded to the United States by the arbitrators on the *Alabama* claims, etc.,—Sept. 14.

SAN JUAN BOUNDARY dispute decided in favor of the United States ; San Juan Island to the United States,—Oct. 21.

FIRE AT BOSTON, Mass. ; estimated loss, $100,000,-000,—Nov. 9–10.

MODOC WAR in California began,—Nov. 29.

1873. CRÉDIT MOBILIER COMMITTEE appointed, Dec. 2, 1872, to investigate frauds in the construction of the Pacific Railroad reported,—Feb. 24.

"SALARY GRAB" act passed,—March 3.

GRANT began second presidential term,—March 4.

1875. ACT providing for specie payments on Jan. 1, 1879, approved,—Jan. 14.

DEATH OF VICE-PRESIDENT WILSON, at Washington, D. C.,—Nov. 22.

THOMAS W. FERRY, president *pro tempore* of the senate.

1876. CENTENNIAL EXHIBITION opened at Philadelphia, May 10, closed Nov. 10.

COLORADO admitted into the Union,—Aug. 1.

PRESIDENTIAL ELECTION,—Nov. 7. (Contest between the Republican and Democratic parties as to its validity.)

1877. ELECTORAL COMMISSION provided for by act of Jan. 29.

HAYES AND WHEELER declared elected by congress,—March 2.

RUTHERFORD B. HAYES inaugurated president,—
March 5.

PRESIDENT HAYES' civil-service order issued,—
June 22.

RAILROAD RIOTS at Pittsburg, Albany, Chicago,
St. Louis, etc.,—July 22–24.

1878. YELLOW FEVER in Louisiana, Mississippi, Tennessee, Kentucky, etc.

SILVER DOLLAR made legal tender over president's
veto,—Feb. 28.

GOLD sells at par in Wall street,—Dec. 17.

1879. RESUMPTION of specie payments; Act of Jan. 14,
1875,—Jan. 1.

Jeannette sails from San Francisco for North Pole,
—July 9.

1880. INCREASING IMMIGRATION,—456,000 immigrants arrived during year ending Dec. 31.

POPULATION of United States over 50,000,000,—
Tenth census.

1881. JAMES A. GARFIELD inaugurated president,—
March 4.

PRESIDENT GARFIELD shot at Washington, D. C.,
—July 2.

DEATH OF PRESIDENT GARFIELD at Long Branch,
N. J.,—Sept. 19.

CHESTER A. ARTHUR inaugurated president at New
York City,—Sept. 19.

560,000 IMMIGRANTS arrived in the United States
during the nine months ending Sept. 30.

CENTENNIAL CELEBRATION at Yorktown, — Oct.
10.

SURVIVORS of *Jeannette* heard from,—Dec. 20.

1882. TERRIBLE ACCIDENT at Spuyten Duyvil, N. Y.,
—Jan. 18.

GUITEAU, the assassin, found guilty, Jan. 25. Hanged June 30.

TRANSIT OF VENUS,—Dec. 6.

1883. NEW YORK AND BROOKLYN BRIDGE opened May 24.

GREAT STRIKE of Telegraphers' Brotherhood in the United States,—July 19 to Aug. 18.

NORTHERN PACIFIC RAILROAD open for traffic, —Sept. 8.

TWO-CENT LETTER POSTAGE went into effect throughout the United States,—Oct. 1.

LORD LANSDOWNE inaugurated Governor-General of Canada vice the Marquis of Lorne,—Oct. 23.

1884. BODIES of *Jeannette* explorers arrived in New York, —Feb. 22.

WASHINGTON MONUMENT completed,—Dec. 6.

OPENING of "World's Fair and Cotton Centennial Exposition" in New Orleans,—Dec. 16.

1885. DEDICATION of Washington Monument,—Feb. 21.

GROVER CLEVELAND inaugurated president, — March 4.

REBELLION in Saskatchewan, British America, began, March 23; Riel captured, May 15, and executed at Regina,—Nov. 16.

REVISED OLD TESTAMENT published,—May 15.

BARTHOLDI STATUE OF LIBERTY arrived in New York,—June 19.

NIAGARA PARK thrown open to the public,—July 15.

GENERAL U. S. GRANT died at Mount McGregor, N. Y., July 23, and buried at Riverside Park, N. Y.,—Aug. 8.

FLOOD ROCK, East River, blown up,—Oct. 10.

GEN. GEORGE B. McCLELLAN died,—Oct. 29.

VICE-PRESIDENT THOMAS A. HENDRICKS died,— Nov. 25.

WILLIAM H. VANDERBILT, the noted millionaire, died,—Dec. 8.

UNITED STATES SENATE passed the Presidential Succession bill,—Dec. 17.

1886. GEN. WINFIELD S. HANCOCK died,—Feb. 9.

HORATIO SEYMOUR died,—Feb. 12.

JOHN B. GOUGH, noted temperance lecturer, died, —Feb. 18.

GREAT LABOR AGITATIONS throughout the United States,—May 1.

RAILROAD STRIKE in the Southwest ended,—May 4.

ANARCHISTS explode a dynamite bomb, killing and wounding many policemen and rioters, at Haymarket Square, Chicago,—May 4.

ODELL, ILL., wrecked by the wind,—May 12.

GROVER CLEVELAND, president of United States, married to Miss Frances Folsom,—June 2.

JUDGE DAVID DAVIS died at Bloomington, Ill., —June 26.

SAMUEL J. TILDEN died,—Aug. 4.

THE GREAT ANARCHIST TRIAL commenced at Chicago, Ill., at 10 A. M., June 21, and ended at 10 A. M., Aug. 20. (The jury brought in a verdict of murder in the first degree in the case of seven of defendants, and of fifteen years in prison for the eighth.)

DEDICATION of the famous Bartholdi Statue of "Liberty Enlightening the World,"—Oct. 28.

DEATH of ex-President Chester A. Arthur,—Nov. 18.

DEATH of General John A. Logan,—Dec. 26.

1887. THE INTER-STATE COMMERCE BILL passed the senate, —Jan. 14.

THE PRESIDENT signed the Inter-state Commerce Bill,—Feb. 4.

REV. HENRY WARD BEECHER died,—March 8.

WILLIAM A. WHEELER, ex-vice-president of United States, died,—June 4.

TERRIBLE RAILROAD ACCIDENT near Chatsworth, Ill.,—nearly 100 killed,—Aug. 10.

GOVERNOR OGLESBY commuted the sentence of Samuel Fielden and Michael Schwab, the Chicago Anarchists, to imprisonment for life, —Nov. 10.

LOUIS LINGG committed suicide,—Nov. 10; August Spies, A. R. Parsons, Adolph Fischer and Geo. Engel, executed,—Nov. 11.

1888. TERRIBLE BLIZZARD in New York and vicinity,— March 13–15.

EX-SENATOR ROSCOE CONKLING died,—April 18.

DEMOCRATIC NATIONAL CONVENTION at St. Louis, nominated Grover Cleveland, of New York, for president, and Allan G. Thurman, of Ohio, for vice-president,—June 6.

REPUBLICAN NATIONAL CONVENTION at Chicago nominated Benjamin Harrison, of Indiana, for president, and Levi P. Morton, vice-president, —June 25.

PHILIP H. SHERIDAN, general of United States army, died,—Aug. 5.

THE PRESIDENT signed the Chinese Exclusion Bill, —Oct. 1.

THE PRESIDENTIAL AND CONGRESSIONAL ELECTIONS were held. Benjamin Harrison was elected president of United States, and Levi P. Morton vice-president,—Nov. 6.

1889. THE PRESIDENT signed a bill, making the following new States: North Dakota, South Dakota, Montana and Washington,—Feb. 22.

PRESIDENT BENJAMIN HARRISON and Vice-President Levi P. Morton inaugurated,—March 4.

THE PROCLAMATION opening the Territory of Oklahoma was issued by the president, March 27, the proclamation to take effect April 22 at high noon.

CENTENNIAL CELEBRATION throughout the United States,—April 30.

TERRIBLE FLOOD at Johnstown, Pa., caused by the bursting of a reservoir; the entire valley of the Conemaugh flooded; loss of life estimated about 5,000; loss of property almost incalculable,—May 31–June 1.

THE BUSINESS PORTION of Seattle, Washington,—destroyed by fire,—June 6.

DISASTROUS FIRE at Spokane Falls, Washington, Aug. 4.

THE CRONIN TRIAL began August 30, ended December 16; John F. Beggs was acquitted; John Kunze found guilty of manslaughter, and sentenced to three years, and Daniel Coughlin, Patrick O'Sullivan and Martin Burk received life sentences.

1890. TERRIBLE STORM passed over the Mississippi valley, —March 27.

SAMUEL J. RANDALL died,—April 13.

GREAT FLOODS in Mississippi valley during April.

THE WORLD'S FAIR BILL passed the senate,—April 21.

PRESIDENT HARRISON signed the World's Fair Bill, —April 25.

MONUMENT to Robert E. Lee was unveiled at Richmond, Va.,—May 29.

IDAHO became a State,—July 3.

WYOMING became a State,—July 10.

DEATH of Gen. Clinton B. Fisk,—July 9.

DEATH of Major-General John C. Fremont,—July 13.

THE McKINLEY TARIFF BILL signed by President Harrison,—Oct. 1.

NEW TARIFF BILL went into effect,—Oct. 6.

OUTBREAK of the Indians,—December.

DEATH of Sitting Bull,—Dec. 15.

THE PRESIDENT issued a proclamation announcing the fact that the World's Fair would be held in Chicago in 1893,—Dec. 24.

DEATH of Gen. F. E. Spinner, ex-treasurer of United States,—Dec. 31.

1891. DEATH of William Windom, secretary of the treasury,—Jan. 29.

DEATH of Admiral David D. Porter,—Feb. 13.

DEATH of Gen. W. T. Sherman,—Feb. 14.

A MOB in New Orleans attacked the jail and killed eleven Italians who were indicted for the murder of David Hennessey; intense excitement all over the country,—March 14.

DEATH of P. T. Barnum, the great showman,—April 7.

GROUND broken for the first exhibition building at World's Fair grounds,—the Woman's Building,—July 9.

1892. UNITED STATES REGULARS and Texas Rangers opposed the movements of Garza, the Mexican revolutionist on the Texas border,—Jan. 2.

CYCLONES devastated several towns in Georgia and Florida,—Jan. 6.

TERRIFIC EXPLOSION at the Osage Coal-Mining Company's mine at Krebs, I. T., resulting in great loss of life and property,—Jan. 7.

THE eminent American sculptor, Randolph Rogers, died at Rome, Italy,—Jan. 15.

FREE SILVER-COINAGE DEBATE in congress,—March 22–24.

GROVER CLEVELAND elected a second time president of the United States,—November.

1893. EX-PRESIDENT RUTHERFORD B. HAYES died,—Jan. 16.

GEN. BENJAMIN F. BUTLER died,—Jan. 11.

HON. JAMES G. BLAINE died,—Jan. 27.

GENERAL BEAUREGARD died,—February.

GROVER CLEVELAND inaugurated President of the United States,—March 4.

FINANCIAL DEPRESSION began; Secretary Carlisle conferred with bank presidents,—April 27.

THE DUKE OF VERAGUA (a descendant of Columbus) arrived in Chicago,—April 29.

WORLD'S COLUMBIAN EXPOSITION formally opened, —May 1.

PANIC OF 1893 began with several failures in New York,—May 4.

JAMES K. BLOUNT appointed by President Cleveland envoy extraordinary and minister plenipotentiary to Hawaii,—May 10.

GOVERNOR MCKINLEY renominated for governor of Ohio,—June 8.

GOVERNOR ALTGELD, of Illinois, pardoned the Chicago anarchists Fielden, Schwab, and Neebe, —June 26.

PRESIDENT convened congress in extra session to consider the repeal of the Sherman Silver Law, —Aug. 7.

PARLIAMENT OF RELIGIONS in session in Chicago, —September.

CARTER HARRISON, Mayor of Chicago, assassinated by an ex-policeman,—Oct. 28.

WORLD'S FAIR closed, Oct. 30.

SHERMAN SILVER LAW repealed, Nov. 1.

FALL ELECTIONS—Great Republican victories in New York and Ohio; Governor McKinley reelected by nearly ninety thousand majority,— Nov. 7.

PRESIDENT CLEVELAND, through the Secretary of State, announced his intention to restore the monarchy in Hawaii —Nov. 10.

STEPS TAKEN to erect a monument on the birthplace of Washington at Wakefield, Virginia,— Nov. 16.

GREAT STRIKE on Lehigh Valley Railroad began,— Nov. 16.

STATUE OF NATHAN HALE unveiled at City Hall Park, New York City,—Nov. 25.

NEW TARIFF BILL to change McKinley Law sent to Ways and Means Committee,—Nov. 27.

CPSIA information can be obtained
at www.ICGtesting.com
Printed in the USA
BVHW041449160819
555975BV00046B/1252/P

9 781318 690305